LEARNING LIFE PRINCIPLES
FROM THE KINGS OF
THE OLD TESTAMENT

LEARNING LIFE PRINCIPLES FROM THE KINGS OF THE OLD TESTAMENT

A Bible Study by

Wayne Barber

Eddie Rasnake

Richard Shepherd

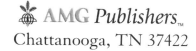
AMG *Publishers*™

Chattanooga, TN 37422

Following God

LEARNING LIFE PRINCIPLES FROM THE KINGS OF THE OLD TESTAMENT

© 1998 by Wayne A. Barber, Eddie Rasnake, and Richard L. Shepherd
Fifth Printing, 2009

ISBN 10 : 0-89957-301-0

ISBN 13 : 978-0-89957-301-4

Unless otherwise noted,
Scripture is taken from the *New American Standard Bible*®.
Copyright © 1960, 1962, 1963, 1968, 1971, 1972, 1973, 1975, 1977
by The Lockman Foundation.
Used by permission.

Quotations also appear from the following used by permission:

Portions appear from *The Complete Word Study Old Testament*
Copyright © 1994 by AMG Publishers.
Used by permission.

Cover Design by Phillip Rodgers

Printed in Canada.
12 11 10 09 –T– 10 9 8 7 6 5

With love and gratitude
we dedicate this book to our parents:
Claude and Myrtle Barber
Fred E. Rasnake and Janet C. Lundy
Lawson and Alice Shepherd

Acknowledgments

This work goes forth with great appreciation to those who have encouraged us in the publication of the first book *Following God: Life Principles from the Old Testament*. We are especially grateful to the body of believers at Woodland Park Baptist Church in Chattanooga, Tennessee, who have walked through many of these studies with us and have been a continual source of encouragement as the writing of new studies progresses. Special thanks to Jennifer Ould and Troy Renfrow for polishing the product. Thanks to the folks at AMG, especially Trevor Overcash, Dale Anderson, and Warren Baker. Thanks to Robin Currier for her help with proofreading. Most of all we remain grateful to the Lord Jesus our King who continues to teach us and lead us in what it means to follow Him with a whole heart.

 THE AUTHORS

Wayne Barber

Wayne Barber is the Senior Pastor of Hoffmantown Church, Albuquerque, NewMexico. A renowned national and international conference ministry speaker, the primary goal of Wayne's ministry is in spreading the message of "the sufficiency of Christ." People around the world connect with Wayne's unique ability to make God's Word come alive through his honest and open "real-life" experiences. Wayne has authored or co-authored several books, and his most recent book, *Living Grace*, was published in 2005. He also authors a regular column in AMG's *Pulpit Helps* monthly magazine. For eighteen years he served as Senior Pastor-Teacher of Woodland Park Baptist Church, in Chattanooga, Tennessee, and for many of those years in Chattanooga, Wayne co-taught with noted author Kay Arthur of Precept Ministries and has studied under Dr. Spiros Zodhiates, one of the world's leading Greek scholars. Wayne and his wife Diana have two grown children and now make their home in Albuquerque.

Rick Shepherd

Richard L. Shepherd has been engaged in some form of ministry for more than twenty years, focusing on areas of teaching, discipleship, and prayer. He has served in churches in Alabama, Florida, Texas, and Tennessee and now serves as Director of Prayer and Spiritual Awakening with the Florida Baptist Convention. For nearly seventeen years (1983–2000), Rick served as an associate pastor at Woodland Park Baptist Church in Chattanooga, Tennessee. The Lord's ministry has taken him to several countries, including Haiti, Romania, Ukraine, Moldova, Italy, Israel, England, and Greece, where he has been involved in training pastors, church leaders, and congregations. Rick has also lectured on college and seminary campuses. He graduated with honors from the University of Mobile and holds a Master of Divinity and a Ph.D. from Southwestern Baptist Theological Seminary in Fort Worth, Texas. He and his wife Linda Gail have four children and make their home in Jacksonville, Florida.

Eddie Rasnake

EDDIE RASNAKE met Christ in 1976 as a freshman in college. He graduated with honors from East Tennessee State University in 1980. He and his wife, Michele, served for nearly seven years on the staff of Campus Crusade for Christ. Their first assignment was the University of Virginia, and while there they also started a Campus Crusade ministry at James Madison University. Eddie then served four years as campus director of the Campus Crusade ministry at the University of Tennessee. In 1989, Eddie left Campus Crusade to join Wayne Barber at Woodland Park Baptist Church as the Associate Pastor of Discipleship and Training. He has been ministering in Eastern Europe in the role of equipping local believers for more than a decade and has published materials in Albanian, German, Greek, Italian, Romanian, and Russian. Eddie serves on the boards of directors of the Center for Christian Leadership in Tirana, Albania, and the Bible Training Center in Eleuthera, Bahamas. He also serves as chaplain for the Chattanooga Lookouts (Cincinnati Reds AA affiliate) baseball team. Eddie and his wife Michele live in Chattanooga, Tennessee, with their four children.

THE SERIES:

Three authors and fellow ministers, Wayne Barber, Eddie Rasnake, and Rick Shepherd, teamed up in 1998 to write a character-based Bible study for AMG Publishers. Their collaboration developed into the title, *Life Principles from the Old Testament*. Since 1998 these same authors and AMG Publishers have produced six more character-based studies—each consisting of twelve lessons geared around a five-day study of a particular Bible personality. In recent years, several topical-based studies have been added in the Christian Living, Discipleship, and Through the Bible categories. However, the interactive study format that readers have come to love remains constant with each new release. As new titles are being planned, our focus remains the same: to provide excellent Bible study materials that point people to God's Word in ways that allow them to apply truths to their own lives. More information on this groundbreaking series can be found on the following web page:

www.amgpublishers.com

Preface

We were created to follow—to follow God—and to discover the adventure of a journey through time into eternity. It is the journey of a family experiencing the love of our Father, of a people discovering the wonders of surrender and service to our awesome King.

It is evident as one observes families, communities, and nations, that we become like those we follow. God wants us to follow Him as our Lord and King and discover for ourselves the security and peace trusting Him can bring. As we do, we begin to discover how to lead others, how to walk in a trustworthy manner, and how to help others do the same. As we learn the value of being a faithful follower, we can lead others to be faithful followers. To use the picture painted by the apostle John, as we walk in the light with the Lord Jesus, we avoid walking in the darkness, and we lead others out of darkness into the light. As we follow, we lead so that others might follow more fully and more faithfully.

This truth is vital to our walk with the Lord, and it applies to every area of life—not just the spiritual dimension, but to business, economics, labor, government, education, philosophy, even recreation. In every area, we become like those we follow.

Leadership is the power of influence, and influence can be very powerful. We are all influenced to follow someone or some idea, and we influence others in the same way. Our character will determine the kind of influence we have, whether for good or for evil. When we look at the nation of Israel, these truths become even more evident. The kings of Israel and Judah provide us with many lessons in following and leading, in being influenced and influencing others—some lessons hard to swallow, some gratefully received.

God's design and call for leadership is to follow Him and His Word. When the kings of Israel or Judah did that, the people followed them, and the land enjoyed the peace and rest God desired. That is always true when we follow the wisdom from above. God's wisdom is always full of purity, peace, and order, even in the midst of trials. When the kings and the people did not follow God, disharmony, strife, and disorder began to prevail. That is typical of the wisdom of man apart from God.

These kings can teach us how to follow God with a whole heart and, in so doing, we can learn how to lead with character and integrity. That is the crying need of the world today whether in business, in government, in education, or in the church. Will someone lead the way? Any "someone" can . . . if he will follow God.

Following Him,

Wayne A. Barber

WAYNE A. BARBER

Richard L. Shepherd

RICHARD L. SHEPHERD

Eddie Rasnake

EDDIE RASNAKE

Table of Contents

xiii

The Lineage of the Kings of Israel and Judah

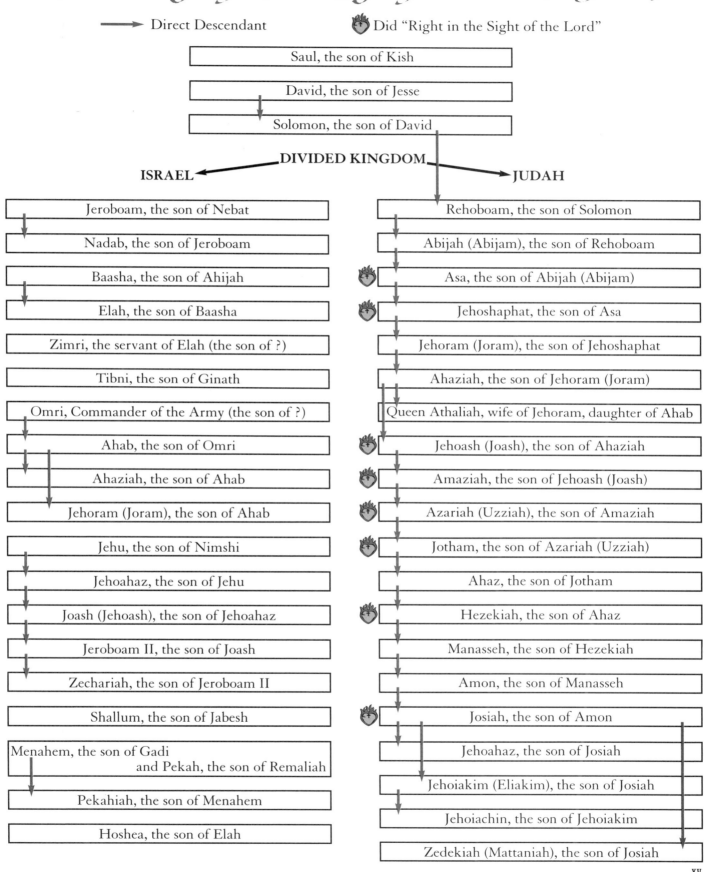

⟶ Direct Descendant   🛡 Did "Right in the Sight of the Lord"

Saul, the son of Kish

David, the son of Jesse

Solomon, the son of David

DIVIDED KINGDOM

ISRAEL ⟵   ⟶ **JUDAH**

ISRAEL	JUDAH
Jeroboam, the son of Nebat	Rehoboam, the son of Solomon
Nadab, the son of Jeroboam	Abijah (Abijam), the son of Rehoboam
Baasha, the son of Ahijah	🛡 Asa, the son of Abijah (Abijam)
Elah, the son of Baasha	🛡 Jehoshaphat, the son of Asa
Zimri, the servant of Elah (the son of ?)	Jehoram (Joram), the son of Jehoshaphat
Tibni, the son of Ginath	Ahaziah, the son of Jehoram (Joram)
Omri, Commander of the Army (the son of ?)	Queen Athaliah, wife of Jehoram, daughter of Ahab
Ahab, the son of Omri	🛡 Jehoash (Joash), the son of Ahaziah
Ahaziah, the son of Ahab	🛡 Amaziah, the son of Jehoash (Joash)
Jehoram (Joram), the son of Ahab	🛡 Azariah (Uzziah), the son of Amaziah
Jehu, the son of Nimshi	🛡 Jotham, the son of Azariah (Uzziah)
Jehoahaz, the son of Jehu	Ahaz, the son of Jotham
Joash (Jehoash), the son of Jehoahaz	🛡 Hezekiah, the son of Ahaz
Jeroboam II, the son of Joash	Manasseh, the son of Hezekiah
Zechariah, the son of Jeroboam II	Amon, the son of Manasseh
Shallum, the son of Jabesh	🛡 Josiah, the son of Amon
Menahem, the son of Gadi and Pekah, the son of Remaliah	Jehoahaz, the son of Josiah
Pekahiah, the son of Menahem	Jehoiakim (Eliakim), the son of Josiah
Hoshea, the son of Elah	Jehoiachin, the son of Jehoiakim
	Zedekiah (Mattaniah), the son of Josiah

Timeline of the Kings

■ United Kingdom ■ Southern Kingdom (Judah) ■ Northern Kingdom (Israel)

The names in purple are kings in Israel or Judah. The names in all caps are PROPHETS.

1050 — 850

1050	1000	950	900	850

SAMUEL   GAD
Judge and Prophet   NATHAN

SHEMAIAH IDDO   Hanani the Seer
ODED
AZARIAH   OBADIAH JOEL
Jahaziel the Levite

Saul
1051–1011

David
1011–971

Solomon
971–931

Rehoboam
931–913

Asa
911–870

Abijam
913–911

Jehoshaphat
873–848

Jehoram
(Joram)
853–841

Ahaziah
841
Athaliah
841–835

Joash
835–796

Ishbosheth ruled over Israel
1011–1004

960—Temple finished

Jeroboam I
931–910

Nadab
910–909

Elah
886–885

Zimri
885

Ahaziah
853–852

Jehu
841–814

David ruled over Judah from Hebron
1011–1004

Baasha
909–886

Tibni
885–880

Ahab
874–853

Jehoram
(Joram)
852–841

Omri
885–874

David ruled over all Israel and Judah from Jerusalem
1004–971

AHIJAH the Shilonite
"A man of God from Judah"
A prophet from Samaria in Bethel

JEHU, son of Hanani
MICAIAH

ELIJAH   ELISHA

Hiram I of Tyre
981–947

Benhadad I of Syria
900–860

Benhadad II of Syria
860–841

800 — 600

800	750	700	650	600

"A Prophet"
(sent to Amaziah)

ISAIAH
MICAH

NAHUM ZEPHANIAH HABAKKUK
HULDAH (a prophetess)
JEREMIAH

Amaziah
796–767
Azariah (Uzziah)
790–739

Jotham
750–735

Ahaz
735–715

Manasseh
697–642

Amon
642–640

Josiah
640–609

Jehoahaz
(Jeconiah)
609

Jehoiachin
598–597

Jehoiakim
609–598

Zedekiah
597–586

Hezekiah
715–686

Jehoahaz
814–798

Joash
(Jehoash)
798–782

Jeroboam II
793–753

Zechariah
753–752

Menahem
752–742

Hoshea
732–722

Shallum
752

Pekahiah
742–740

Pekah
752–732

JONAH

AMOS   ODED
HOSEA

*There are no more kings or prophets in the Northern Kingdom.
Foreign peoples are resettled into the land.*

605—1st Captivity
DANIEL
Hananiah
Mishael
Azariah
597—2d Captivity
EZEKIEL
Nebuchadnezzar
605–562

Tiglath-pileser I
745–727

722—Assyria takes Israel into captivity

Shalmaneser V
727–722

Sennacherib
705–681

612—Fall of Nineveh

550 — 400

550	500	450	400

HAGGAI
ZECHARIAH

MALACHI

Zerubbabel
536—First Return
536—Rebuilding the Temple
516—Temple completed

Ezra
458—Second Return
Rebuilding the people

Nehemiah
445—Third Return
Rebuilding the walls
and the city of Jerusalem

586—Final Captivity
Jerusalem and Temple destroyed

*The Jews are without a king
or a prophet, living under the
dominion of foreign rulers, and*
AWAITING THE MESSIAH,
THE TRUE KING OF ISRAEL.

538–Decree of Cyrus to return

Queen Esther

Amel-Marduk
(Evil-Merodach)
562–560

Cyrus
539–530

Darius I
522–486

Xerxes
486–464

Artaxerxes
464–423

Socrates
470–399

Plato
428–348

Aristotle
384–322

THE FOLLY OF NOT FOLLOWING GOD

Saul, the son of Kish of the tribe of Benjamin, was the first king of united Israel. He reigned from 1051 to 1011 BC. Samuel prophesied in his reign.

God created man to reflect His image, to reproduce a godly heritage, and to reign in life, but sin has stained all of that, and marred God's purpose. After sin, the image of God can no longer be clearly seen in mankind. The stains of sin are reflected not only in leaders, but also in the desires of the people. When Israel begins to clamor for a king, it is not out of a desire to follow God but a desire to be like the other nations. Even their choice of a king is not who God would pick. In Samuel we saw the transition from judges ruling Israel to prophets and kings. This week we want to look at the first king of Israel. Unfortunately, in Saul we do not find a positive example of following God. Yet there is much to be learned from even a negative example. If we are wise, we will learn from Israel's mistakes in their selection of this king, and we will learn from Saul's mistakes along the way. This week in king Saul and next week in king David we will see the wrong way and the right way to deal with sin as we follow God. Let's look into the Word and see what God wants to say to us from the life of king Saul.

In Saul we do not find a positive example of following God. Yet, there is much to be learned even from this negative example.

WHEN DID HE REIGN?

1050	1000	950	900	850
SAMUEL GAD			SHEMAIAH IDDO Hanani the Seer	OBADIAH JOEL
Judge and Prophet NATHAN			ODED	Jahaziel the Levite
			AZARIAH	
			Rehoboam Asa	Jehoshaphat Jehoram Ahaziah Joash
Saul	David Solomon		931–913 911–870	873–848 (Joram) 841 835–796
1051–1011	1011–971 971–931		Abijam	853–841 Athaliah
			913–911	841–835
	Ishbosheth ruled over Israel		Jeroboam I Nadab Elah Zimri	Ahaziah Jehu
	1011–1004 960—Temple finished		931–910 910–909 886–885 885	853–852 841–814
			Baasha Tibni Ahab Jehoram
	David ruled over Judah from Hebron		909–886 885–880 874–853 (Joram)
	1011–1004		Omri 852–841
			885–874	
			AHIJAH the Shilonite	
			"A man of God from Judah" JEHU, son of Hanani	
	David ruled over all Israel and Judah from Jerusalem		A prophet from Samaria in Bethel MICAIAH	
	1004–971		ELIJAH ELISHA	
	Hiram I of Tyre		Benhadad I of Syria Benhadad II of Syria	
	981–947		900–860 860–841	

WANTING A KING LIKE ALL THE NATIONS

The kingship of Saul was born out of a dark time in Israel—a time characterized by the people following their own sinful desires rather than following God. It falls on the heels of the period of the Judges whose dismal refrain was, "*. . . there was no king in Israel; every man did what was right in his own eyes*" (Judges 17:6; 18:1; 19:1; 21:25). Without spiritual authority and leadership, Israel wandered greatly. Unfortunately, though there was nothing wrong with Israel wanting a king, their demand for Saul flowed from wrong motives. God, who sees into the hearts of man, says they were rejecting Him as their King. Today we want to begin investigating what led to Israel's desire for a king.

📖 Read 1 Samuel 8. Why did the request in verse 5 to "*appoint a king for us . . . like all the nations,*" displease Samuel (vv. 12–20)?

_____

_____

_____

> "Appoint a king for us to judge us like all the nations."
> 1 Samuel 8:5

The statement of concern is the phrase at the end of verse 5, "*. . . like all the nations.*" Verses 19–20 also tell us that Israel wanted to "*be like all the nations.*" Instead of following God, Israel was following the world. The world's system does not follow God and is never to be imitated by God's people.

Why was God displeased with Israel's request for a king (v. 7)?

_____

_____

_____

Sometimes God's greatest judgment is giving us what we think we want so we can see that it isn't really what we wanted at all. The Lord told Samuel that Israel's request for a king was a rejection of God as their king. The Law made provision for the appointment of a king (Genesis 49:10; Numbers 24:17; Deuteronomy 17:14–20), but until Israel recognized God's lordship and rule in their lives, a king would not meet their needs.

> Sometimes God's greatest judgment is giving us what we want so we can see that it isn't really what we want.

📖 If asking for a king in the manner that Israel did was a rejection of God as their king, why do you think the Lord tells Samuel three times (vv. 7, 9, 22) to "*listen to their voice?*"

_____

_____

_____

There is no clear-cut answer to this question, but it would seem that God gave Israel what they wanted in a king so He could use the negative experience of Saul to teach them to start wanting what God wants. Then He would provide them His king. As we will see more clearly next week, David was a man after God's own heart. God was teaching Israel to follow Him instead of the world.

In 1 Samuel 12 we see Samuel's farewell address as the last of the judges of Israel. Though he was no longer to be a ruler over them, he continued his priestly and prophetic activities.

📖 Read chapter 12, verses 1–19. Who chose Saul as king, according to Samuel (v. 13)?

_____

Samuel presented Saul as the king Israel had chosen and Israel had asked for. He added that the Lord has *"set a king over you."* You can almost hear Samuel saying, "You asked for it, and now you've got it."

What is the promise and its conditions revealed in verse 14 by Samuel?

Promise:

_____

_____

_____

Conditions:

_____

_____

_____

_____

Samuel exhorted the people, *"If you will fear the LORD and serve Him, and listen to His voice and not rebel against the command of the LORD, then both you and also the king who reigns over you will **follow** the LORD your God"* (emphasis added). Remember, "following God" is what we, too, are trying to learn.

Verse 15 indicates that if Israel would not follow God (evidenced by not listening to God and rebelling against His command), then the hand of the Lord would be against them just as it was against their fathers (v. 9). As if to add an exclamation point, God sent a thunderstorm (an uncommon occurrence during the wheat harvest season of May-June) as a sign. In verses 20–25 Samuel closed out his exhortation with an invitation to return to following God.

📖 Read 1 Samuel 12:20–25. In the space provided, list each verse with the corresponding spiritual principle.

Verse

_____ God placed people in their paths who would instruct them as to where God was leading so they could follow.

_____ Even though their request for a king was sinful, that didn't mean they could never follow God again.

_____ God's gracious commitment to His people does not mean there are no consequences for those who choose not to follow Him.

_____ If they didn't follow God, they would be going after futile things which could not profit or deliver.

Following God means following His Word.

Put Yourself in Their Shoes

WAS IT WRONG FOR ISRAEL TO WANT A KING?

Israel's request for a king was not wrong in and of itself. In fact, the Law made provision for the appointment of a king. In Genesis 49:10, Jacob prophesied that kings from Judah would one day rule over Israel. In Numbers 24:17, Balaam prophesied that a king from Israel would even rule over other nations. In Deuteronomy 17:14–15, the issue comes into balance. There the assumption is made that Israel would want a king, and instructions are given on how to select a king and what he should be like. The most important thing we see there is that God is to select the king.

_____The Lord's commitment to them was because of His character, not because of how they followed Him.

_____The Lord has already shown again and again that He is worth following.

(Your answers should be placed in this order: 23, 20, 25, 21, 22, 24)

There is a key here to following God. It means letting go of the things you are convinced will take care of your needs and problems, and letting God give you His solution. Many times we are blinded to what God wants to do in our lives by what we can see. We are so entrenched in our own opinions that we say no to God, foolishly insisting on our own way. And when He gives it to us, we take that to mean we were in His will all along. But disobedience is costly, and our way comes with a high price tag.

Saul DAY TWO

The people were impressed with Saul because of how he looked on the outside, but God saw the heart.

SAUL, THE CHOICE OF A NEW GENERATION

Once it was settled that Israel, for better or worse, was going to have a king, all that was left to do was to figure out who he would be. As we will see, not only has Israel's desire for a king been tainted by sin, but the type of king they were looking for was stained as well. In Saul we will see that God gave them exactly what they wanted, even though it was not what He wanted. Today we want to look at the process by which Saul was chosen, and see what we can learn about following God.

📖 Read 1 Samuel 9:1–2. Write down three things that Saul had going for him that would attract Israel (with their wrong motives) to him as a king.

_____

_____

_____

First, we see that Saul came from a good family—his father was *"a mighty man of valor."* He was good looking (*"a choice and handsome man"*), and he was tall and impressive for battle (*"from his shoulders and up, he was taller than any of the people"*). On the outside, he looked like a king, and he certainly had the right resumé. The people were impressed with Saul because of how he looked on the outside, but God saw the heart.

📖 Read 1 Samuel 10:14–22. Saul exhibited some unusual behavior in these verses. You may not understand why Saul did these things, but identify the aspects of his conduct that don't seem quite right.

_____

_____

_____

_____

In verse 16, Saul does not tell his uncle about Samuel's prophecy concerning Saul's future kingship. Then in verse 22 we see that at the moment Samuel reveals to the nation God's selection of Saul as king, Saul hides himself with the baggage.

Why do you think Saul did these things?

_____

_____

_____

_____

Both of the actions recorded here suggest Saul's insecurity and lack of self-confidence. This suggestion is confirmed in 1 Samuel 15:17 where we are told that Saul was *". . . little in* [his] *own eyes."* These revelations did not bode well for the nation he would be leading.

In 1 Samuel 10, Saul is given specific instructions from the Lord by way of Samuel. One of those instructions included waiting at Gilgal for Samuel to come and offer sacrifices and show him what to do.

📖 Read 1 Samuel 13:1–12. How well did Saul follow God's instructions?

_____

_____

Why did Saul say he did what he did?

_____

_____

Saul's first test was a miserable failure. Instead of continuing to wait for Samuel to come with instructions from God, he saw the people scattering and took matters into his own hands. He usurped the priestly role and offered a burnt offering to unite the people and prepare for war. It was a classic example of situational ethics. Saul believed the situation warranted ignoring God's explicit instructions. But if we will simply walk in trusting obedience, we can trust the outcome to God.

📖 Read Samuel's indictment of Saul in verses 13, 14. What did Samuel say about Saul's actions (v. 13)?

_____

_____

What would be the consequences of Saul's actions (v. 14)?

_____

_____

_____

Samuel clearly identified Saul's actions as foolish disobedience. The result was Saul's rejection as a permanent leader. The clear indication is that Saul was not *"a man after* [God's] *own heart."*

Saul had the outside appearance of a king, but he lacked the right stuff on the inside. His poor self-image, his jealousy, his vengeful attitudes, all speak

Waiting on God means more than time. One of the most important factors in God's ways is obedience and trust in His timing.

 **DAY THREE**

Eventually, what is inside a man comes out—time reveals character.

of a man who would rule out of self-interest instead of serving the people by leading them in following God.

This biblical account speaks words of warning to us all. If fleshly desires rule in our hearts, we will look for the wrong kind of leaders. In 2 Timothy 4:3 Paul warns that a time will come when people will not endure sound doctrine, but *"they will accumulate for themselves teachers* **in accordance to their own desires***"* (emphasis added). I used to get mad at the preachers teaching heresy on television and radio, until the Lord reminded me that they wouldn't have the apparent success they enjoy unless people wanted to hear what they were saying. Saul is a sober reminder of the consequences of not following God.

SAUL'S IMPRUDENCE

Saul's reign as king began with some mighty military victories, but sadly, the farther his reign progressed, the more he revealed his true heart. In his war with the Philistines, he reveals again and again his lack of commitment to really seeking God.

In 1 Samuel 13 we saw that, instead of waiting in Gilgal until Samuel got there, Saul took matters into his own hands and usurped the priestly role by sacrificing the burnt offerings himself. When Samuel confronted him, Saul offered excuses but no valid reasons for his disobedience. He showed no evidence of remorse or repentance. Today we want to focus in on Saul's foolishness and see what we can learn from his mistakes.

📖 Read 1 Samuel 14. Identify from verse 24 the oath Saul required from his soldiers.

_____

_____

_____

From your knowledge of Saul so far, what do you think his motive was for requiring this oath?

_____

_____

_____

Saul was so intent on conquering the Philistines that he neglected the needs of his own men with a poorly conceived oath not to eat until evening comes and the battle is completely won. Saul probably thought that they shouldn't waste time on food when they had the chance to wipe out his enemies. In fact, lack of food probably made his troops less able to complete the task.

Saul's own son, Jonathan, unaware of his father's rash oath, ate some honey in front of the people. As we will see in a moment, Saul's foolishness would come back to haunt him.

📖 Look at verses 28–32. What were the results to the people of Saul's harsh oath?

_____

_____

_____

_____

Verse 28 indicates the people were weary, and verse 31 says they were *"very weary."* Jonathan accused his father of having *"troubled the land."* He indicates their success was not as great as it would have been if the people had been allowed to eat. At the end of the day, the men were so physically weakened that they rushed to the captured animals and began eating them with the blood still in them, a violation of the Law (Leviticus 17:10–14). Remember that people are a reflection of their leadership, and though the men feared violating the edict of the king to eat, they had fewer scruples about transgressing God's law.

As tired as his men were, Saul wanted to spend all night raiding the Philistine camps for the spoils of battle.

📖 Look at verse 36. Whose idea was it to ask God about the plan?

_____

It wasn't until after the priest suggested Saul seek God that he made inquiry of the Lord. This public request left Saul little choice but to comply. Notice that he had already told the people of his plan before he ever asked God about it.

When Saul finally sought God's direction about the plan for a night raid, God's silence caused Saul to look for sin in the camp. The drawing of lots singled out Jonathan, and once again we see Saul's impulsiveness. Saul declared a curse on himself if he didn't kill his son. He was more concerned about how his leadership was perceived than about truth and justice.

What had Jonathan done (v. 43)?

_____

_____

What had he violated?

_____

Had Jonathan done anything in violation of God's law that would warrant a sentence of death?

_____

What do you think would have been accomplished by his death?

_____

_____

Did You Know?
CASTING LOTS

Lots were sometimes used in the Middle East to determine matters of justice or in decision making. It was used in Joshua 7 in discovering the sin of Achan, in I Samuel 10 in the choice of Saul as king, and in one instance with Jonathan (I Samuel 14:36–46). Proverbs 16:33 and 18:18 speak of lots used in making decisions. Centuries later we read of it in the incident with the prophet Jonah on board the ship in the storm, and we see it in the New Testament in the choice of Matthias to replace Judas (Acts 1).

To seek God was not Saul's first thought. It was an afterthought.

Jonathan acted in innocent ignorance of Saul's foolish oath. He was not worthy of death before God. It was not God's righteousness, but only his father's pride, which must be satisfied. According to verse 45, the people recognized that Jonathan had *"worked with God"* to bring about their deliverance.

Again and again we see Saul's selfish pursuit of glory and success getting in the way of his following God. We would do well to take his life as a warning to ourselves.

Placed in a position beyond his abilities, Saul felt it was his responsibility to make sure everything was successful. God expects love and obedience from us, and obedience to Him will never negate what He wants to accomplish through our lives. Doing God's will God's way glorifies God. Trying to accomplish a work for Him in our own strength leads only to frustration and empty success.

If we only obey God when it fits with our plans, we really aren't obeying God, but our own desires.

Word Study
DEVOTED

The Hebrew word *charam* or *cherem* means "devoted" or "under the ban." Something "put under the ban" referred to something set aside totally for God's purposes. The spoils of Jericho were "devoted" or literally, "under the ban"— set apart, as it were, as firstfruits belonging to the Lord (Joshua 7). Leviticus 27:28 speaks of a devoted offering, and 27:29 speaks of a person under the ban, meaning that person was set apart for judgment to be executed for his sin. Amalek was among those under the ban ("utterly destroy"—I Samuel 15:3, 8–9, 18, 20) whose crimes merited execution as did the Canaanites of Joshua's day.

THE PERIL OF PARTIAL OBEDIENCE

Several years have passed in the reign of Saul, and he has been allowed by God to pursue his own ambitions. In 1 Samuel 15 we see God placing a new test in front of him—a new opportunity for him to demonstrate a willingness to fully follow God. The Amalekites were perhaps the most savage and inhumane of all the Canaanites, and during Israel's wilderness journey, they cruelly attacked God's people from the rear, killing the weak and elderly stragglers (Exodus 17:8–13). Verse 33 of 1 Samuel 15 indicates children were among their victims. Though five hundred years have passed since they were placed under divine judgment, God has not forgotten their wickedness. Saul was assigned the task of utterly destroying them (literally, "put under a ban"). This involved destroying the cities, killing all the inhabitants, and even destroying all their animals and possessions. Though quite severe, this was a just punishment, as God considered the land so stained by their sin that nothing was to be spared.

📖 Read 1 Samuel 15. According to verses 7–9, how much of God's command in verse 3 does Saul fulfill?

_____

_____

_____

Saul killed all the people except for Agag, the king, and he destroyed everything worthless, but saved the valuable things because, as the text says, *"Saul and the people . . . were not willing to destroy them utterly."* Saul probably saved Agag as a trophy of his victory, a common practice of the pagan nations. The greatest boast a conquering king could have would be to bring the vanquished king back in chains to be mocked and displayed.

📖 To us it appears that Saul was only partially obedient, but how did God view Saul's actions (v. 11)?

_____

_____

God says Saul has "...*turned back from* **following Me**, *and has not carried out My commands.*" Notice, God does not say that Saul only carried out part of His commands. What we would call partial obedience, God calls disobedience.

In verse 12 we see Saul's selfish focus reflected in the fact that he "*set up a monument for himself.*" His first comment when he saw Samuel the prophet was to affirm his obedience to God. Samuel, who already knew about Saul's disobedience, gave him an opportunity to repent by asking about the animal noises in the background.

📖 Look at verses 15, 20 and 21, and identify who Saul blames and how he excuses his disobedience.

_____

_____

_____

_____

In verse 15, trying to explain away the animals that should have been destroyed, we see Saul say "they" have brought them. He says "the people" spared the best, and then tries to excuse it by indicating their intent to use them for sacrifices. In verse 20 Saul proclaims his own obedience while again throwing the blame on the people in verse 21.

📖 What is Samuel's response in verses 22–23 to Saul's explanation of his lack of obedience?

_____

_____

_____

_____

Samuel made it clear that saving the animals for sacrifice was not the offering the Lord desired. God would rather have had Saul's obedience than his religious offerings. Animal sacrifices were simply an excuse, for as we saw in verse 9, the real problem was that Saul and the people "*were not willing*" to utterly destroy the animals. The fact that they saw value in them shows that they did not have God's perspective about sin.

Let's not be too quick to cast a judging eye on Saul and Israel. How often do we offer up our sacrifices of time, money, and praise on Sunday, when we have not been obedient throughout the week? It's easy to think we're doing fine because our actions fit the religious requirement, when our hearts are still full of sinful stubborn willfulness.

 Are there areas in your life in which you have been trying to substitute good things for obedience to the Lord?

Samuel's response makes it clear that the "sacrifice" excuse was unacceptable. The Lord prefers obedience over sacrifices, and it must not be forgotten that these animals were "under the ban." This means that they were so stained by sin that God would not allow Israel to keep them even though they were valuable. How could something under the ban have possibly been an acceptable

Partial obedience is disobedience.

"Has the Lord as much delight in burnt offerings and sacrifices as in obeying the voice of the Lord? Behold, to obey is better than sacrifice, and to heed than the fat of rams."
1 Samuel 15:22

sacrifice, when offerings were to be without blemish? Samuel equated Saul's rebellion with "divination," or witchcraft and his insubordination with "idolatry." Truly, failing to submit to God is idolatry, for it places our will over His and is practically a form of worshiping self. Even the good things in our life are worthless when they are corrupted by our willfulness.

📖 Read verses 24, 25 and 30. What signs do you see of Saul's repentance or lack of repentance in these verses?

_____

_____

_____

_____

We cannot look into Saul's heart, but we can observe his actions. His confession in verse 24, instead of including remorse, is couched with an excuse (again blaming the people). It is significant that Saul asks Samuel to pardon his sin, rather than asking God. Verse 30 reveals Saul cared more about his standing with the people than his standing with God. Notice he says "...that I may worship the LORD **your** God" (emphasis added).

Saul stands in stark contrast to king David, who though he sinned greatly, prayed that God might "create" in him a clean heart (Psalm 51:10). Saul only wanted his actions pardoned. We must not mistake remorse over the consequences of sin with true repentance. Saul acknowledged that he "transgressed the command of the LORD," but there is no indication that he saw himself as wrong in doing so. Quite to the contrary, he defended his actions. True confession is agreeing with God that an action is wrong and repenting of it. This is tragically absent in Saul.

If we are wise, we will learn from the mistakes of Saul.

Saul **DAY FIVE**

FOR ME TO FOLLOW GOD

Saul stands as a negative example of what it means to follow God. In his mistakes and the consequences of his wrong choices we have a tutor for our own walk with God. Saul graphically illustrates that we can never lead until we learn how to follow. God has a leadership role for every one of his children. If we are parents, God has placed us as leaders of our children. If we are husbands, he has placed us as leaders of our wives and homes. Sooner or later, we will probably have someone looking to us for leadership in our employment. Even if we never marry or have children, we will someday be the older ones in our churches and communities with the responsibility of leading the younger generation by our words and example. But we will never lead rightly until we learn how to follow God. Looking at the life of Saul, let's ask ourselves the hard questions his life raises as we seek to apply the Word to our lives.

📖 Read the following verses. In each case, where did Saul go wrong?

1 Samuel 10:8; 13:8–10

_____

_____

1 Samuel 15:2, 3, 8, 9

_____

_____

Saul had a basic problem obeying God, but what motivated that disobedience?

📖 Look carefully at each of the following verses. What appears to be behind Saul's disobedience?

1 Samuel 13:7–8

_____

_____

1 Samuel 15:15, 21, 24, 30

_____

_____

_____

Obedience to God seems like perhaps the most obvious, self-evident aspect of following God. But if that's the case, why are we so often disobedient? We don't take God seriously. The things of the world are blinding us from His way. Our own agenda is a greater motivation to us than our desire to follow God's agenda. We care too much what others think of us. Saul's primary motivation seems to be how he could best retain the support of the people. He was willing to sacrifice obedience to God on the altar of the approval of others.

📖 Read 1 Samuel 9:21; 10:21–22; and 15:17. How does it seem Saul viewed himself and his adequacy as king?

_____

_____

_____

_____

It appears that Saul was initially a reluctant king who did not think he was all that qualified for the job, but following God would have made Saul equal to any situation or task. Saul viewed success in the eyes of people rather than in the eyes of God. And Israel saw the same thing: strength in a king they could see and touch, a king that looked good to them and the surrounding nations. Because Saul's confidence was not in God to begin with, he was left on the shaky ground of gaining his confidence from the people he was supposed to be leading. Rather than leading the people by following God, Saul was continually being driven by public opinion.

This is not God's way. God outvotes public opinion. When our confidence is in ourselves and our own abilities rather than God and the work He will do through us, we leave ourselves open to the destructive pressures of the world and our own flesh.

 Have you seen any of these warning signs in your own life? (Check all that apply.)

> **Saul was willing to sacrifice obedience to God on the altar of the approval of others.**

_____You don't think you're good enough.

_____You always seek popular friends.

_____You get depressed when criticized.

_____Your value as a person is based on your achievements.

_____It's always your fault when people misunderstand you.

_____Your decisions are dependent on the approval of others.

_____You are easily intimidated by people and situations.

In our lives "public opinion" is called peer pressure. Maybe we're trying to live up to our spouse's expectations. Maybe we're striving to prove ourselves to a boss. If you are single, maybe you're trying to be good enough to attract a mate. Maybe you're trying to impress your pastor and the people in your church. Or maybe you are a pastor and you're trying to live up to your congregation's expectations!

In any of these cases, we're looking to the wrong people. They will never hold us to a high enough standard. The standard we should be aiming for is God's . . . the impossible standard. But fortunately, He has promised to accomplish it in us.

📖 Read Romans 8:29. What is God's standard for us?

_____

_____

God's standard for us is to *"become conformed to the image of His Son,"* but how is this accomplished?

📖 How does Galatians 2:20 say this happens in our lives?

_____

_____

_____

📖 Read Philippians 2:13. Whose work is this?

_____

_____

📖 According to Philippians 1:6, what will He do?

_____

_____

> **When our confidence is in ourselves and our own abilities rather than in God and the work He will do through us, we leave ourselves open to the destructive pressures of the world and our own flesh.**

Conformity to Christ means more than just imitation of Christ. It means *being* like Him, having His nature. There's no way we can work our way into conformity to Christ. The only way we can be conformed to Him is if He lives His life in and through us, and that requires dying to ourselves—our own agendas and desires. It means dying to our own dreams so God can give us His dreams for our lives.

Accomplishing God's aims for our lives is not in our striving, but in His *"work in [us], both to will and to work for His good pleasure"* (Philippians 2:13). The work that He begins, He will perfect in us. The Greek word translated "perfect," *epiteleo,* means to finish or complete. God is working in our lives to complete us, to make us like Christ.

So what does this mean as we seek to follow God every day? How does it affect our lives so that they will not be marked by the disobedient spirit of Saul? First, we need to get God's perspective on our circumstances.

📖 Read Romans 8:28. What does God say about the situations He allows in our lives?

_____

_____

If we love God and are seeking Him, even when we mess up He'll work it out to our good and His glory.

📖 In Matthew 22:37–39, what does Jesus say should be the priorities in our lives?

_____

_____

By nature, every one of us is the center of our own universe. But God wants our focus off of ourselves and onto Himself first, and others second. Basically, God wants to change *our* perspective to *His* perspective. He wants us to see everything around us with His eyes, and to respond with His heart. He wants our lives to be totally wrapped up in Him.

This is His work, and there is nothing we can do in and of ourselves to accomplish it. But we can open up our hearts and lives to allow Him to work as He wills. Here are a few things that can help us begin to do that:

✓ First, we can realize that it is completely *His* work. God is God and you are not. Stop trying to control your life and give the reins over to Him.

✓ Second, open your heart up to Him in prayer. When your heart is full of love and joy in Him, tell Him so! And when you feel distant from Him and don't want to pray or seek after Him, tell Him that too, and ask Him to change your heart.

✓ Third, renew your mind in His Word. Listen to Him. Make yourself available to Him every day in His Word, and let His Spirit teach you what He will.

As you do these things, He daily changes your perspective to be more and more like His.

Take some time in prayer with your merciful Father right now.

 Lord, forgive me for my distraction with the stuff of the world. I have allowed the opinions of so many others to come before You in my life. Teach me to cherish obedience to You over the acceptance and approval of others. Help me to live daily in the understanding that what You have for my life is so much greater than anything I can imagine. I trust You to bring it to pass. Forgive me for my sin and straying. Teach me to turn to You each morning and follow you all day, every day for the rest of my life. In Jesus' name, Amen.

CHRIST IS PREEMINENT

"All things have been created by Him and for Him [Jesus Christ]. And He is before all things, and in Him all things hold together. He is also head of the body, the church, and He is the beginning, the first-born from the dead; so that He Himself might come to have first place in everything." Colossians 1:16b–18

Write out your own prayer, remembering that God is seeking a relationship with you.

_____

_____

_____

_____

_____

_____

_____

_____

_____

Notes

Notes

A HEART TO FOLLOW GOD

David reigned over all Israel from 1011 to 971 BC. The prophets who ministered in his life and reign include Samuel, Nathan, and Gad.

We have seen that God created man to bear His image, to bear fruit, and to reign, but sin has stained all of that and marred God's purpose. We were created to follow God, to respond always and only to Him. But to give that choice meaning and to keep us from being mere puppets, God also created us with the ability to choose, even to choose not to follow Him. As we saw last week in the life of king Saul, man can choose to follow his own will instead of following God, but when we turn aside from following God, we always end up going after *"futile things which can not profit or deliver"* (1 Samuel 12:21). Whenever we turn away from God, we turn to a lie. When Jesus reached a point in His ministry of teaching the hard truths of God, the Bible says in John 6:66, *"As a result of this many of His disciples withdrew, and were not walking with Him anymore."* Jesus then asked the twelve, *"You do not want to go away also, do you?"* Peter's response speaks wisdom to us also: *"Lord, to whom shall we go? You have words of eternal life."* Whenever I turn from following God, I turn to a lie. This week in the life of king David we see what it means for fallen man to follow God. It is an imperfect pursuit, and yet David was called *"a man after [God's] own heart."* How could this be? How could a man after God's own heart sin? How can a sinner be a man after God's own heart?

Following God is a pursuit, not an arrival.

WHEN DID HE REIGN?

1050		1000	950		900		850	
SAMUEL	GAD			SHEMAIAH	IDDO Hanani the Seer		OBADIAH	JOEL
Judge and Prophet		NATHAN			ODED	Jahaziel the Levite		
					AZARIAH			
				Rehoboam 931–913	Asa 911–870	Jehoshaphat 873–848	Jehoram (Joram)	Ahaziah 841 Joash 835–796
Saul 1051–1011		David 1011–971	Solomon 971–931		Abijam 913–911		853–841 Athaliah 841–835	
				Jeroboam I 931–910	Nadab Elah Zimri 910–909 886–885 885		Ahaziah 853–852	Jehu 841–814
		Ishbosheth ruled over Israel 1011–1004	960—Temple finished		Baasha 909–886	Tibni Ahab 885–880 874–853	Jehoram (Joram)	
		David ruled over Judah from Hebron 1011–1004				Omri 885–874	852–841	
				AHIJAH the Shilonite "A man of God from Judah" A prophet from Samaria in Bethel			JEHU, son of Hanani MICAIAH	
		David ruled over all Israel and Judah from Jerusalem 1004–971					ELIJAH	ELISHA
		Hiram I of Tyre 981–947			Benhadad I of Syria 900–860		Benhadad II of Syria 860–841	

GOD LOOKS AT THE HEART

The reason God rejected the kingship of Saul is the same reason He chose David as his replacement. In 1 Samuel 13:14 we see that God rejects Saul because *"The LORD has sought out for Himself a man after His own heart."* Acts 13:22 puts it this way: *"And after He had removed him, He raised up David to be their king, concerning whom He also testified and said, 'I HAVE FOUND DAVID the son of Jesse, A MAN AFTER MY HEART, who will do all My will.'"*

When Israel wanted a king, they were looking at the outside. They wanted a Saul who was taller than anyone else, better looking than anyone else, and from a better family than anyone else. God gave them what they wanted so He could teach them to start wanting the right things. When Samuel was sent to anoint a new king from Jesse's sons he wanted to pick Eliab, the oldest. But God says in 1 Samuel 16:7, *"Do not look at his appearance or at the height of his stature, because I have rejected him; for God sees not as man sees, for man looks at the outward appearance, but the LORD looks at the heart."*

You may not have as much going for you as the next person. They may be taller and better looking. They may come from a better family. They may be the older and you the younger. But God isn't looking at any of that. All He wants is someone with a heart to follow Him, a heart after His own heart. David was such a man, and each of us can be too. Let's take a closer look at his life.

David and Goliath

While Saul was still king and David was only a youth, a man arose from the Philistines who struck terror in the hearts of the armies of Israel. He was nine and a half feet tall and his armor weighed almost as much as David. Twice a day for more than a month he taunted the soldiers of Saul. When Israel's trained warriors looked at Goliath, they looked up and saw a giant. When David looked at Goliath, he looked higher and saw God. In 1 Samuel 17:26 David responds, *". . . who is this uncircumcised Philistine, that he should taunt the armies of the living God?"* David saw God alone as the one to be reckoned with. Goliath was an uncircumcised (ungodly) pagan who did not stand a chance against the living God. When word reached Saul that there was one who was not afraid of Goliath, he sent for him, but he was doubtful.

📖 Read 1 Samuel 17:23–27 and 31–37. According to David, who was going to kill Goliath and why (vv. 36–37)?

_____

_____

_____

_____

Even though David's victories had never made the newspapers, he had seen God deliver him from both the lion and the bear. David had the wisdom to recognize that it was God who had delivered him then, and he was able to trust that since Goliath was blaspheming God, the Lord would not allow him to prosper in this battle.

A heart to follow God is a heart to do His will.

Why do you think God allowed David to face the lion and the bear?

_____

_____

_____

📖 Read the rest of the story in verses 38–58. What, according to David, was Goliath trusting in for his deliverance (vv. 45–46)?

_____

_____

What was David trusting in, according to these verses?

_____

_____

We can see from what David said that Goliath was trusting in his sword, spear and javelin. This implies that Goliath trusted in his own strength and skill. In contrast, it is evident that David's trust was in *"the name of the LORD of hosts, the God of the armies of Israel."* He was not trusting his slingshot; he was trusting God. He says, *"This day the LORD will deliver you up into my hands."* God had allowed David to face wild animals alone in the wilderness so that he could experience the strength and deliverance of God in his life. Those experiences gave David a rock solid trust in God to rest in—no matter what situation he faced.

APPLY What is the most recent situation God has used in your life to teach you to trust and rely on Him?

_____

_____

_____

How has this affected other areas of your life?

_____

_____

_____

Sometimes God puts experiences in our lives to teach us to trust Him to take us through them. Often, when we're in the midst of a trial or a test, we're so focused on just getting out, that we don't stop to look for God *in* the trial. We're crawling around trying to get out so we can find God, and all the while He's standing right beside us waiting for us to take His hand and follow Him through to the other side. Those are the times when we really get to know God and learn to follow Him with all our hearts.

📖 What is God's message to all the earth through this battle according to verse 46?

_____

_____

_____

Did You Know?
WERE THE WEAPONS OF THE ISRAELITES MORE ADVANCED?

The Philistines were technologically superior to the Israelites who were primarily farmers and herders. They did extensive work in iron and other metals as is evidenced from Goliath's armor. The Israelites had very little armor. The Israelites were no match for their technology, but then God does not depend on technology to accomplish His will, does He?

God delivered David so that *"all the earth may know that there is a God in Israel."* God was giving testimony of himself—He was proving who He is to all who could see.

What was God's message to the armies of Israel in this victory (v. 47)?

_____

_____

_____

God's message to Israel was that He does not deliver by the might of man—*"by sword or by spear."* Victory does not depend on our strengths, abilities or resources. Victory always belongs to God, and it is He who gives it to us. The battles we face do not come to us apart from God, but by His hand for the purpose of glorifying Him.

From what you have observed about David to this point, what evidence do you see that David had a heart after God's heart?

_____

_____

_____

The first sign we see that David has a heart after God is his ability to see that *"the battle is the Lord's."* The focus is on the Lord, not the battle. Following God does not mean fighting great battles for God. It means letting God lead you into the battles He wants so He can show both the world and the people of God what He can do through a yielded heart.

GOD'S WILL GOD'S WAY

One of the greatest evidences of a heart after God's heart is someone who is willing to let God do His will, His way. Human striving is evidence of trust in self. Surrender is evidence of trusting that God can and will do what He intends. We see this principle illustrated in David's ascendancy to the throne of Israel. Immediately after Saul was rejected by God, Samuel anointed David for the first time as a sign that he would be king (1 Samuel 16). But years will pass before God will bring this plan to fruition. Jealousy moved Saul against David, and he repeatedly tried to get rid of him.

You would think that if the tables were turned and David had the chance to do away with Saul, he would. After all, he *was* to replace Saul as king, and Saul *was* trying to kill him: three times he hurled a spear at David (1 Samuel 18:11; 19:10). Saul did everything he could to put him in harm's way with the Philistines (1 Samuel 18:17, 25), and even commanded hit squads to kill David (1 Samuel 19:1, 11, 15). Surely David would be justified in bringing this drama to a quick end. It would practically have been an act of self-defense.

Did You Know?

WHY DOES GOD WORK THROUGH MEN AND WOMEN?

The work of God through Joshua and the Israelites, almost 400 years before, had the same purpose as David's victory over Goliath—"that all the peoples of the earth may know that the hand of the Lord is mighty, so that you may fear the Lord your God forever" (Joshua 4:24). God's work in and through our lives has the same purpose—that through you people will know the Lord is alive and is God.

📖 Read 1 Samuel chapter 24. What reasons did David give for not killing Saul in the following verses?

v. 6 _____

v. 10 _____

v. 12 _____

v. 15 _____

The first reason we see that David chose not to kill Saul was "...*because of the LORD*" (v. 6). We also see that David refused to touch Saul because he was the Lord's anointed—God's appointed authority (vv. 6, 10). When authority does not follow God, the Lord wants us to honor the position even if we can't honor the person. A third reason that David spared Saul is the confidence that the Lord would judge between them (v. 12) and plead David's case (v. 15). Fourth, we see that David understood the Lord would avenge him against Saul (v. 12). "*VENGEANCE IS MINE*," says the Lord, "*I WILL REPAY*" (Hebrews 10:30). When we follow God, we can let Him fight our battles. David recognized that it was not his job, but God's, to make him king.

📖 In 1 Samuel 26 the Lord delivered Saul into David's hands a second time. Read the chapter, and write down the reasons David gave for not killing Saul in the following verses.

v. 9 _____

v. 10 _____

v. 23 _____

v. 24 _____

Again we see that David didn't kill Saul because he was "*the LORD's anointed*" (v. 9) and to do him harm would have brought guilt regardless of how poor a king he was. Second, we see that David acknowledged that it was God's job to bring about Saul's death as He saw fit (v. 10). A third truth here is that David trusted the Lord to repay righteous deeds, such as David's, as well as evil, such as Saul's (v. 23). Finally, David saw God, not self, as his deliverer (v. 24).

We want to look at David's response to the news of Saul's eventual death, remembering all that Saul had done against David. Saul's death freed David from any fear of retribution, and his heart towards Saul shows through.

📖 Read 2 Samuel 1:1–16. What was David's immediate response at the news of Saul's death (vv. 11–12)?

_____

_____

_____

How did David respond to the Amalekite who brought him the news (vv. 13–16)?

_____

_____

_____

> **David recognized that it was not his job, but God's, to make him king.**

It is amazing to see how David responded when he found out that his rival was dead. David mourned the death of Saul, even though Saul had tried to kill him (vv. 11–12). Then we see that David punished the man who claimed to have killed Saul (vv. 13–16) because those actions dishonored the position of the king, *"the LORD's anointed."*

📖 Read 2 Samuel 1:17–27. How did David memorialize Saul and Jonathan (vv. 17–19)?

_____

How did David describe Saul in this song?

_____

_____

_____

_____

David set up a song of remembrance to be taught to the children so Saul and Jonathan would not be forgotten throughout Israel's history (v. 17). There was no sign of the enmity between Saul and David in the song. Saul was described as "mighty," "beloved and pleasant," "swifter than eagles," and "stronger than lions." David credited him with the prosperity of Israel.

📖 Read 2 Samuel 2:4–7. How did David respond to those who buried Saul's body?

_____

_____

_____

David honored and blessed those who gave Saul a proper burial. What a beautiful picture we see in David of someone who trusts God instead of becoming bitter over those who sought to harm him.

APPLY When you are faced with someone who is working against you, and perhaps against God as well, how do you usually respond?

_____

_____

_____

📖 Read Luke 6:27–35. How does Jesus tell us to respond to our enemies?

_____

_____

_____

_____

This is behavior that seems incomprehensible to the world, and even to many Christians. Our flesh would tell us that we have rights and a reputation to protect. But we are redeemed (purchased) by God, and we are not our own (1 Corinthians 6:19–20). The rights and reputation are God's, and He is fully able to protect them.

KEEP A GOOD CONSCIENCE

"Keep your behavior excellent among the Gentiles, so that in the thing in which they slander you as evildoers, they may on account of your good deeds, as they observe them, glorify God in the day of visitation. . . . And keep a good conscience so that in the thing in which you are slandered, those who revile your good behavior in Christ may be put to shame. For it is better, if God should will it so, that you suffer for doing what is right rather than for doing what is wrong" (1 Peter 2:12; 3:16–17).

📖 Saul was dead, and David knew that he is the Lord's anointed as the next king. Look at 2 Samuel 2:1–4 and identify what David does first.

_____

_____

Instead of taking matters into his own hands, David's first response after the death of Saul is to inquire of the Lord. He is following God, not following his own ambition, or even following God's plan. Often, we act as if God's primary interest is in us accomplishing His plan, when in fact, He wants us simply to follow Him. The results are in His hands. There is a difference between following God and following God's plan. We must seek for God's will to be done in God's way, and that is what David did.

Unlike the battle with Goliath, the battle for the crown of Israel was not one God had called David to fight. And David followed God in this as well, even though it meant not striking out in defense of himself or of God's revealed plan for his life. David's heart sought God for God's sake, not just because it seemed right, or for the blessings and benefits he might receive.

FALLEN MAN FOLLOWING GOD

 *David* DAY THREE

David was now king. It took years for God's plan to come to fruition, but there is no doubt in anyone's mind that God did it, not David. Unlike Saul, David was a man after God's own heart. But like the rest of us, he was a fallen man. A heart after God's own heart did not mean that he would not sin, but it did mean that when he did sin, he dealt with it God's way. As we paint the portrait of this man of God, we are going to see some very candid snapshots of his life, and some of them are not so flattering. But even in seeing this very human side of David, we will see a heart to follow God.

The first incident we want to look at is David's moving of the ark of God to Jerusalem. His initial attempt ended in abject failure because he didn't do it God's way. The Law was explicit that the ark was only to be moved by priests carrying it by poles in the rings on the sides. But in 2 Samuel 6 we see David and his company placed the ark on a new cart. Where do you suppose David got the idea of using a cart? Perhaps he got it from the Philistines who had captured the ark more than a century earlier (1 Samuel 4, 5). But the ark had brought only peril and plague to them, so, we are told in 1 Samuel 6:7, the Philistines sent it back to Israel on a new cart. Placing efficiency above strict obedience, David apparently tried to save time by using this Philistine method to move the ark. But then the cart hit a bump in the road, the ark tipped, and Uzzah took hold of it, another violation of the Law. God struck him dead for his irreverence. This would have never happened if David had done things God's way. After three months of waiting, David made a second attempt to move the ark.

📖 Read 2 Samuel 6 and identify how the ark is transported the second time. You'll have to look closely.

_____

_____

Verse 13 speaks of *"the bearers of the ark."* This verse also tells us they had gone six "paces" or steps. Apparently David had learned his lesson. Now we see that the ark was being carried by hand as the Law required, instead of hauled on a cart as the Philistines had done.

APPLY What does this incident tell you about how having a heart after God's heart will affect the way you handle mistakes?

_____

_____

_____

_____

A heart after God does not mean the absence of mistakes, but it does mean that we are quick to correct our mistakes. Spiritual health is reflected more in how we handle our mistakes than in the mistakes themselves. A man with a heart after God's heart will always keep coming back to follow God.

The next incident we want to observe in David's life moves us ahead a few years. The kingdom was prospering under David's reign. In the spring of the year when kings were supposed to go into battle, David decided to take a vacation. He must have been staying up late and sleeping in, for 2 Samuel 11:2 tells us *". . . when evening came David arose from his bed."* He went for a stroll and temptation found him in the form of Bathsheba taking a bath. He lusted after her and used his kingly influence to lay with her. To make matters worse, when he found out she was pregnant, he first tried to bring her husband home from the war to sleep with her so none would be the wiser. But Uriah was too good a soldier to seek wifely pleasures when he should have been back at the battle. When David realized his plan had failed, he had Uriah sent on a suicide mission, effectively committing murder. Now he was free to take Bathsheba as his wife, but his sin was not hidden from God. When Nathan the prophet confronted him, he acknowledged his sin.

But there were still consequences to David's sin even though he was repentant, for the child born to Bathsheba was stricken by the Lord and died. David's response to the news of his son's death tells us much about his heart.

📖 Look at 2 Samuel 12:19–20. How did David respond to the child's death?

_____

_____

After David learned of his son's death, he went into the house of the Lord and worshiped. He was not bitter against God, but accepted the outcome.

📖 Read verses 24–25. Who was David's second son with Bathsheba?

_____

_____

What was God's response to this child?

_____

> *Spiritual health is reflected more in how we handle our mistakes than in the mistakes themselves. A man with a heart after God's heart will always keep coming back to follow God.*

What does this tell you about grace?

_____

_____

_____

How amazing it is that God would choose for the kingly line to be continued through Bathsheba and not one of David's other wives. So precious to God is this son, Solomon, that He sent word through Nathan the prophet and renamed him "Jedidiah" (beloved of the Lord).

APPLY Write out the last time God, in His grace, took sin in your life and worked it to His purpose and your good.

_____

_____

_____

_____

Sometimes, because of our sins and failures, we want to write off a part of our lives. But God wants to work in and through those very things. The birth of Solomon did not erase David and Bathsheba's sin, but their repentant hearts allowed God to work in the situation and the result was Israel's wisest king. God, in His sovereignty, takes the pieces of our lives marred by sin but offered freely to Him and works them together to good.

One final incident from David's life will give us yet another look at how he dealt with his failures. In 2 Samuel 24 we find David calling his military leaders to take a census of the nation in order to determine how big of an army he had. Joab, his chief of staff, counseled him against this, perceiving a trust in numbers instead of a trust in God, but David did it anyway. The result was a plague that killed seventy thousand people.

📖 Read 2 Samuel 24, and identify David's response to his sin in each of the verses below:

v. 10 _____

_____

v. 14 _____

_____

v. 17 _____

_____

vv. 24–25_____

_____

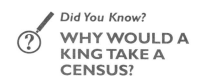

Did You Know?

WHY WOULD A KING TAKE A CENSUS?

A census of a nation's armed forces was a way to assess one's strength, to boast in one's might, or to prepare for further military campaigns. God wanted David to do none of these things.

In verse 10 we see that although David made a foolish mistake, he was troubled about his sin and confessed it. No prophet was needed to point it out. In verse 14, David trusted himself and the nation to God. In verse 17, further evidence that David's repentance was from the heart is the fact that he asked God to pour His wrath on him instead of the people. Finally, we see in verses 24, 25 that David refused to worship the Lord in a manner that cost him nothing.

Having a heart after God's heart means that even a sinner can follow God so long as he is willing to face his sin and deal with it God's way. That is what separated David from king Saul—a repentant heart, a heart that turns from sin to God. There is much we can learn about following God from this shepherd boy turned king of Israel.

David DAY FOUR

CREATE IN ME A CLEAN HEART

Perhaps nowhere is David's heart for God seen more clearly than in Psalm 51, the psalm of repentance he wrote after his sin with Bath-sheba. As we seek to see what it takes to have a heart after God's heart, this contrite sinner's prayer for pardon will give us a more detailed look at how a sinner can keep following God—by dealing with his sin. Sin could not be swept under the rug, it must be put under the mercy of the blood.

📖 To start today, read through Psalm 51. Take your time—it would even be a good idea to read it twice.

One of the marks of genuine repentance is taking full responsibility for our own choices. As we saw repeatedly, king Saul when confronted with his sin was quick to "pass the buck" by blaming others. He had a victim mentality. How was David's heart different?

📖 Read Psalm 51:3–4. How did David view his sin?

_____

_____

_____

_____

David took full responsibility for his sin and blamed no one else. Even though his sin affected others, he recognized that it was God's law he had violated and that it was God he had offended. He offered no defense or excuses. An important part of repentance is agreeing with God about our sin. And as we begin to see the sin in our lives the way God sees it and repent, we will also begin to see the sin that confronts us with temptation each day the way God sees it and learn to turn from that temptation.

📖 Look at each of the following verses. What was David asking God to do in his life?

v. 2 _____

_____

v. 7 _____

_____

v. 10 _____

_____

v. 11 _____

_____

v. 12 _____

_____

It is important to see that David was not merely asking that his sin be for-given. In verse 2 he asked to be washed thoroughly and "cleansed." In verse 7 he requested the priestly purification of hyssop and literally says, "mayest Thou wash me." Verse 10 is most significant, for he called on God to create *a clean heart* in him. David was not merely looking for removal of the con-sequences; he wanted his heart changed to what God wanted it to be.

In verse 11, he sought the presence of God in his life, and in verse 12 he asked God to sustain in him *a willing spirit,* pliable to God's work in his life. David wanted a restored relationship with God, and he knew his sin was a barrier to that relationship. But he also knew that God in His abun-dant mercy could restore and sustain that relationship.

📖 Identify from verses 16–19 the kind of sacrifice God desires for our sins.

_____

_____

_____

God is not interested in religious compensation for our sins. He wants bro-kenness. When our hearts are made right, then and only then do our offer-ings and sacrifices—and our works of service—have any meaning to God.

📖 Read Micah 6:6–8. What does the Lord require of us?

_____

_____

We will not win God's heart with mere acts of service, but with a heart that loves what He loves (justice and kindness) and humbly seeks His presence. A heart after God's heart—that is the goal. It is this kind of heart that God desires, and only God can make this kind of heart. That is why we see David calling on God to *"create in me a clean heart."* Following God is not an arrival where the journey is completed. It is a pursuit we keep returning to, and each time our hearts are stained with sin, we must call on God to recreate His heart in us.

Did You Know?
WHAT IS THE SIGNIFICANCE OF HYSSOP?

Hyssop was used to dip the blood of the Passover lamb out of the basin and to place it on the lintel and doorposts of Israelite homes on the night of the first Passover in Egypt (Exodus 12:21–28). It was used by the priests in the cleansing ceremony for a healed leper (Leviticus 14:1–9). It was part of the mixture burned with the red heifer to create the ashes used for cleansing (Numbers 19:6), and its leafy branch was also used for sprinkling that ash mixture mixed with water for ceremonial cleansing (Numbers 19:18). David knew that hys-sop spoke of cleansing.

FOR ME TO FOLLOW GOD

David **DAY FIVE**

David . . . the man after God's own heart. Let's look back and review some of what that meant in David's life.

As a youth with no experience in battle, David volunteered to fight the giant, Goliath. King Saul was skeptical, but he allowed David to represent Israel.

Read 1 Samuel 17:37, 45–47. On what one thing was David focused?

_____

_____

Victory in this situation depends upon (choose one):

_____David's skills

_____Goliath's weakness

_____David's courage

_____God

_____The support of the king

_____David's faithful life

David was looking to God for the victory. He was focused on the Lord rather than on the battle. The circumstances didn't matter as long as God was in the picture. David's heart attitude was one of reliance on God. His own abilities were irrelevant to the outcome—he was simply a willing instrument for God to use.

APPLY What does it mean to have a heart after God's own heart? Choose one.

_____Getting the job done for God.

_____Working harder and smarter than normal.

_____Focusing on God, allowing Him to do His work through you.

God has given each of us gifts and abilities. They are not there for our benefit, but for His glory. It is important for us to keep our focus and trust on our Provider, and not the circumstances or even His provision.

Years later, Saul became threatened by David's popularity and the blessing of God on his life and sought to kill him. David had already been anointed by Samuel as the future king, so how did he handle this persecution?

Read 1 Samuel 24:12, 15. What did David believe God would do?

_____

_____

_____

What did he see that he was responsible to do?

_____

_____

Read 1 Samuel 26:23–24. What did David trust the Lord to do?

_____

_____

David trusted God to work out His will His way.

David trusted God to work out His will His way. God's will for David's life was not something David had to accomplish or make happen. David was only responsible to faithfully follow God day by day and let God take care of the outcome. David's heart was more interested in following after God's heart than any ambitions he might have, and he was willing to wait for God's time.

But David didn't always faithfully follow God. When he followed his own selfish desire for Bathsheba he fell into great sin. A heart after God's heart is not perfect, but we can learn much from his response to God in this situation.

📖 Read 2 Samuel 12:13 and Psalm 51:4. Who did David say his sin was against?

_____

Look closely at verse 4. By what has David determined the evil he has done?

_____

David was agreeing with God about his sin. He was learning to see sin from God's perspective. This is what 1 John 1:9 is telling us to do when it instructs us to "confess" our sins. The Greek word used means "to speak the same with, or consent to the desire of another." The heart following God will name the sin in our lives as He names it and share His attitude in dealing with it.

🛑 APPLY Is there sin in your life which you have hesitated to acknowledge for what it is? If so, stop now and bring it before the Lord. Psalm 51:6 says, *"Thou dost desire truth in the innermost being, And in the hidden part Thou wilt make me know wisdom."* God wants us to be honest with ourselves and Him about our sin, and He is willing to help us. Ask Him to give you His perspective.

📖 Read Psalm 51:7. Who will purify and cleanse the heart stained by sin?

_____

_____

There is nothing we can do to cleanse our own hearts. All the determination in the world to do better will get us nowhere. Determination is not the answer. Surrender is the answer, surrender of our hearts, wills and lives to God. His is the washing that truly cleans our hearts.

📖 Read Psalm 51:10–12. How is David going to continue in God's ways?

_____

_____

It is God who sustains in us His spirit of obedience, God who holds us steadfast. Following God doesn't come to a dead halt when we mess up and then start all over again at the beginning. Following God is a learning process that only grows as we allow God to teach us to deal with sin His way.

In each of these situations, David sought God's will and way, not what would appear to be safe, comfortable, or in his own best interest. He trusted God with the final outcome. But these attitudes are simply evidences of David's heart for God, for God referred to him as *"a man after My own heart,"* before we were even introduced to David in Scripture (1 Samuel 13:14). The evidence of David's heart after God's heart was seen in David's focus on God rather than on his circumstances, in his waiting on God to accomplish His will in His way and time, and in his repentant attitude when he sinned. What motivated David to live this way? A personal, intimate relationship with God. Let's look at what David himself had to say about that relationship.

Put Yourself in Their Shoes
TRUTHFULNESS IN THE INNER MAN

God has always wanted truthfulness in the innermost part of a man or woman. The first question posed to Adam was "where are you?" meaning more than location. The Lord wanted Adam to admit where he was in his relationship with the Lord. Why was he hiding and covering himself with fig leaves? "Where are you? What is true of you, Adam, in the inner man?" John 4 reminds us that the Father seeks those who *"will worship Him in spirit and truth"*—from the heart with a cleansed conscience. That also means those who are truthful in spirit. Ephesians 6 tells us the first piece of armor is the belt of truth which implies truthfulness—an open, honest heart. God wants truthfulness in the innermost being. David understood that.

📖 Read Psalm 63:1–8. What heart attitudes do you see David expressing to God?

_____

_____

_____

_____

✎ _Did You Know?_

WHERE DO YOU TURN WHEN YOUR NEED IS GREAT?

Psalm 63 was written by David out of his experience in the barren Judean wilderness in a time of great need. It was written either when he was running from Saul (1 Samuel 23) or when he was running from Absalom (2 Samuel 15)—in either case David was seeking to follow the Lord with a whole heart.

We see here, better than perhaps anywhere else, the yearning of David's heart for God. He had found in God the satisfaction of his soul, and he would cling to Him. David had a relationship with God that was marked by intimacy, and that kind of relationship is available to each of us today.

None of us follow God perfectly: we all bear the consequences of a stubborn sin nature, and David was no exception. His sin was on an even grander scale than many of us can comprehend. And yet He was beloved of God, _"a man after My own heart,"_ the Lord said. And if you're much like me, those words tug at your heart, and you feel like there's some elusive part of the equation that you're missing in your relationship with God. There seems to be such intimacy between God and David. How can we have that? How can somebody as imperfect as I am have that kind of relationship with the infinitely perfect God of the universe?

The only thing that makes that relationship possible is the fact that God seeks it with us. It is because of His powerful grace and mercy that we can _"walk humbly with_ [our] _God"_ (Micah 6:8). And there are some steps He has given us to help us get started.

- ✓ First, realize that God is God and you're not. We often give God lip-service but act as if the outcome, in reality, depends on us. God is fully capable of accomplishing His will His way, and He invites us to come along for the ride.

- ✓ Second, He has revealed Himself to us in His Word, the Bible. A heart seeking His heart will saturate itself in His Word daily, seeking to make God's truth the foundation of his life.

- ✓ Third, as we continually seek Him in prayer, He will guide us into that intimate relationship with Him which will be evidenced outwardly in our lives for all around us to see.

What does it take to be a man or woman after God's own heart? A heart wholly seeking Him. For He has promised that if we seek Him, we will find Him. _"And you will seek Me and find Me, when you search for Me with all your heart"_ (Jeremiah 29:13).

Spend some time in prayer with the Lord right now.

 Father, I want a heart after Your heart. More than I want to do great service for You, I want to know You and simply follow You. Make me sensitive to the sin that leads me astray. I want to see it with Your eyes. Renew my mind and heart, and lead me in Your ways. Teach me to trust you when circumstances are against me. May my entire life be a response of praise and surrender to You alone. In Jesus' name, Amen.

JEO

Write out your own prayer. Ask Him to give you a heart to follow Him.

_____

_____

_____

_____

_____

_____

_____

_____

_____

_____

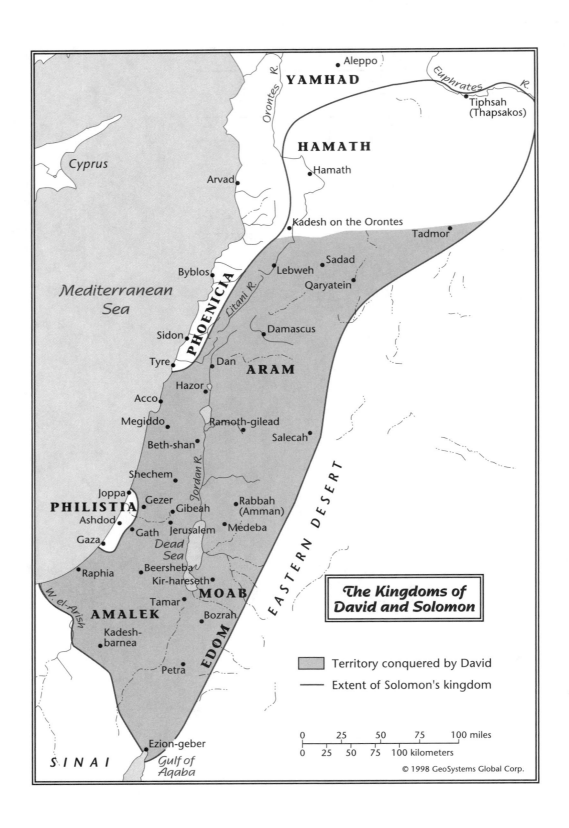

Cyprus

Mediterranean Sea

YAMHAD

Aleppo

Orontes R.

Euphrates R.

Tiphsah
(Thapsakos)

HAMATH

Hamath

Arvad

Kadesh on the Orontes

Tadmor

Byblos

Lebweh
Sadad
Qaryatein

Litani R.

PHOENICIA

Sidon

Damascus

Tyre

Dan

ARAM

Hazor

Acco

Megiddo

Ramoth-gilead

Salecah

Beth-shan

Jordan R.

EASTERN DESERT

Shechem

Joppa

Gezer

Rabbah
(Amman)

PHILISTIA

Gibeah

Ashdod

Jerusalem

Medeba

Gaza

Gath

Dead Sea

Raphia

Beersheba

Kir-hareseth

W. el-Arish

Tamar

MOAB

AMALEK

Bozrah

Kadesh-barnea

EDOM

Petra

Ezion-geber

SINAI

Gulf of Aqaba

The Kingdoms of David and Solomon

Territory conquered by David

Extent of Solomon's kingdom

0   25   50   75   100 miles
0 25 50 75 100 kilometers

© 1998 GeoSystems Global Corp.

Notes

Notes

Solomon

FOLLOWING GOD: GUARDING YOUR HEART

The life of Solomon is one of the most unique in all of Scripture and history as well. Acclaimed as the richest king to ever rule, he has some things to teach us about riches. Proclaimed in his own day as the wisest ruler, he has some things to show us about wisdom—what it can do and what it cannot do. The Temple he built is still spoken of as one of the most beautiful structures ever built. His life speaks to us about the works of God and with that, about the worship of the one true God and the folly of any detours into idolatry. A look at the walk of Solomon and how he followed God will instruct us in the paths we take and the way we follow Him. One thing is certain, Solomon would tell us to hear God's Word and guard our hearts with all diligence if we are to follow God and enjoy our walk with Him.

Despite his great wisdom, Solomon gradually forsook the one true God and the blessings God had poured out upon him, exchanging them for fleshly lusts and idolatry. We must remember that riches and wisdom cannot buy righteousness, nor can they be used to buy back our souls from wickedness.

Solomon, the second son of David and Bathsheba, reigned over united Israel from 971 to 931 BC. Interestingly, there is no record of a prophet ministering in the time of Solomon until the very end of his reign when Ahijah prophesied the division of the Kingdom.

"The conclusion, when all has been heard, is: fear God and keep His commandments, because this applies to every person. For God will bring every act to judgment, everything which is hidden, whether it is good or evil."

Ecclesiastes 12:13–14

WHEN DID HE REIGN?

1050	1000	950	900	850
SAMUEL GAD	NATHAN		SHEMAIAH IDDO Hanani the Seer	OBADIAH JOEL
Judge and Prophet			ODED Jahaziel the Levite	
			AZARIAH	
			Rehoboam Asa	Jehoshaphat Jehoram Ahaziah Joash
			931–913 911–870	873–848 (Joram) 841 835–796
Saul	David	Solomon	Abijam	853–841 Athaliah
1051–1011	1011–971	971–931	913–911	841–835
			Jeroboam I Nadab Elah Zimri	Ahaziah Jehu
	Ishbosheth ruled over Israel		931–910 910–909 886–885 885	853–852 841–814
	1011–1004 960—Temple finished		Baasha Tibni Ahab	Jehoram
			909–886 885–880 874–853	(Joram)
	David ruled over Judah from Hebron		Omri	852–841
	1011–1004		885–874	
			AHIJAH the Shilonite	
	David ruled over all Israel and Judah from Jerusalem		"A man of God from Judah" JEHU, son of Hanani	
	1004–971		A prophet from Samaria in Bethel MICAIAH	
			ELIJAH ELISHA	
	Hiram I of Tyre		Benhadad I of Syria Benhadad II of Syria	
	981–947		900–860 860–841	

FOLLOWING THE WORD OF GOD WITH AN OBEDIENT HEART

Since Adam in the Garden of Eden, God has wanted man to follow Him by paying heed to His Word. That was His desire for His covenant people, Israel, and for those who would lead them. With Saul that seldom happened. With David we see a man who had a heart to follow God and His Word, however imperfectly. How well would the next king follow? Let's look to the record of Scripture and see. First of all, let's look at the principles God gave for the kings of Israel.

📖 Read Deuteronomy 17:14–17. What three basic instructions are given for a king of Israel to follow?

1. _____

_____

2. _____

_____

3. _____

_____

"Guard your heart with all diligence."
Proverbs 4:23

If Israel would be the people God desired them to be, they must be led by His Word. If they were to have the leadership they needed and that God desired for them, they must follow Him in the choice of who would be king. This was not an office a man would choose for himself. God wanted them to have a king He would choose. That is of utmost importance. The Lord gave other guidelines as well. They must choose an Israelite, not a foreigner. The king himself was not to be a self-seeking man. He should not, first, seek military might by multiplying horses nor, second, political might by the alliances that came with many wives. With many wives also came the danger of the compromises of idolatry—the heart turning away from the Lord to his wives and their ways. Third, neither should his goal be personal wealth. The Lord wanted a man who would seek Him, not money and power. That meant following Him through **His Word**.

📖 Read Deuteronomy 17:18–20. What was the one thing the king is instructed to do for himself—by implication, the most important thing?

_____

_____

_____

One of the most crucial acts of his reign would come in writing *for himself* a copy of the Law, in making sure to keep that copy with him and in reading that copy all his life. The results of knowing the law of the Lord would be the fear of the Lord—through obedience, a walk in humility not pride, as well as a walk that was consistent rather than veering away into wrong paths. If he did this, he could experience a long reign for himself and his sons. Implied in this is a blessed reign with benefits for all of Israel.

David followed the counsel and wisdom of the Lord in much of his life and reign. He had a heart for God and sought to follow Him. When Solomon was born, David sought to teach him the ways of the Lord that he might walk in those ways as he grew. We know some of what he was taught, because it is given in Proverbs 4:1–9, as Solomon testifies of what David taught him in his youth.

📖 Read Proverbs 4:1–9. What are the main points of David's counsel?

_____

_____

_____

What will be the results if his advice is followed (vv. 6, 8–9)?

_____

_____

_____

How do you think this would prepare Solomon for life and for being the kind of king God wanted?

_____

_____

From David, Solomon learned that his heart must *"hold fast"* the words of wisdom and *"acquire understanding."* If he would obey those words, his path would be guarded and his life would be honored. Those words would serve Solomon well as king, *if* he would listen to them.

When David desired to build a house for the Lord and began making plans, the Lord intervened and spoke to him. What He said affected the whole future of who would be king after David. God was still setting the stage for His choice of king.

📖 Read 2 Samuel 7:1–17. What do verses 12–16 say about the next king?

_____

_____

_____

_____

The Lord planned for one of David's sons to be king. The Lord would establish his kingdom and promised to be a father to him, to correct him with *"the rod of men and the strokes of the sons of men,"* and to show lovingkindness to him. Ultimately, the promise to David would be fulfilled in the one greater than Solomon, the Lord Jesus Christ (Luke 1:32–33; 11:31).

Second Samuel 12:24–25 records that Solomon was born to David and Bathsheba soon after the death of their first son. David named him Solomon ("peaceful"), and Nathan the prophet named him Jedidiah ("beloved of the Lord") because *"the LORD loved him."*

Word Study
LET YOUR HEART HOLD FAST

The Hebrew word for heart, *lev*, is often used to refer to thinking, feeling, and choosing—mind, emotions, and will. For Solomon to hold fast to the words of his father with his "heart" meant that he would meditate fully, embrace warmly, and make his choices consistently in line with those words.

Read 1 Chronicles 22:6–13. What was David's charge to Solomon (v. 6)?

_____

How was Solomon to fulfill his tasks (v. 11)?

_____

_____

What was at the heart of David's instructions (v. 13)?

_____

_____

The Lord had promised David he would have a son who would be a man of peace ruling in a land of peace. That son would build the Temple David longed to build, and the Lord Himself would establish his kingdom forever (referring ultimately to the Messiah to come who would rule forever). David charged his son to obey the Lord's call to build, to rule by the wisdom and discernment of the Lord, and to follow His Word.

With the land at peace, what was to be the focus of Solomon and the people according to 1 Chronicles 22:17–19?

_____

_____

_____

The focus of Solomon and the nation was to seek the Lord. Building the Temple would be a tangible way to focus on the one true God and on true worship. Through the Temple they could better focus on their relationship to God as His covenant people.

David gathered all the officials and leaders of the nation of Israel in Jerusalem, and spoke to them of the Lord's choice of Solomon as king (1 Chronicles 28:5) and of the task of building the Temple. He gave Solomon the plans the Lord had given him (28:11–19). He testified of his own joy in giving generously, and called on the people to give themselves and their gifts to help build the Temple. The people did so and rejoiced in the ways and workings of the Lord. They honored David, and amidst the sacrifices of worship, *"they ate and drank that day before the Lord with great gladness"* (1 Chronicles 29:22).

David prayed for the people and for his son Solomon that they would have a heart focused on and loyal to the Lord (1 Chronicles 29:18–19). That would come as they obeyed the Word of the Lord. David desired more than anything that Solomon have a heart to follow God and His Word, and with that, he would build the Temple as God had directed.

The book of First Kings opens in the final days of King David. He is seventy years of age and ready to turn over the reins of the kingdom to his son Solomon. After a failed attempt to take the throne by his then oldest son Adonijah, David ordered Zadok the priest and Nathan the prophet to take Solomon, anoint him as king, and proclaim *"Long live King Solomon!"* (see 1 Kings 1:5–37). With that accomplished, David gave a charge to his son Solomon and died soon after (1 Kings 2:1–12).

📖 Read 1 Kings 2:2–4. What is the most important thing for Solomon to know if he would be the man God desired him to be and the type of king who would rule as God wanted?

_____

_____

_____

If a man would be the kind of man God wants, he must listen to God's Word and walk in His ways. For Solomon, the law of Moses would guide him in all he needed to know to walk with God. As a result, Solomon could expect to succeed God's way in all that he did and wherever he turned. True success is always tied to following God, not to following the world's definitions of success.

APPLY Are God and His Word the foundation of your belief system?

_____

How does that practically affect your life? How should it?

_____

_____

_____

_____

THE NECESSITY OF A HEARING HEART

Solomon DAY TWO

Solomon came to the throne probably at the age of twenty or twenty-one and ruled for forty years (971–931 BC). In his first year as king, Solomon traveled to Gibeon where the Tabernacle was located. There he offered a thousand burnt offerings, and there the Lord appeared to him in a dream and asked him what he wanted (1 Kings 3:5).

📖 Read 1 Kings 3:5–14. What did the Lord say (v. 5)?

_____

_____

For what did Solomon ask (v. 9)?

_____

_____

Why did he ask for wisdom (vv. 7–9)?

_____

_____

_____

Did You Know?
? A HEARING HEART

The Lord was delighted that Solomon asked for "a hearing heart." Isaiah 50:4 prophesied that the Messiah would have a listening, teachable ear. When Jesus came, He said, "I speak these things as the Father taught Me" (John 8:28–29). The Father told Peter, James, and John on the Mount of Transfiguration, "Listen to Him (the Lord Jesus)" (Matthew 17:5). That was the heart of Mary of Bethany when she was seated at the Lord's feet "listening to the Lord's word"—She had "chosen the good part" (Luke 10:42). God delights in a hearing heart.

The Lord asked Solomon what he wanted Him to do for him. Solomon responded in genuine humility admitting that he considered himself but a little child needing instruction in how to go out and come in. He knew he must judge the people with wisdom and justice. Therefore, he went straight to the source. If he would have wisdom, he must be able to hear God. He must have *a hearing heart*. God gladly gave that to him. Solomon's wisdom was soon tested.

APPLY If you were given the ability to ask for whatever you wanted, what would it be?

_____

_____

_____

We are given that ability—we can take our petitions straight to the throne room of God. But how often do we ask for wisdom? James tells us, *"But if any of you lacks wisdom, let him ask of God, who gives to all men generously and without reproach, and it will be given to him"* (James 1:5).

📖 Read 1 Kings 3:16–28. What predicament did Solomon face?

_____

_____

_____

_____

How did Solomon decide the case?

_____

_____

_____

How did the people of Israel respond to this judgment (v. 28)?

_____

_____

_____

Solomon understood human nature and the heart of a mother. He applied what he knew, and the truth surfaced so that justice could be administered. As a result, the people of Israel recognized the superior wisdom of God. They *"feared the king"*—their respect for him became a settled issue. They knew God was with him and that he could be trusted.

📖 News of Solomon's wisdom continued to spread. Read the summary in 1 Kings 4:29–34, and list the details of his well-known wisdom.

_____

_____

_____

_____

Did You Know?

SOLOMON THE WRITER

Solomon wrote The Song of Solomon, the book of Ecclesiastes, and most of the book of Proverbs (chapters 1–29), as well as Psalm 72 and Psalm 127.

Solomon's wisdom came from God. It is compared to the sand on the seashore in its breadth. Solomon was greater than the wise men of his day—the sons of the east, the wisdom of Egypt, and all other men of wisdom. Solomon's name spread to the surrounding nations. He recorded 3,000 proverbs along with 1,005 songs. His wisdom included insights about trees, plants, animals, birds, creeping things, and fish. Because of his wisdom, people came from all around to hear him, and it is recorded for us to read and to benefit.

The Lord had instructed David that he was not to build the Temple, but that his son Solomon would. David had given Solomon the responsibility, the resources, and the very plans God Himself had revealed to David (1 Chronicles 22:6–10; 28:11–19). In the fourth year of Solomon's reign, he began the construction and completed it in seven and a half years (1 Kings 6:1, 37–38). He did so with the help of Hiram, King of Tyre, and 183,300 men from the land of Israel who gathered and transported timber from the forests and cut stone from the quarry (1 Kings 5:8, 13–18; 6:7). The vast amount of materials and the incredible stores of gold, silver, bronze, and iron along with the best timbers and well-cut stones assured that this would be no ordinary building. In the midst of building the Temple the Lord spoke to Solomon.

📖 Read 1 Kings 6:11–13. What is most important in the Lord's sight?

_____

_____

_____

That which was most important to the Lord was not the externals of wealth, gold, silver, etc., but the internal heart of Solomon and the people of Israel. He wanted them to obey because His commands reflect the purity and holiness of His heart. As they walked in obedience they would experience what He had promised as well as the joy of His presence. With that they could know His power and provision for their needs. God's concern was and is the heart relationship with Him, hearing Him and walking with Him, not the building, as important as it was.

When the Temple was completed, Solomon brought in all the furnishings, and the priests brought the Ark of the Covenant into the Holy of Holies.

📖 According to 2 Chronicles 5:11–14 (also 1 Kings 8:10–11), what happened, and why is it significant?

_____

_____

_____

Jesus Christ came and "tabernacled" with us that each of us might know Immanuel "God with us" (Matthew 1:23; John 1:1, 14, 18).

The cloud of glory filled the Temple so that the priests could not minister—the same glory cloud that had led the children of Israel out of Egypt 487 years before (1 Kings 6:1), through the Wilderness, and into the Promised Land. The Lord was emphasizing His covenant relationship with His people. When they obeyed His Word, they could experience the joy of His presence—life as it was meant to be.

📖 Read Solomon's response in 1 Kings 8:12–53 and 2 Chronicles 6:40–42—his address to the people and his prayer of dedication and intercession. What do you see in his heart?

_____

_____

_____

_____

Solomon acknowledged the faithfulness of the Covenant God in His promises to David, and prayed for God to hear and answer his cry, not only on that day, but on any day the people cried out to the Lord. He prayed that God would have mercy on all those who cried out to Him in repentance of sin, for defeat of the enemy He led them against, or for relief in drought or famine. Solomon knew God was just and compassionate toward His people and prayed in the light of that truth.

📖 What was the response of the Lord and the people according to 2 Chronicles 7:1–3?

The Lord (vv. 1–2) _____

_____

_____

The people (v. 3)_____

_____

When he finished praying, the fire of God came down and consumed the sacrifices, and the glory of the Lord again filled the Lord's House. The people worshiped the Lord with great reverence and awe.

📖 Read 1 Kings 8:54–61. What does Solomon say about following God?

_____

_____

_____

God wants us to follow Him first and only.

In this benediction Solomon acknowledged God's gift of rest to His people in the land of Israel. He prayed that the people would fulfill the desire of God's heart and _"walk in all His ways"_ (8:58), _"so that all the peoples of the earth may know that the Lord is God; there is no one else"_ (8:60). That could be a reality for the people of Israel if they would be _"wholly devoted to the Lord . . . to walk"_ in His Word (8:61).

After Solomon blessed the people of Israel and blessed the Lord, he and the people offered thousands of oxen and sheep (2 Chronicles 7:4–7). The celebration lasted fourteen days—seven in dedication of the Temple followed by the seven-day Feast of Tabernacles. Second Chronicles 7:8–11 and 1 Kings 8:66 report that in the middle—on the eighth day, after a solemn assembly—the people _"went to their tents joyful and glad of heart for all the goodness that the Lord had shown to David His servant and to Israel His people."_ That stands as a picture of a life of following God, walking with Him, knowing His Presence.

THE DETOURS OF A DIVIDED HEART

After Solomon finished the Temple the Lord appeared to him a second time as He had at Gibeon. It was a time to steady his course on following God and His Word.

📖 Read 2 Chronicles 7:11–22. (Another account is also given in 1 Kings 9:1–9). What does God say about the people of Israel (vv. 13–14, 22)?

_____

_____

_____

_____

What does He say about the Temple (vv. 12, 15–16)?

_____

_____

_____

_____

And what does He say to Solomon (vv. 17–22)?

_____

_____

_____

_____

_____

The Lord spoke to Solomon concerning His people first. If calamity came to Israel, it would be because of the sin of the people, and repentance would bring healing (7:14). God promised to hear the prayers offered in the Temple, the place He had chosen for Himself. He also commanded Solomon to walk before Him like David had in *"integrity of heart and uprightness"* (1 Kings 9:4). The Lord promised His blessings for obedience and His judgment for disobedience. The people would be uprooted from their land, and the Temple would become *"a heap of ruins"* (1 Kings 9:8), if the people turned away from the Lord and turned to idols.

After this Solomon continued his course of building, and he amassed vast wealth (see 1 Kings 9:27–28; 10:11–12, 14–29; 2 Chronicles 9:13–28). His yearly collection of gold alone amounted to 666 talents (about 25 tons). His trade included horses from Egypt, Kue, and other nations as well as chariots from Egypt. He exported these to the Hittites and to the kings of the Arameans (area of Syria). He amassed great trade revenues from traders and merchants from around the Middle East. Many sought Solomon for his wisdom and brought him great riches year after year (*"silver and gold, garments, weapons, spices, horses, and mules,"* 1 Kings 10:25). Every three years the ships of Tarshish (possibly from Spain or the mines of the area around Ezion-geber) brought gold, silver, ivory, apes, and peacocks. All his drinking vessels were of pure gold, *"none was of silver; it was not considered valuable in the days of Solomon"* (1 Kings 10:21). Verse 27 adds *"and the king made silver as common as stones in Jerusalem."* When the Queen of Sheba came to see this kingdom and test the wisdom of Solomon, she left declaring, *"I did not believe the reports, until I came and my eyes had seen it. And behold, the half was not told me"* (1 Kings 10:1–10, 13).

But all was not well in the midst of Solomon's grand kingdom. In spite of his wisdom, some very foundational truths were being ignored.

📖 Read 1 Kings 11:1–2. What do you find out about Solomon?

_____

_____

_____

_____

The Lord made it clear in His Law that the nation of Israel was not to associate with the nations around them. They were certainly not to intermarry (see Exodus 23:31–33; 34:12–16; Deuteronomy 7:1–11). Solomon, however, loved these foreign women and side-stepped God's Word as well as the warnings He had given him.

📖 Read 1 Kings 11:3–8. What did Solomon do as a result?

_____

_____

_____

_____

_____

When we listen too long to the noises of the world, our hearing becomes dull.

Solomon's heart first turned away from the Lord and His Word to his seven hundred wives and three hundred concubines. Apparently, their voices became louder than the Lord's voice and Solomon's "hearing" became dull. Then his heart turned to their idols and to the detestable worship of those idols.

Solomon's idolatry was not a one-time event. He began a practice that led from one god to another. The list included Ashtoreth (the goddess of the Sidonians) who was the female partner of Baal. This idol was linked to the evening star and was considered the goddess of fertility (called Ishtar in Babylon, Athtart in Aram, Aphrodite in Greece, Venus in Rome). Worship included immoral and lascivious rites. Solomon also worshiped *"Milcom the detestable idol of the Ammonites"* (1 Kings 11:5, 7) also known as Molech. Solomon built an altar to Molech in the Valley of the Son of Hinnom (New Testament—Gehenna). Worship of this idol sometimes included child sacrifice in the fires of the altar of this god. Ironically, Molech or Milcom was considered as a protective father to the Ammonites. Solomon also built a high place on the Mount of Olives for Chemosh, a Moabite idol whose worship also sometimes included child sacrifice (2 Kings 3:26–27). This high place was called the Mount/Hill of Corruption or Destruction in 2 Kings 23:13.

📖 Read 1 Kings 11:9–13. How did the Lord respond?

_____

_____

_____

_____

_____

The Lord was very angry with Solomon. Solomon had been commanded about this very thing and ignored God's Word to him. As a result the kingdom was to be given to his servant after his death. In the midst of this judgment God amazingly still showed mercy for the sake of David and for the sake of Jerusalem, His chosen city.

📖 Read 1 Kings 11:14–40 and 2 Samuel 7:14. What happened as part of the Lord's judgment?

_____

_____

_____

_____

_____

Just as the Lord had promised, He chastened Solomon with *"the rod of men and the strokes of the sons of men"* (2 Samuel 7:14). During his reign God raised up three main adversaries—**1)** Hadad the Edomite (1 Kings 11:14–22), **2)** Rezon the son of Eliada (11:23–25), and **3)** Solomon's servant, Jeroboam the son of Nebat (11:26–40). Because of the sin of Solomon and the people of Israel, the kingdom would be torn in two at Solomon's death. Jeroboam would rule over the ten northern tribes of Israel in opposition to Rehoboam (Solomon's son) in Judah (the Southern Kingdom). God dealt seriously with idolatry. He knew it was absolutely destructive. It eventually led to the dispersion of the ten northern tribes in 722 BC, the uprooting of the people of Israel to Babylon for seventy years of captivity (605–536 BC), and the destruction of Solomon's Temple (586 BC).

THE WISDOM OF A GUARDED HEART

Solomon DAY FOUR

What would Solomon say to us today about *following God*? By God's wisdom and providence we can know because he has written it down. First, Solomon has given some insights into life on a solely material level without the abundant life of God in the picture.

📖 Read Ecclesiastes 2:4–11, 17–19 (it is helpful to read it in more than one translation). What did Solomon come to see about all he had achieved?

_____

_____

Solomon's divided heart led to a divided kingdom.

_____

_____

_____

All that Solomon did, all the wealth he amassed, all the experiences he had were meaningless without a right relationship to God. His idolatry sapped the life out of his heart. He drank from a poison well and found his heart sick because of it. Jesus said a man's life does not consist in the possessions he accumulates (Luke 12:13–31). Life is found only in Him—in knowing Him, following Him, walking with Him, obeying His Words which are spirit and life (John 6:63).

📖 Look at Ecclesiastes 12:1, 9–14, and summarize Solomon's conclusions.

_____

_____

_____

_____

_____

Solomon urged his readers to first remember their Creator in the days of youth. It would make a difference for all of life. Then he commended the value of wise teaching—of hearing and heeding wisdom from the One Shepherd. That was how Solomon started his reign as king, with a prayer for a hearing heart. With a hearing heart one can know God's Word and follow Him faithfully. Solomon knew to watch out for the many words of many books. His conclusion was in a few words—*"fear God and keep His commandments"*—listen carefully to His Word, and follow what He says. He realized too, that everyone is accountable to God, whether king or slave.

📖 There is one other word that Solomon would say. Read Proverbs 4:20–27 (note especially v. 23). What was Solomon's counsel to his son and to us (This comes immediately after the account of his father David's word to him as a young son [4:1–9])?

_____

_____

_____

Idolatry saps the joy of life out of the heart of a man or woman.

Did You Know?
24-HOUR GUARD

In order to guard your heart, you must also

• Guard your relationships.

• Guard your time.

Solomon saw that the words of wisdom must be kept in the heart every day and applied to every circumstance. He also recognized that the heart must be guarded *"with all diligence."* The ways of sin, flesh, the world, and the devil all come to attack and overtake the heart and destroy the life. Watch the path of your feet. Do not veer to the right nor to the left. Turn away from evil. Stay focused on the Lord and His truth; listen to Him, look to Him, guard all He says. Don't let it escape from your heart. Guard your heart watching over it with diligence.

Solomon would say "Guard your heart." Perhaps we could add two other words of admonition that serve as fitting companions to that: **1)** "Guard your relationships" and **2)** "Guard your time."

📖 Read Matthew 5:16, 23–24 and Acts 24:16. What do these verses teach concerning relationships?

_____

_____

_____

_____

_____

📖 What does Ephesians 5:15–16 teach concerning time?

_____

_____

_____

_____

Solomon failed to guard his time and his relationships and left his heart open to destructive thoughts, choices, and actions. Solomon serves as an example and a warning to every believer. He would be the first to echo the warning of the wise and aged apostle John in 1 John 5:21, *"Little children, guard yourselves from idols."* Be ever watchful and ever diligent in guarding your heart, for truly the dangers are real and affect all of life, for from the heart *"flow the springs of life"* (Proverbs 4:23).

FOR ME TO FOLLOW GOD

 *Solomon* DAY FIVE

Solomon was given the unenviable task of succeeding David as king of Israel. He was about twenty or twenty-one years old when he came to the throne, and he reigned for forty years. Imagine what he must have felt like. He would have been excited about the honor—yet fearful of the responsibility. As he began to reign, he was marked by an appropriate humility. When he traveled to Gibeon in the first year of his reign, to worship at the Tabernacle, God met with him in a special way with an unusual offer: *"Ask what you wish me to give you"* (1 Kings 3:5). All of us have dreamt of a magic genie offering to grant our wishes, but here is God extending such an offer to Solomon. Anything his heart desired, God would give. In Solomon's answer we see gratitude mingled with fear and great humility (*". . . yet I am but a child; I do not know how to go out or come in"* [1 Kings 3:7]). It says much of the new king's heart that instead of asking for riches or honor or military victories, he asks, *". . . give Thy servant an understanding heart to judge Thy people to discern between good and evil."*

Not only does God affirm and grant Solomon's request, but He adds to it some important advice: *". . . if you walk in My ways, keeping My statutes and commandments . . . then I will prolong your days"* (1 Kings 3:14). In this divine counsel we see the seeds of warning for a problem looming on the horizon. It is one thing to possess wisdom and yet another to apply it to our lives. Solomon was given greater wisdom than anyone before or since (1 Kings 3:12), yet even this was no guarantee of godliness.

Ours is a society which places a premium on knowledge and education. Learning is viewed as the key to bettering oneself in life. Yet in 1 Corinthians 8:1 we are warned of knowledge's limitations: *"Knowledge makes arrogant, but love edifies."* Knowledge alone is not enough. It is not what we know that defines us, but what we do with what we know.

Thinking back through this week's lessons, where do you think the turning point was in Solomon's following God—where he began to have a divided heart?

_____

_____

_____

_____

_____

Knowledge alone is not enough. It is not what we know that defines us, but what we do with what we know.

Solomon began well, with a humble, dependent heart. He recognized the magnitude of the task both of leading Israel and of building the Temple. He saw himself as unable to get the job done apart from God. But along the way, as he began to see success after success, he became self-confident instead of God-dependent. It appears that in his heart, pride began to grow, and he started taking credit for all that God in His grace had done. In 1 Kings 10:23–24 we get a glimpse of where the turning point might have been rooted: *"So King Solomon became greater than all the kings of the earth in riches and in wisdom. And all the earth was seeking the presence of Solomon, to hear his wisdom which God had put in his heart."*

From the second time God met with Solomon after the dedication of the temple, until the end of his life, there is no record of Solomon giving glory to God for all the success he enjoyed. Although he religiously continued to offer burnt offerings and peace offerings three times a year until his construction projects were finished (1 Kings 9:25), by the end of his life those offerings were being given to the Canaanite gods.

APPLY Can you think of any examples in your own life where you failed to acknowledge God for your successes?

_____

_____

_____

_____

_____

What resulted from this failure?

_____

_____

_____

_____

_____

As Solomon became proud, it appears that he began to view himself as above the law of God. In violation of that law, he multiplied wives, and not just any women, but those Canaanite women explicitly forbidden because of the gods they worshiped. Perhaps Solomon thought God's favor meant obedience was not required of him, or perhaps he thought his superior wisdom would protect him from the dangers of wives who served other gods. Whatever the reason for his decline, the king who had more wisdom than any before or since began to live foolishly. The law of God he had copied by hand at the beginning of his reign, was disregarded at the end of it. Solomon's greatest achievement—building the Temple of God in Jerusalem—was overshadowed by the many pagan altars he erected in Israel. In 1 Kings 11:1 we are told, *"Now King Solomon loved many foreign women . . ."* That he "loved" foreign women who worshiped other gods speaks of the division in his heart. That he loved "many" women speaks of the rampant indulgence of his fleshly desires. That he ignored the admonition of God against these things, speaks of his pride and arrogance. Solomon, who contributed to so many books of wisdom in Scripture (writing some of the Psalms and most of Proverbs as well as Ecclesiastes and Song of Solomon) failed to follow the wisdom given to him by God.

APPLY It was Solomon's making room in his heart for those who didn't love God that began to erode his own devotion to the Lord. Who are the people in your life that offer that same danger to you?

_____

_____

_____

_____

_____

What do you need to do to guard your heart?

_____

_____

_____

_____

_____

When our heart becomes divided, we are susceptible to idols. Read 1 John 5:21. Write that verse in the space below, and then write your observations about John's words to Christians.

_____

_____

_____

_____

_____

An idol is not simply a statue of an imagined god. It is anything that usurps the preeminent place God should have in our hearts and lives. As you evaluate your own heart, check the things which are prone to move toward being idols in your life.

In Scripture, right hearing equals fully obeying.

The Lust of the Eyes

___ Fancy Cars	___ Home	___ Furnishings
___ Clothing	___ Boat	___ Grown-up "toys"
___ Jewelry	___ Other:_____	

The Lust of the Flesh

___ Food	___ Sex	___ Beauty
___ Leisure	___ Hobbies	___ Experiences/Vacations
___ Other:_____		

The Boastful Pride of Life

___ Awards	___ Competition	___ Athletic Achievement
___ Job Advancement	___ Positions	___ Performance
___ Knowledge	___ Accomplishments	___ Child's Performance
___ Other:_____		

What do you need to do to guard yourself from these areas becoming idols in your life?

_____

_____

_____

_____

_____

Perhaps the summary problem we see in Solomon's life is that he knew a lot of truth, but he didn't always apply it. In 1 Kings 11:9–10 we read this indictment from the Lord against Solomon: *"Now the Lord was angry with Solomon because his heart was turned away from the Lord . . . who had . . . commanded this thing, that he should not go after other gods; but he **did not observe** what the Lord had commanded"* (emphasis added). It is a remarkable thing to think that the wisest man who ever lived could wind up being a fool. It rocks the foundation of our world to recognize that knowledge will not "prodigal proof" our hearts. Although we are not endowed with the wisdom Solomon had, even we are in danger of not applying all that we know.

📖 Read James 1:22–25, and record what you learn there about this issue of applying what we know.

_____

_____

_____

_____

_____

James warns us of the need to be a "doer" and not merely a hearer. It is scary to realize that greater truth brings greater accountability before God. In fact, what James tells us here is that knowledge that isn't applied not only does not help us, but may actually hinder us. He says it can be a "deluding" influence in our lives. It can deceive us into thinking we are spiritual because of how much we know instead of how we live.

Did You Know?

THE MARKS OF IDOLATRY

Idols and idolatry always involve:

• Deception

• Distortion

• Abomination

• Distraction

• Abhorrence

• Destruction

How would you rate yourself on the chart below in your "doing" of the word of God?

Hearer Only ⟵ 1 2 3 4 5 6 7 8 9 10 ⟶ Doer of the Word

As you have studied this week's lesson, has the Lord been putting His finger on a part of your life where you know the right thing to do and aren't doing it? What do you need to do differently?

_____

_____

_____

_____

_____

Because the Lord is God and we are not, He has every right to make demands on our lives. It is arrogant and foolish for us to ignore the will of God and live as we please. Perhaps the most important lesson from the life of Solomon is the necessity of obedience. Yet obedience in our own strength is impossible. That is why the most important word in the Christian life is not "commitment" (what I do by gritting my teeth and trying hard), but "surrender" letting God be in control of every area of my life so that He can live in and through me.

Remember, there are always consequences to not obeying what we know. Solomon's divided heart led to a divided kingdom. In the same way, divided allegiance to the Lord—worshiping of the idols of our own desires—will lead to divided relationships, divided families, divided communities. Deal with any glimpse you see of a divided heart.

Take some time to cement these applications through prayer.

Lord, I know that I am not living all that I have learned. In my heart there are idols of possessions, idols of pleasure, and idols of pride. Unite my heart to follow you. Show me the truth I am not living—convict me of neglected obedience to you. And grant me courage to choose obedience even when I don't feel like it. Help me to "watch my heart with all diligence" since the streams of my life flow from there. Most of all, may all the kingdom of my heart be yours alone to rule. Amen.

Record your own prayer of surrender in the space below.

_____

_____

_____

_____

_____

_____

_____

_____

_____

_____

_____

_____

_____

_____

The Kingdoms of Israel and Judah

0 10 20 30 40 miles
0 10 20 30 40 kilometers

Beirut

Sidon

PHOENICIA

Tyre

Acco

Mt. Carmel

Mediterranean
Sea

Megiddo

Taanach

Ibleam

Dan

Kedesh

J. Jarmuk

Hazor

Mt. Hermon

Damascus

Abana R.

Litani R.

Pharpar R.

ARAM

Sea of
Galilee

Ashtaroth

Mt.
Tabor

Mt. Moreh

Beth-shan

Mt.
Gilboa

Kishon R.

Yarmuk R.

Jordan R.

Edrei

Ramoth-gilead

Jabesh-gilead?

Tirzah

Samaria

Mt. Ebal

Mt. Gerizim

Schechem

Succoth?

Penuel?

Mahanaim?

Jabbok R.

Yarkon R.

Aphek

Shiloh

ISRAEL

Rabbah
(Amman)

AMMON

Joppa

Bethel

Jericho

Gezer

Aijalon

Jerusalem

Bethlehem

Mt. Nebo

Heshbon

Medeba

Ashdod

Gath

Mareshah

Hebron

Dead
Sea

Arnon R.

Dibon

Ashkelon

Gaza

Gerar

Besor Br.

JUDAH

Beersheba

MOAB

Kir-hareseth

Raphia

PHILISTIA

Zered Br.

WILDERNESS

W. el-Arish

Region
periodically
contested
by Judah
and Edom

Bozrah

EDOM

Kadesh-
barnea

WILDERNESS

© 1999 MapQuest.com, Inc

Notes

Jeroboam I

THE RUIN OF FOLLOWING THE DEVICES OF ONE'S OWN HEART

*S*olomon's reign ended in 931 BC. Because of the idolatry and corruption that accompanied it, God chose to judge Israel for a time. He allowed the division among the people that had begun under Solomon to blossom. Only the tribe of Judah would be ruled by a descendant of David; hence, the Southern Kingdom is known as Judah. The Northern Kingdom of ten tribes would be known as Israel and would be ruled by a man chosen by God. That man, Jeroboam, would have the opportunity to follow God as David had done and establish his name and the nation of Israel on a foundation of following God.

Instead, Jeroboam's life presents to us the tragedy of grace offered and grace foolishly refused. It is the account of a man consumed with himself and the devices of his own heart. Jeroboam had the opportunity to bring healing to a nation weary with the idolatry and harsh labor of the latter days of Solomon's rule, but instead led the people further down the road of idolatry with all its deception, decay, and destruction. He was the headwaters of a river of wickedness that flowed in Israel for the next 210 years and eventually emptied over a precipice into destruction. In 722 BC the nation of Israel was taken captive by the Assyrians, and was never restored. The ways of Jeroboam should be a flashing beacon to us: "Danger Ahead," and should guide us back onto the path of following God and His ways.

Jeroboam I, the son of Nebat of the tribe of Ephraim, reigned over the ten tribes of the Northern Kingdom of Israel from 931 to 910 BC. The prophets who spoke during his reign were Ahijah and "a man of God from Judah," as well as an unnamed prophet in Bethel. Rehoboam, the son of Solomon, reigned in the Southern Kingdom of Judah at the same time (931–913 BC).

The life of Jeroboam presents to us the tragedy of grace offered and grace foolishly refused.

WHEN DID HE REIGN?

1050	1000	950	900	850
SAMUEL Judge and Prophet	GAD NATHAN		SHEMAIAH IDDO Hanani the Seer ODED AZARIAH	OBADIAH JOEL Jahaziel the Levite
			Rehoboam 931–913	Asa 911–870		Jehoshaphat Jehoram Ahaziah Joash 873–848 (Joram) 841 835–796
Saul 1051–1011	David 1011–971	Solomon 971–931	Abijam 913–911	853–841 Athaliah 841–835
	Ishbosheth ruled over Israel 1011–1004 960—Temple finished	Jeroboam 931–910 Nadab Elah Zimri 910–909 886–885 885	Ahaziah Jehu 853–852 841–814
	David ruled over Judah from Hebron 1011–1004	Baasha 909–886 Tibni Ahab 885–880 874–853 Omri 885–874	Jehoram (Joram) 852–841
		AHIJAH the Shilonite "A man of God from Judah" A prophet from Samaria in Bethel	JEHU, son of Hanani MICAIAH ELIJAH	ELISHA
	Hiram I of Tyre 981–947		Benhadad I of Syria 900–860	Benhadad II of Syria 860–841

THE OPPORTUNITY TO FOLLOW GOD

Jeroboam was born at the end of king David's reign or during the first part of the reign of king Solomon. First Kings 11:26 tells us he was born to Nebat and Zeruah in the town of Zeredah in the territory allotted to the tribe of Ephraim. At some point in his early years his father had died, leaving him to support his widowed mother. What else do we know about Jeroboam? What kind of man was he? The Scriptures paint a clear picture for us.

Read 1 Kings 11:26. What was Jeroboam's occupation?

_____

According to 1 Kings 11:28, what marked Jeroboam's service? How well did he do?

_____

_____

_____

Beware of walking in foolish ways.

It would be helpful at this point to understand the chronology of 1 Kings 11 and where these verses fit into the big picture. We know from the context of chapter 11 that Solomon has gone astray into idolatry following the ways of his foreign wives. He imposed forced labor on the people for many of his projects. One of his servants was a young man named Jeroboam. The order of the verses pertaining to Jeroboam should be as follows: **1)** He began working as one of Solomon's servants (v. 26a). **2)** He was a valiant warrior and distinguished himself as "industrious" (v. 28). **3)** Solomon appointed him as an overseer *"over all the forced labor of the house of Joseph"* (v. 28). That included both the tribe of Manasseh and the favored tribe of Ephraim (Jeroboam's tribe).

Read 1 Kings 11:29–39. What happened *"at that time"* (v. 29), after Jeroboam was appointed an overseer (vv. 29–31)?

_____

_____

_____

_____

According to verse 33, why was this taking place? List the reasons given.

_____

_____

_____

_____

_____

What was the promise given to Jeroboam in verses 35–38? What kind of opportunity did this give him?

_____

_____

_____

_____

After Jeroboam was appointed an overseer, the prophet Ahijah met him on the road outside Jerusalem and gave him the prophecy concerning the division of the nation into two kingdoms, with one tribe under the house of David and ten tribes under Jeroboam. Because of the idolatry of Solomon and the nation under him, the Lord was tearing ten tribes out of the hand of Solomon and giving them to Jeroboam to rule.

Jeroboam had the opportunity to reign over whatever he desired and, with that, the opportunity to know the presence of the Lord (*"I will be with you"*) as well as the promise of a lasting heritage (*"an enduring house"*) and the honor and privilege of ruling in Israel (v. 38). It was simple. All he had to do was keep on listening to what the Lord commanded, keep on learning by walking in His ways, and keep on doing what is right in His sight. It meant giving up his own "wisdom," his own ways, his own opinions of what was right in order to fully embrace the Lord and His will. The reward would be rich, good, and lasting for Jeroboam—for his family and for the nation.

📖 Verse 26 tells us what happened after he had been appointed as an overseer and heard the prophecy of verses 29–39. In that position and with those promises, how did Jeroboam lead?

_____

_____

_____

Why do you think he would choose to lead in this way?

_____

_____

_____

📖 According to verse 40, what happened as a result?

_____

_____

_____

_____

Did You Know?
WHERE IS THE TWELFTH TRIBE OF ISRAEL?

Ten Tribes to the North—One Tribe to the South with the house of David. Where is the Twelfth tribe of Israel? As the division of Israel worked out, there were ten tribes that sided with Jeroboam (Reuben, Simeon, Zebulun, Issachar, Dan, Gad, Asher, Naphtali, Ephraim, and Manasseh). Levi, the priestly tribe, was not numbered with them since they were spread throughout all the tribes, though most moved to Judah favoring the house of David. Judah was the one tribe allotted to the house of David. For the most part Benjamin, the twelfth tribe, sided with Judah so that the Southern Kingdom was Judah and Benjamin. However, some of the territory of Benjamin was part of the Northern Kingdom, particularly Bethel.

As a "valiant warrior" and an "industrious" leader, Jeroboam apparently believed he knew the best route to take to claim what God had promised. He took things into his own hands and rebelled against the king. It appears he wanted his "desire" now without waiting on God's timing. He would take by force what God had already promised him. As a result, Solomon sought to kill him, so Jeroboam fled to Egypt where he lived under the protection of Shishak the king. Jeroboam refused the opportunity to follow God and God's ways and allied himself with the people and ways of Egypt.

JEROBOAM'S CHOICE TO FOLLOW THE DEVICES OF HIS OWN HEART

First Kings 12:1 tells us that at Solomon's death, his son, Rehoboam went to Shechem to be made king over all Israel. Jeroboam heard of Solomon's death and of Rehoboam's expectation to reign in his father's place as king. The men of Israel *"sent and called"* for Jeroboam and he came to Shechem. What do we learn about Rehoboam and his leadership? What role did Jeroboam play in the meetings that followed? How did he fit into this scenario?

📖 Read 1 Kings 12:1–14. What did the people ask Rehoboam (v. 4)?

_____

_____

_____

Whose advice did Rehoboam seek (vv. 6, 8)?

_____

Summarize the advice each group gave him:

The elder's (v. 7): _____

_____

The young men (vv. 10–11): _____

_____

Which advice did he follow (vv. 13–14)?

_____

When presented with an opportunity to exhibit godly leadership, Rehoboam showed the foolishness of his heart. He proudly tried to show a strong hand instead of humbly seeking to serve the people of Israel, as the elders who served with his father had advised. He refused to listen to good counsel and instead listened to the foolish counsel of his young counselors. He showed the people what kind of leader he would be.

First Kings 12:15 states that this was *"a turn of events from the LORD, that He might establish His word,"* that is, the prophecy God had given through Ahijah to Jeroboam. Rehoboam did not have the wisdom of the Lord in his decision-making process. On the human side, Rehoboam did not walk in the fear of the Lord. He did not want nor seek the wisdom and counsel of the Lord. On the divine side of these events at Shechem, God withheld His wisdom from Rehoboam in judgment on the house of David for Solomon's idolatrous ways. The Lord allowed him to have what he wanted. That is often His way of judging sin, by pouring out a measure of His wrath to deal with the selfishness and foolishness of man. Rehoboam experienced this first hand.

The ways of God often include both a divine side and a human side. In this He is ever working all things according to the purposes He wants to accomplish.

📖 Read 1 Kings 12:16–19. What was Israel's response to Rehoboam?

_____

_____

_____

Again we see a human side and a divine side. How does God characterize their response in verse 19?

_____

_____

The men of Israel saw that their pleas to lighten the burdens Solomon had imposed were rejected; therefore, they wanted nothing to do with the house of David. Their cry in verse 16 was a repeat of the cry of Sheba the son of Bichri, when he rebelled against king David and led the ten northern tribes to withdraw from David and those of the tribe of Judah. That rebellion was subdued by the death of Sheba (2 Samuel 20). But this inter-tribal rivalry—ten tribes versus Judah—simmered under the surface of the nation for the next several years, ultimately erupting in the division of the nation under Rehoboam.

First Kings 12:19 states it as a case of rebellion against the house of David, the place of God's covenant promises and blessings. Through David the Lord would bless all of Israel and all the earth, and his throne would endure by the hand of God (2 Samuel 7:12–28; Luke 1:32–33). From the human side the ten northern tribes refused to live under the rule of the house of David, thus rejecting God's covenant promises made to David. From the divine side, the Lord was allowing their hearts to carry out His judgment on the idolatry of Solomon and the foolishness of Rehoboam.

📖 Read 1 Kings 12:3, 12, 20 and 2 Chronicles 13:4–7. What role did Jeroboam play in all that occurred?

_____

_____

What kind of influence did he have, according to these verses?

_____

_____

When Israel called Jeroboam to Shechem out of Egypt, he came there as their spokesman before Rehoboam. There were several "worthless men" who gathered about Jeroboam and stood with him against Rehoboam. The people of Israel agreed in this rebellion and rejected Rehoboam. When they did, they accepted Jeroboam as their king and proclaimed it at the assembly at Shechem.

Jeroboam established himself as king by first building up Shechem in Ephraim and then Penuel in Gilead east of the Jordan River. He thus fortified his position in the central part of the Northern Kingdom and in the eastern territory between Syria and Israel. But that is not all he did to establish himself. With his counselors, very likely some of the same "worthless men" who stood with him at Shechem, he devised a way to maintain his throne.

Did You Know?
A COVENANT OF SALT

In Israel, salt was used as a preservative and a purifier. Salt spoke of that which would not decay or rot, that which remained good and beneficial and so communicated the idea of loyalty, faithfulness, and dependability. Such is the character of God, and such is the covenant He made with Abraham and later with Israel. In 2 Chronicles 13:5 we find that the Lord gave the rule over Israel forever to David and his sons by a covenant of salt, a guarantee from the Lord. Leviticus 2:13 required that salt be included in the grain offering and was called "the salt of the covenant of your God." It was linked to the covenant with Israel and spoke of the faithfulness God expected from Israel. In Numbers 18:19 by "an everlasting covenant of salt," the Lord promised the priests their provisions of food from the sacrifices given by the people. It was a guarantee of provision. God guaranteed the throne to the seed of David.

Read 1 Kings 12:26–33. What did Jeroboam perceive to be the threat to his throne (vv. 26–27)?

_____

_____

_____

What did he do about it?

_____

_____

_____

_____

Jeroboam feared that Israel would return to the house of David, so he consulted with his counselors and devised a plan to keep Israel away from Jerusalem, the seat of religious worship and the heart of the tribe of Judah and the house of David. He made two golden calves and set them up at Dan (the northern area) and at Bethel (the southern area), and called Israel to worship them as their gods, a direct violation of the first two of the Ten Commandments. This was sin for the people of Israel, for they worshiped at these altars.

What does verse 33 indicate Jeroboam was following?

_____

Jeroboam was worshiping the devices of his own heart—his own plans and accomplishments—and leading the people to do the same. How tragic it is when our leaders follow their own hearts rather than following after God's heart!

Building altars at Dan and Bethel and placing the golden calves there was not enough. Jeroboam wanted to further establish himself and his rule in Israel.

Read 2 Chronicles 11:13–17 and 1 Kings 12:30–31. What did Jeroboam do (vv. 14–15)?

_____

_____

_____

What were the different responses of the people?

_____

_____

_____

Jeroboam excluded the Levites from serving in their God-ordained place—as priests to the Lord. Instead, he established priests of his own from among all the tribes except Levi. These priests were "*for the high places, for the satyrs, and for the calves which he had made*" (2 Chronicles 11:15). The Levites therefore fled to Judah along with all those from the various tribes "*who set their*

Put Yourself In Their Shoes

JEROBOAM'S LEGACY

The people were led into greater and greater sin and bondage by Jeroboam's deception and dishonesty. This legacy to them included:

- False gods
- False altars
- False praise
- False worship
- False priests
- False incense and prayer
- False feasts

hearts on seeking the LORD God of Israel" (11:16). This greatly strengthened the kingdom of Judah because they were following God. Most of the people of Israel were led into sin in worshiping idols in Dan and Bethel as the Northern Kingdom continued in its course of corruption.

In addition to these atrocities, Jeroboam established a feast on the fifteenth day of the eighth month *"like the feast which is in Judah"* (1 Kings 12:32–33). The Feast of Tabernacles or Booths was celebrated in Judah on the fifteenth day of the seventh month to commemorate the time Israel spent in the wilderness and to rejoice over the harvests of the land (Leviticus 23:33–44; Numbers 29:12–40). Jeroboam compromised this as well, perhaps to accommodate the later harvests of the north, but certainly to further strengthen his control of the ten northern tribes. The feast was used as a time to burn incense and sacrifice to the calves he had set up before the altars at Dan and Bethel, a practice that totally corrupted their understanding of prayer, sacrifice and worship, and ultimately their view of the Lord God.

Jeroboam followed the devices of his own heart and led Israel with him along that path, a path that would surely lead to judgment if not stopped. God in His mercy sought to do just that.

GOD'S WARNING TO JEROBOAM

Jeroboam was leading Israel down the wrong path, worshiping the golden calves he made at Dan and Bethel. The Word of God had clearly revealed the right way to worship God, and His prophets proclaimed the will of God. Would Jeroboam listen to either?

📖 What had God said about where and how to worship? Read Deuteronomy 12:1–14; 1 Kings 11:36; and 2 Chronicles 7:11–16. What do you find about . . .

the **place** of worship?

_____

_____

_____

_____

the **attitude** or **spirit** that God desired in that place?

_____

_____

_____

Just before Israel entered the land of Canaan, the Lord through Moses gave specific instructions concerning any and every place of worship dedicated to false gods. Any and every altar or idol of the land was to be torn down and destroyed. God wanted Israel to *"seek the LORD at the place which the LORD your God shall choose"* (Deuteronomy 12:5). For many years, that place was wherever the Tabernacle rested. Then it was Jerusalem where Solomon

Did You Know?
THE PLACE OF WORSHIP

God was clear about where He wanted Israel to come and worship Him—"You shall seek the Lord at the place [Jerusalem] which the Lord your God shall choose from all your tribes [Judah], to establish His name there for His dwelling [the Temple], and there you shall come" (Deuteronomy 12:5).

built the glorious Temple, the Temple Jeroboam himself had seen and, in all likelihood, where he had worshiped. God expected His people to worship there, in humility seeking Him. Jeroboam knew it was God's chosen place of worship and sacrifice, but he ignored the Word of God and chose against the will of God.

📖 What was the message of the *"man of God from Judah"* according to 1 Kings 13:1–3?

_____

_____

_____

_____

An unidentified *"man of God"* was sent from Judah to cry out against the altar at Bethel and all it stood for. His message was a message of judgment. There would be born a king in Judah named Josiah who would execute judgment on the priests of the high places and on the very bones of those who had given their service to this idolatrous place. Not only that, but, for the present, the altar would be split apart so that the ashes would spill out—thus defiling the altar (Leviticus 4:12; 6:8–11) and that place of false worship.

📖 Read 1 Kings 13:4–6. What was Jeroboam's response (v. 4)?

_____

_____

How did God confront him personally (vv. 4–6)?

_____

_____

_____

_____

Jeroboam no doubt recognized that the man of God was speaking out against not only the altar but against him and his wicked ways. He lashed out against the man of God from Judah, revealing the attitude of his self-occupied heart. God struck him with a withered hand, the altar split apart, and the ashes of the false sacrifices were spilt.

Jeroboam personally experienced the chastening hand of God. He was struck by the authority and power of the man of God and the seriousness of the message and cried out for deliverance from the chastening hand of *"your God."* The man of God prayed, and Jeroboam's hand was restored. How did Jeroboam respond at this turn of events? Would this mark a change in his heart?

📖 First Kings 13:7 records that Jeroboam invited the man to come home to be refreshed and receive a reward. Read 1 Kings 13:7–10. How did the man from Judah respond?

_____

_____

God is faithful to get His message across. He waits to see if we will hear and obey.

Why did he respond in this way?

_____

_____

What do you think his thoughts were in this incident?

_____

_____

_____

The man refused both refreshment and reward. Most likely he recognized that he needed no fellowship with such a king and certainly was not dependent on him for favors, payment, or reward. Surely he saw the priests and worshipers of that place and recognized the kind of men, their character, and conduct, who were already on Jeroboam's payroll. It would be an opportunity to see the subtle snares of fellowship with such worshipers. The Lord had already told the prophet that he must not eat bread or drink water in Bethel nor even return the same way he had come. He obeyed and departed, but another snare awaited him.

First Kings 13:11–32 records the compromise of the man of God based on a "new" word from God, a supposed message from an angel to an old prophet living in Bethel. It was, in fact, a lie. Believing the lie, the man disobeyed what God had told him and ate and drank in Bethel. On his return to Judah he met his death from an attack by a lion. The seriousness of his original message was underscored by this severe judgment from God. The old prophet of Bethel recognized that God was speaking loudly in all the incidents surrounding the mission of the man from Judah. The old prophet confirmed that the message was indeed from God and would come to pass.

But how did the incidents surrounding the man of God from Judah impact Jeroboam? What difference would this make in his life and in his reign? Would he respond in repentance?

📖 Read 1 Kings 13:33–34. How did Jeroboam respond to the whole incident?

_____

_____

What significance would that have (v. 34)?

_____

_____

God's message of judgment emphasized the seriousness of Jeroboam's sin.

Jeroboam did not turn from his evil ways. He gathered and established more priests for the high places, not from the priestly tribe of Levi, but from any of the tribes, any of the people willing to serve regardless of the directions and prohibitions of the Word of God. The NKJV translates the latter part of verse 33, *"and he* [Jeroboam] *became one of the priests of the high places."* This reveals even more his self-occupied, self-exalting attitude, rebelling in the face of God's clear will. As a result of his attitudes, actions, and ways, a sentence of death was passed on him and upon his entire house.

GOD'S JUDGMENT ON JEROBOAM

Jeroboam persisted in wanting to rule his way. God had spoken through His Word. He had spoken personally through the prophet Ahijah, offering Jeroboam the blessings of an enduring house if he would follow God the way David had. When he took things into his own hands and established his own religious rituals and festivities, God came with a clear warning. With the death of the man from Judah, he saw the seriousness of God about true worship. But Jeroboam would listen to none of it. He would not follow God. He wanted to rule his own life, so God let him. But he soon found that he was powerless in many ways.

📖 Read 1 Kings 14:1–4. How did Jeroboam try to handle this crisis in his family?

_____

_____

Why do you think he acted this way?

_____

_____

_____

Did You Know?
GETTING THE NAMES STRAIGHT

There are two Abijah's and one Ahijah during this period. In Judah, Rehoboam had a son named Abijah, while in Israel, Jeroboam I had a son with the same name. There was also a prophet in Israel named Ahijah the Shilonite.

Jeroboam's son Abijah became sick, apparently very seriously ill. Jeroboam had received a true prophecy from Ahijah before he became king, and now he hoped for another word from the prophet concerning his son. To find out what would happen to his son, Jeroboam convinced his wife to disguise herself and go to Ahijah with an offering, the offering of a common man or woman. Why would Jeroboam want her disguised as a common woman? Perhaps he did not want the people to know he was seeking help from a prophet of the Lord. Perhaps he was too proud to admit the evil of his ways and humble himself before the Lord and one of His true servants. His actions admitted that he was powerless to bring healing to his son. All his man-made rituals and self-appointed priests were helpless and useless.

The Lord spoke to Ahijah as Jeroboam's wife approached and gave him the message to speak concerning Jeroboam, his house, and his son (14:5–16). What was that message?

_____

_____

📖 Read 1 Kings 14:5–9. The Lord contrasts David and Jeroboam giving three characteristics of David and three of Jeroboam. List those characteristics as given in verses 8 and 9.

David	Jeroboam
1. _____	1. ___
2. _____	2. ___
3. _____	3. ___

David followed the Lord with a whole heart, keeping His commandments, and doing what was right in *God's* sight. Jeroboam did not follow the Lord. In fact, he cast Him behind his back, turning away from Him and His ways to follow after the desires and devices of his own heart. Jeroboam set up idols and accomplished more evil than any of his predecessors.

📖 What was the judgment on Jeroboam (1 Kings 14:10–14, 17–18)?

_____

_____

_____

📖 Read 1 Kings 14:15–16. What was the judgment on Israel?

_____

_____

Why was Israel judged also?

_____

_____

_____

The Lord was angered by Jeroboam's actions and brought His judgment on Jeroboam and his house. The Lord spoke of making *"a clean sweep of the house of Jeroboam, as one sweeps away dung until it is all gone"* (14:10). Jeroboam had so corrupted himself and his house that he was compared to dung, the physical waste product of flesh. In Philippians 3:3–8, Paul spoke of all his human accomplishments apart from Christ as "rubbish" or dung, worthy only to be thrown away.

This judgment included the dishonor of no proper burial, rather the one dying in the city would be eaten by scavenging dogs, and the one dying in the fields would be eaten by the birds. This was true for all but Abijah, Jeroboam's son. He was the one exception in the house of Jeroboam, the one who had a heart to follow God. *"In him something good was found toward the LORD God of Israel in the house of Jeroboam"* (14:13).

In the midst of the corruption of those around him, Abijah was pleasing to the Lord. Apparently, he had a heart that honored God as God, that was surrendered to Him, and that desired to follow and obey Him. It also appears that he had accomplished what God wanted in his life. God chose that the time for his death had come. His death would serve to call attention to the evil of his father and of the nation, as well as reveal the righteous ways of the Lord. In mourning for Abijah, perhaps some would be brought to repentance and to the kind of surrender found in the heart of Abijah.

In his prophecy, Ahijah also proclaimed that the people of Israel would one day face God's judgment for their turning away from the Lord to follow after their idols and the evil desires of their hearts. In His perfect holiness, God would not allow the corruption of the land to continue, especially in His covenant people. He would "strike" them, "uproot" them, and "scatter" them, all part of removing them from the place of covenant blessing to the place of judgment. If they did not want to follow God, if they did not want to live in His presence, then He would give them what they wanted.

In His perfect holiness, God would not allow the corruption of the land to continue, especially in His covenant people.

> **Jeroboam was ever seeking for himself; self-occupied, self-centered, rebelling against the Lord and His ways, ever fighting to insure the accomplishment of his will, his way.**

Jeroboam was ever seeking for himself. He did not hesitate to go to war to get what he wanted (James 3:14–16; 4:1–2). First Kings 14:30 notes *"there was war between Rehoboam and Jeroboam continually"* (Rehoboam reigned ca. 931–914 BC). In 2 Chronicles 13:1–20, we find the account of one of Jeroboam's later attempts to conquer: during the three-year reign of Abijah, Rehoboam's son, over Judah (ca. 913–911 BC), Jeroboam attacked with 800,000 troops. What do we discover in this incident?

📖 Read the account in 2 Chronicles 13:1–20. What is at the heart of this battle according to verse 12?

_____

_____

_____

What three specific things did God do according to verses 15–20?

_____

_____

_____

This battle was a picture of the life and reign of Jeroboam; self-occupied, self-centered, rebelling against the Lord and His ways, ever fighting to insure the accomplishment of his will, his way. We find a great contrast in Abijah and his men. They came to the battle and went into the fight trusting the Lord. In the midst of the battle *"they cried to the LORD,"* and saw God smite Jeroboam and his troops (v. 14). They captured several towns and villages from Jeroboam's realm giving Jeroboam a great defeat and greatly weakening him. Soon after this *"the LORD struck him and he died"* (v. 20), the beginning of the end of the house of Jeroboam.

📖 Nadab the son of Jeroboam became king in his place. Read 1 Kings 15:25–28. How long did he reign?

_____

What kind of reign did Nadab have (v. 26)?

_____

_____

Nadab only reigned for two years, and he followed in the ways of Jeroboam, including the evils of idolatry.

📖 Read 1 Kings 15:28–30. What happens to Jeroboam's family (v. 29)?

_____

_____

According to verses 29 and 30, why did this happen?

_____

_____

_____

_____

📖 Read 2 Kings 23:15–18. What happens to the altars of Jeroboam?

_____

_____

_____

_____

Why did this happen (v. 16)?

_____

_____

God fulfills His word. He deals with sin and rebellion. He destroyed all the house of Jeroboam through king Baasha around 909 BC, about two years after the death of Jeroboam. All of this was because of the sins of Jeroboam which he committed and because of the way he led Israel into sin. The Lord dealt with him and his house in anger after many warnings and calls to repentance. In the reign of king Josiah of Judah (640–609 BC), the altar and the high place at Bethel were destroyed along with their idols. Josiah also burned the bones of the false priests of that place just as the man of God had prophesied.

The life of Jeroboam should instruct us. There comes a point when God says, "Enough!" Many times His judgment comes in giving men what they want, releasing them to chase after their lusts and attaining the desires of their heart. That is the picture painted in Romans chapter one. At other times, He brings about an abrupt end to the wickedness of a man, a family, or a nation as in the case of Pharaoh in Moses' day (Exodus 14), or in the flood of Noah's day (Genesis 6–8). God spoke to Jeroboam several times. He offered him the multiplied blessings of following God. When he chose to follow the devices of his own heart, God warned him more than once. Faithful to His word He brought judgment.

God desires that we walk with Him in mercy, not judgment. When He brings sin to the surface, He wants us to repent and receive forgiveness. The desire of His heart is that we be restored to oneness and harmony with Himself, that we follow Him with a whole heart. Jeroboam chose to turn his back on God, His mercy, and all He offered. And God let him have what he wanted. For us, He calls us to come, follow Him, and discover the joys of His kind of life. May we not follow the foolish devices of our own heart, but rather the wise and loving ways of the heart of our Lord Jesus Christ.

The life of Jeroboam should instruct us. Though God wants us to walk with Him in mercy, not judgment, there comes a point when He says "Enough!"

FOR ME TO FOLLOW GOD

Jeroboam I **DAY FIVE**

God desires that we walk with Him in mercy, not judgment. When He makes us aware of our sin, the Lord wants us to repent and receive forgiveness so that we can be restored to oneness and harmony with Him. It is His will that we follow Him with a whole heart. Jeroboam was given the opportunity to be used greatly by the Lord—to play a prominent role in the workings of God in his day. He was offered the throne of the Northern Kingdom of Israel (the ten northern tribes), and if he would follow God, that throne would become an enduring opportunity for his descendants. God made it clear through the prophet Ahijah that He was not going to bring this to pass in Solomon's lifetime, but when his son would take the throne (1 Kings 11:34–35). But instead of seeking God and waiting on God's will to be done in God's way, Jeroboam tried to take Solomon's throne by force while he was still alive (1 Kings 11:26). As a result he had to flee to Egypt for the rest of Solomon's reign. Yet, in grace, God still gave the throne to him. Look at the promise God gave to Jeroboam:

". . . if you listen to all that I command you and walk in My ways, and do what is right in My sight by observing My statutes and My commandments, as My servant David did, then I will be with you and build you an enduring house as I built for David, and I will give Israel to you." (1 Kings 11:38)

All that was required of Jeroboam was "following God" and his family line would be established like Abraham's and David's were before him. But Jeroboam chose to turn his back on God, His mercy, and all He offered. He followed the foolish devices of his own heart instead of following God.

📖 Think back to the opportunity God gave to Jeroboam (see Day One). Why do you think he turned his back on that opportunity?

_____

_____

_____

What do you see about Jeroboam's heart that is a warning to you?

_____

_____

_____

Jeroboam, along with his wicked companions, sought to gain for themselves all that power and position made available to them. Instead of using his God-given position to serve God and His people, Jeroboam chose to serve himself—to follow the devices of his own heart. He misused the servant position of being a leader, and instead, became a harsh master more concerned with pleasing himself than pleasing God. He surrounded himself with "worthless men" and "scoundrels" (2 Chronicles 13:7), who counseled him to turn the entire nation of Israel to idolatry (1 Kings 12:28). Even then, God did not give up on Jeroboam. He faithfully sent warning after warning, but Jeroboam refused to listen to the Lord who placed him on the throne.

Each of us are leaders in some arena of life. God has placed us in positions to lead others either by our words or our example. Consider the list below, and identify each area where God has made you a leader of others.

> **Are you living a life filled with the devices of your own heart, or are you seeking to follow the desires of the heart of God?**

___ Employer	___ Trainer	___ Club officer
___ Elder or Deacon	___ Board member	___ Employee with seniority
___ Upperclassman	___ Parent	___ Teacher
___ Older sibling	___ Supervisor	___ Manager
___ Public official	___ Senior citizen	___ Spokesperson for others
___ Other leadership position:_____		

Are you using your superior position to serve the Lord and those you lead, or to serve yourself and the devices of your own heart?

Use Leadership Positions to Serve God:

___ Always   ___ Often   ___ Usually   ___ Seldom   ___ Never

Use Leadership Positions to Serve Others:

___ Always   ___ Often   ___ Usually   ___ Seldom   ___ Never

Use Leadership Positions to Serve Self:

___ Always   ___ Often   ___ Usually   ___ Seldom   ___ Never

Since God is faithfully committed to us, He warns us when we stray from Him. We see this clearly illustrated in the life of Jeroboam. Time and again God let him know he was not what he should be. But sadly, he did not listen.

📖 In each of the passages below, God sends a warning to king Jeroboam. In your own words, summarize what you think the warning is and whether God is warning by a divine circumstance of judgment given to Jeroboam, a judging consequence given to someone around him, or a specific word from God to him.

1 Kings 11:29–35 _____

_____

_____

_____

1 Kings 13:1–2 _____

_____

_____

_____

1 Kings 13:3, 5 _____

_____

_____

_____

1 Kings 13:4 _____

_____

_____

_____

1 Kings 13:14–25 _____

_____

_____

_____

1 Kings 14:1 _____

_____

_____

_____

1 Kings 14:6–18 _____

_____

_____

_____

Although God warned Jeroboam in every way imaginable, he would not listen. God warned him through His judgment of Solomon. God warned him by a direct rebuke via "the man of God from Judah." God warned Jeroboam by breaking in two the pagan altar he had built. God warned him by withering his hand when it was raised against the prophet. God warned him by judging that prophet when he disobeyed God's instruction. God warned him through the illness and eventual death of his son. God warned him through another direct message via the prophet, Ahijah. What powerful evidence of God's longsuffering patience! Yet still Jeroboam would not listen and repent. His stubborn, rebellious heart is reflected in the statement of 1 Kings 13:33–34,

> *After this event Jeroboam did not return from his evil way, but again he made priests of the high places from among all the people; any who would, he ordained, to be priests of the high places. And this event became sin to the house of Jeroboam, even to blot it out and destroy it from off the face of the earth.*

Looking honestly at your own life, has God been trying to get your attention about a matter? Are you listening? Are there any warnings from God yet to be heeded? One benefit we have that Jeroboam did not have is the whole Word of God in both the Old and New Testaments. Yet this greater privilege brings with it greater accountability. God judged Jeroboam with increasing harshness as he rejected the divine warnings. When Jeroboam didn't learn from the calamity of others, the calamity fell upon him. God made an example of him by destroying his household and ending his family line. That example was a warning to the people of his day, but it is also a warning to us today. God is faithful to warn us when we stray, and to judge us when we do not heed his warnings.

Look at these different areas, and ask the Lord to make you sensitive to any words of warning you see.

Are there any warnings for you in the judgment God has meted out to those around you?

_____

_____

_____

_____

Are there any warnings from God in the words of people He has sent to you?

_____

_____

_____

_____

Are there some warnings from God to be seen in calamities He has brought into your life?

_____

_____

_____

Are there any warnings that God is giving you directly from the Scriptures?

_____

_____

_____

God is faithful to pursue us even when we stray. He will warn us when judgment is coming, and thankfully, He will hear our cries for repentance. Psalm 86:15 says, *"But Thou, O Lord, art a God merciful and gracious, slow to anger and abundant in lovingkindness and truth."* What an awesome truth there is to be seen that when Jeroboam, wicked as he was, repented of raising his hand against the prophet of God, his withered hand was healed. There is mercy with God, but that mercy cannot be overlooked. Mercy spurned is a prelude to sure and swift judgment. Jeroboam could have followed God and avoided this judgment.

Maybe the greatest application of this week's lesson is not of unheeded warnings in your own life. Perhaps God wants you to be that prophet's voice in someone else's life. Perhaps there is someone you need to speak to in a spirit of humility and gentleness (Galatians 6:1), to bring them to restoration.

Write down the name of anyone you sense God wants you to lovingly confront about sin and rebellion. Maybe you can be an agent of mercy in calling them to repentance.

_____

_____

One final word of warning from the life of Jeroboam: Regardless of our choices, others will follow our example. A phrase you see repeated about virtually every king of the northern ten tribes, is that they *"followed in the sins of Jeroboam, son of Nebat."* Fifteen kings are specifically mentioned in this way. If we do not heed the warnings of God, we may be setting an example by our lives that will cause others to stumble.

Take some time to pray about this week's lesson.

 Lord, I thank You that *"Thou, O Lord, art a God merciful and gracious, slow to anger and abundant in lovingkindness and truth."* Thank You for the many ways You have shown mercy and grace to me, and for the many times You have been slow to anger even though I was rebellious. Thank You for being faithful to send warning my way through Your Word, through faithful servants, through judging others in ways I can see, and even for sending judging circumstances to me when I am stubborn and rebellious. Lord, soften my heart. Do whatever it takes to get my attention when I need to be called back to You. And make me an instrument of warning to those in my life who need loving confrontation. Amen.

> "But Thou, O Lord, art a God merciful and gracious, slow to anger and abundant in lovingkindness and truth."
>
> **Psalm 86:15**

Now, write out your own prayer to the Lord from what you have learned this week from the life of Jeroboam.

_____

_____

_____

_____

_____

_____

_____

_____

_____

_____

The Life of Jeroboam I and His Impact on Israel

DATE	EVENTS	SCRIPTURE
	Jeroboam was born to Nebat and Zeruah in Zereda in the territory of Ephraim.	1 Kings 11:26
	His father died and Zeruah became a widow.	1 Kings 11:26
971–931 BC	Most likely he grew up under the reign of king Solomon. Jeroboam was one of Solomon's servants during part of that time.	1 Kings 11:26
After 946	He was distinguished as "industrious" and was made an officer/overseer over forced labor of the house of Joseph (Ephraim and Manasseh) building the Millo and repairing the city of David. [For the chronology of these building projects, see 1 Kings 6:37; 7:1; 9:10, 15, 22, 24.]	1 Kings 11:27–28
	Ahijah prophesied of the kingdom being torn apart. The tribe of Judah served as the Southern Kingdom with Rehoboam as king, and the ten tribes served as the Northern Kingdom with Jeroboam I as king.	1 Kings 11:29–39
	Jeroboam rebelled against Solomon and Solomon sought to kill him.	1 Kings 11:26, 40
	Jeroboam sought asylum in Egypt under Shishak, king of Egypt. [Probable influence of Egyptian thinking, laws, and religion/gods.]	1 Kings 11:40
931	King Solomon died.	1 Kings 11:40–43
931	Jeroboam returned to Israel.	1 Kings 12:2–3; 2 Chronicles 10:2
931	Jeroboam served as spokesman for the ten tribes, meeting with Rehoboam at Shechem.	1 Kings 12:3–16 2 Chronicles 10:3
931	The men Jeroboam relied on for counsel were "worthless" and "scoundrels" (literally, "sons of Belial").	2 Chronicles 13:6–7
931	Jeroboam was made king over Israel, the ten northern tribes, at Shechem.	1 Kings 12:20
931	Jeroboam made his capital at Shechem.	1 Kings 12:25
931	Jeroboam built Penuel east of the Jordan River on the Jabbok River.	1 Kings 12:25
931	Jeroboam made two golden calves and set them up at Dan and Bethel.	1 Kings 12:26–30
	Beginning in 931, Jeroboam rejected all priests from the tribe of Levi (Levites) from serving as priests. Many moved to Judah.	2 Chronicles 11:13–14, 16–17
	Jeroboam appointed false priests from any tribe (not just Levi).	1 Kings 12:31
	Jeroboam also set up idols of satyrs/goats in many "high places" in Israel.	2 Chronicles 11:15
931–928	Many of the faithful in Israel moved to Judah.	2 Chronicles 11:16–17
	Jeroboam created a false feast to be celebrated on the eighth month, fifteenth day, one month after the Feast of Tabernacles/Booths in Jerusalem.	1 Kings 12:32–33
	A prophet from Judah spoke against the altar in Bethel, concerning its future destruction by Joash and the sign of the altar splitting and the ashes spilling that day.	1 Kings 13:1–3
	Jeroboam stood against the prophet, and the Lord withered his hand.	1 Kings 13:4
	The altar at Bethel cracked, and the ashes spilled out, thus defiling the altar. [On God's instructions for the ashes of the altar, see Leviticus 4:12; 6:10–11; 16:27.]	1 Kings 13:5
	Jeroboam asked him to entreat the Lord to restore his hand and arm. The Lord granted his request.	1 Kings 13:6
	The prophet from Judah left Bethel, but failed to follow the Lord's direction, and was slain by a lion after heeding a false prophecy.	1 Kings 13:7–31
	The old prophet of Bethel confirmed the word of the man of God from Judah against the altar at Bethel and against the high places.	1 Kings 13:32
	After all the warnings of the prophet, Jeroboam persisted in his wickedness by ordaining any who desired the office as priests of the high places, and he became a priest himself.	1 Kings 13:33–34
	Jeroboam's son Abijah (probable heir to the throne) became ill, and Jeroboam sent his wife under disguise to Ahijah the prophet on behalf of his son.	1 Kings 14:1–4
	The Lord informed the prophet of what Jeroboam was doing and gave him a message to give Jeroboam's wife concerning the child's death, concerning certain judgment on the entire house of Jeroboam, and concerning judgment on Israel for following the sins of Jeroboam.	1 Kings 14:5–16
	When Jeroboam's wife returned to her house, the child died as she crossed the threshold, as the prophet had said. All Israel mourned for him.	1 Kings 14:17–18

DATE	EVENTS	SCRIPTURE
931–914	Jeroboam had continual war with Rehoboam, king of Judah.	1 Kings 14:30; 15:6
913–911	Jeroboam of Israel, who had 800,000 troops, waged war with Abijam (Abijah), king of Judah and son of Rehoboam, who had only 400,000 troops. However, 500,000 of Israel's troops fell. Abijam (Abijah) pursued Jeroboam and captured several cities from Israel.	1 Kings 15:7; 2 Chronicles 13:2–19
910	Jeroboam did not recover strength after the war with Abijam (Abijah). *"The LORD struck him and he died"* (13:20). This was the end of the reign of Jeroboam I, but not the end of his wickedness. Many walked in the sins of Jeroboam.	2 Chronicles 13:20; 1 Kings 14:19–20
ca. 909	About two years after Jeroboam's death, the house of Jeroboam was slain by Baasha, king of Israel, fulfilling the word of the Lord concerning God's judgment on Jeroboam I.	1 Kings 15:28–30
640–609	During his reign, king Josiah destroyed the altars at Bethel in fulfillment of the word of the Lord through the man of God from Judah.	1 Kings 13:2; 2 Kings 23:15–18

The Impact of the Sin of Jeroboam I on Future Generations in Israel

DATE	REIGN	SCRIPTURE	
910–909 BC	In the reign of Nadab, son of Jeroboam I. Slain by Baasha	1 Kings 15:25–28	
909–886	In the reign of Baasha, son of Ahijah	1 Kings 15:30, 34; 16:1–4, 7, 11–13	
885 BC	In the reign of Zimri, commander of half the chariots of king Elah, son of Baasha. Zimri killed the drunken Elah and all the house of Baasha and, soon after, died a tragic death. He reigned only 7 days.	1 Kings 16:8–20	
885–874	In the reign of Omri, commander of the army of Israel under Elah.	1 Kings 16:16–28	
874–853	In the reign of Ahab, son of Omri	1 Kings 16:30–33; 17:1; 21:17–26, 29; 2 Kings 10:10–11, 17	
853–852	In the reign of Ahaziah, son of Ahab	1 Kings 22:52–53; 2 Kings 1:4, 17	
852–841	In the reign of Jehoram (Joram), son of Ahab	2 Kings 9:5–10, 22–26	
841–814	In the reign of Jehu, son of Jehoshaphat	2 Kings 9:2, 3; 10:29, 31	2 Kings 17:7–23
814–798	In the reign of Jehoahaz, son of Jehu	2 Kings 13:1–2, 6, 11	2 Kings 17:7–23
798–782	In the reign of Jehoash (Joash), son of Jehoahaz	2 Kings 13:10–11	2 Kings 17:7–23
793–753	In the reign of Jeroboam II, son of Joash	2 Kings 14:23–24	2 Kings 17:7–23
753	In the reign of Zechariah, son of Jeroboam II	2 Kings 15:8–9	2 Kings 17:7–23
752–742	In the reign of Menahem, son of Gadi	2 Kings 15:17–18	2 Kings 17:7–23
742–740	In the reign of Pekahiah, son of Menahem	2 Kings 15:23–24	2 Kings 17:7–23
752–732	In the reign of Pekah, son of Remaliah	2 Kings 15:27–28	2 Kings 17:7–23

The Impact of the Ways of Israel and Jeroboam I on the Kings of Judah

DATE	REIGN	SIN AND ITS JUDGMENT
735–715	In the reign of Ahaz, son of Jotham in Judah	2 Kings 16:2–4
695–642	In the reign of Manasseh, son of Hezekiah in Judah	2 Kings 21:1–18; see also 24:3–4
642–640	In the reign of Amon, son of Manasseh in Judah	2 Kings 21:19–24
609	In the reign of Jehoahaz, son of Josiah in Judah. He reigned 3 months.	2 Kings 23:31–34
609–597	In the reign of Jehoioakim/Eliakim, son of Josiah in Judah.	2 Kings 23:34, 37; 24:1–4
597	In the reign of Jehoiachin, son of Jehoiakim in Judah. He reigned 3 months.	2 Kings 24:8–9

Notes

Notes

"THE LORD IS WITH YOU WHEN YOU ARE WITH HIM"

We are told in 2 Chronicles 14:2, *"Asa did good and right in the sight of the LORD his God."* This statement stands in stark contrast to the family in which he grew up. His father, Abijah, and his grandfather, Rehoboam, were sinful men who led Judah away from the Lord. The queen mother (it is uncertain, but apparently she was his grandmother) was a shame to him and the nation, setting up a horrid image as an Asherah, a Canaanite goddess. Yet Asa reigned for forty-one years as one of Judah's most godly kings. He was a reformer, leading the Southern Kingdom back to the worship of the one true God. So effective were his reforms, that many from Israel (the northern ten tribes) defected to his kingdom and joined in the revival of his days. At the end, however, Asa stumbled, and the last five years of his reign were out of step with the godliness that had characterized it up to that point. The civil war with Israel resurfaced, and instead of trusting God, he trusted in an alliance with the pagan king of Aram. The words of Azariah the prophet, spoken to him early in his reign, speak loudly to us as well —*"the LORD is with you when you are with Him. And if you seek Him, He will let you find Him; but if you forsake Him, He will forsake you"* (2 Chronicles 15:2). In Asa's life we see both sides of this promise—when he sought the Lord, he found Him and was prospered, but when he forsook the Lord, he was forsaken.

Asa reigned over Judah for 41 years (911 to 870 BC). Azariah, Oded, and also Hanani the seer prophesied in Judah during his reign. During these 41 years, eight kings reigned in the Northern Kingdom. They include Jeroboam I, Nadab, Baasha, Elah, Zimri, Tibni, Omri, and Ahab. Jehu, Elijah, and Micaiah prophesied in the Northern Kingdom at some time during this period.

WHEN DID HE REIGN?

1050		1000		950		900					850		
SAMUEL	GAD					SHEMAIAH	IDDO	Hanani the Seer				OBADIAH	JOEL
Judge and Prophet		NATHAN					ODED				Jahaziel the Levite		
								AZARIAH					
						Rehoboam	Asa				Jehoshaphat	Jehoram	Ahaziah Joash
						931–913	911–870				873–848	(Joram)	841 835–796
Saul		David		Solomon			Abijam					853–841	Athaliah
1051–1011		1011–971		971–931			913–911						841–835
						Jeroboam I	Nadab	Elah Zimri				Ahaziah	Jehu
		Ishbosheth ruled over Israel				931–910	910–909	886–885 885				853–852	841–814
		1011–1004		960—Temple finished			Baasha	Tibni Ahab				Jehoram	
							909–886	885–880 874–853				(Joram)	
		David ruled over Judah from Hebron						Omri				852–841	
		1011–1004						885–874					
						AHIJAH the Shilonite							
						"A man of God from Judah"				JEHU, son of Hanani			
		David ruled over all Israel and Judah from Jerusalem				A prophet from Samaria in Bethel				MICAIAH			
		1004–971							ELIJAH				ELISHA
		Hiram I of Tyre						Benhadad I of Syria			Benhadad II of Syria		
		981–947						900–860			860–841		

"OUT OF A DYSFUNCTIONAL FAMILY COMES A GODLY KING"

That Asa was such a godly king stands in sharp contrast to the family in which he had been raised. His heart toward God was much more like his great-great grandfather David than any of the preceding kings he would have known personally. It was said of him that he did *"what was good and right in the sight of the LORD his God."* The interesting thing about this statement is that last phrase: *". . . in the sight of the LORD."* Most of the kings of Israel and Judah followed the pattern of the nation during the dismal period of the Judges when *"there was no king in Israel and every man did what was right in his own eyes."* They invented their own standards of goodness and rightness, adapted to their own convenience, desires, and ambitions. But Asa was concerned about what was right in the sight of the Lord. Implied in this simple statement is the necessity that, in order to know what was good and right in the sight of the Lord, Asa had spent a lot of time seeking God and His will. Lest we wrongly believe the worldly philosophies of our day which teach us a man's character is determined by his environment, we want to begin our study of Asa by looking at the environment in which he grew up.

The godly line of David had a tremendous beginning. Though he made mistakes, his devotion to God and quickness to repent marked David as *"a man after God's own heart."* Solomon, his son, started well and ruled Israel with God-given wisdom, but as he multiplied wives, his wives turned his heart away from the Lord, and, in the end, he was far from godly. His son, Rehoboam reigned foolishly, laying heavy burdens on the people and not listening to the wise counsel God placed around him. As a result, the kingdom split and Rehoboam retained power over only the two southern tribes of Judah and Benjamin. His reign was a disappointment, and yet God still was faithful to His covenant with David. Rehoboam was succeeded by his favorite son, Abijam, whose short reign of three years continued Rehoboam's half-hearted devotion to the Lord. But when Asa took the throne, a new day dawned in Judah.

We want to begin by looking at the reign of Asa's grandfather, Rehoboam.

📖 Read 2 Chronicles 10:1–19 and summarize the foolish choices of Rehoboam that led to the division of the kingdom of Israel (vv. 8, 13–15).

_____

_____

_____

_____

Rehoboam stands as a beacon of warning to all who would lead. His foolishness in not listening to the people God had called him to serve, kept him from being the king he should have been. In fact, one could rightly say that his biggest mistake was his inability to listen. Not only did he fail to listen to

> **Following God means seeking Him and His will, listening to His Word and the wisdom of godly men and women around us.**

the concerns of the people, but as verse 13 states, *"Rehoboam forsook the counsel of the elders."* Instead, he listened to his peers, a group of "yes men" who undoubtedly told him what he wanted to hear. As a result, instead of relaxing the heavy rule of his father, he made it worse and lost most of his kingdom, though he did reign seventeen years over Judah.

Now we want to look at the reign of Asa's father, Abijah. Though there are some details of his short reign in 2 Chronicles, the best summary can be found in 1 Kings.

📖 Read 1 Kings 15:1–8, 12. What characterized the reign of Abijah (also called *"Abijam"*)?

_____

_____

_____

_____

Abijah only reigned for three years, and it would seem that the main thing he accomplished was bringing Asa into the world. Sadly, in his reign, Abijah walked *". . . in the sins of his father which he had committed before him."* We know from other passages and from the problems Asa had to deal with in verse 12, that these included male cult prostitutes (homosexual) and the making of idols. Sins are always a reflection of the heart, and in verse 3 we see that the root problem with Abijah is that, like Rehoboam, his heart was not wholly devoted to the Lord his God.

Next we want to look at Maacah. Whether she was Asa's mother or grandmother is uncertain, but most likely she was the wife of Rehoboam and daughter of Absalom who led a revolt against his father, David. Who she was is less important than what she did and how Asa dealt with her. Whether she was mother or grandmother, she served for some time as "queen mother" and no doubt had a hand in the rearing of Asa.

📖 Read 2 Chronicles 15:16. What was the sin of Maacah?

_____

_____

What does that reveal to you about her character?

_____

_____

_____

Maacah, the wicked queen mother, made (the Hebrew word means "to construct, or build") a horrid image (the Hebrew word means "a terror, a hideous idol, a monster, a horrid thing") as an Asherah. Clearly she was no follower of Jehovah. There were no Bible stories told when Asa sat on his grandmother's knee. Whatever their relationship, we know that Asa went against the Oriental culture of the day in banishing her from her position and destroying her work.

God wants our hearts to be like David's heart—"wholly devoted to the LORD," 1 Kings 15:3.

Out of such a family one would hardly expect an Asa. Yet God in His faithfulness raises up a man with a heart for Him. We want to close out our study today by focusing on the contrasting goodness of Asa, set against the backdrop of his family.

📖 Read 2 Chronicles 14:1–7. List the things Asa did in the first ten years of his reign.

_____

_____

_____

_____

_____

_____

The *"good and right"* that Asa did was to remove the foreign (Canaanite) altars and high places. Most likely, these were altars to Baal. In addition, he tore down the sacred pillars and the Asherim. Sacred pillars were associated with Baal worship, and Asherim were images of Asherah, mother of seventy gods, including Baal. Not only did he remove the negative influences of Baal worship, but Asa also commanded Judah to seek the Lord and study His Word (the Law). He also removed the *"high places"* and incense altars. These were not for the worship of other gods, but substitutes for the worship of God at Jerusalem as He had commanded. As a result of Asa's "clean-up" campaign, the land was undisturbed for ten years, and, instead of putting their energies into war, they were able to build the nation's infrastructure.

Asa   DAY TWO

FAITH IS THE VICTORY

Asa had inherited quite an army from his father. In 2 Chronicles 13 we learn that with God's help, the army of Judah, though surrounded, was able to defeat Israel, and, in this one battle, half a million soldiers of Israel were slain. Building on this victory, Abijah fortified his troops and *"became powerful"* (v. 21). Though Abijah's reign was short, he left behind a well-organized and experienced army, but most importantly, an army that had trusted the Lord and seen victory. It is worth noting that in their battle with Israel the soldiers of Judah *"cried to the LORD"* (v. 14), though there is no record of Abijah crying to the Lord, and *"it was God that routed Jeroboam and all Israel."*

📖 Take a look at 2 Chronicles 14:8. What was the make-up of Asa's army?

_____

_____

_____

_____

Not only did Asa boast an army of over half a million men, but it was a well-balanced army. The 300,000 soldiers of Judah were outfitted and adept at hand-to-hand combat. The 280,000 soldiers of Benjamin were trained and equipped for attacking the foe from a distance. Their bows were a decided advantage in that they could attack an opponent before he reached them. The verse closes by indicating that all of them were *"valiant warriors."* As any general would know, what is important is not just how many soldiers you have in the fight, but how much fight you have in your soldiers.

📖 Now read 2 Chronicles 14:9–10. What circumstance faced Asa?

_____

_____

_____

These verses tell us that Zerah the Ethiopian came out against Judah. The verse literally reads Zerah "the Cushite." He was not from modern day Ethiopia, but rather from the region of the Sudan just below Egypt. His army was quite formidable, numbering a million field soldiers plus three hundred chariot teams. He came to Mareshah, a city between Gaza and Jerusalem, belonging to Judah, and the invasion sets the stage for war.

📖 According to 2 Chronicles 14:10–11, how does Asa respond to the threat of Zerah?

_____

_____

_____

_____

Asa prepared for battle, but before he met Zerah, he met with God. What is significant here is not just that he called to the Lord, but through the content of his prayer we see clearly the focus of his trust. Asa makes it clear that he realized only God could bring victory under the circumstances. He characterizes his army as *"those who have no strength"* while describing the Ethiopians as *"the powerful"* and *"this multitude."* In this passage, he is not just asking for God's help in the improbable, he is asking for deliverance in the impossible.

📖 Read 2 Chronicles 14:12–15. What was the outcome of the battle with Zerah?

_____

_____

_____

_____

As a result of their trust in God, Asa and the armies of Judah saw a total victory. The text indicates that the Lord did something initially that put the Ethiopian army to flight (the text literally reads, *"...the LORD struck the Ethiopians"*). Asa and the troops were able to follow and defeat them utterly, bringing back much *"plunder"* or spoils from the battle. The lesson is obvious: when we are dependent on the Lord, we can count on His strong support.

Did You Know?

VICTORY BELONGS TO THE LORD

In his reaction to the attack of the Ethiopians and Egyptians (ruled by Zerah the Ethiopian) around 900 BC, Asa shows us that when we are dependent on the Lord, we can count on His strong support. Twenty-five years before this attack, Shishak of Egypt invaded Judah when Rehoboam ruled. Rehoboam and the people of Judah had abandoned the Lord, so the Lord allowed them to face defeat and servitude. Asa and the people of Judah depended on the Lord, and He gave victory. After Asa's victory, Judah was free of Egyptian interference for 160 years. The Lord honored their trust.

TRUST AND OBEY, FOR THERE IS NO OTHER WAY

After the mighty victory over the Ethiopians, one might expect Asa to let up in his pursuit of God. Sadly, with many of the kings, their victories made them proud, and often led them to trust themselves instead of the Lord. Perhaps Asa, too, was tempted in such a way, and might have fallen to this temptation had it not been for a divine visitor. The Lord follows up the battle by sending the prophet Azariah to Asa with a message of encouragement and direction. Unlike his father Abijah, Asa didn't rest on his laurels after the victory, nor did he try to take credit for what God did. As a result of his faith and obedience, the Lord blesses him with an even greater task than protecting Judah from without. The Lord calls him to purify Judah from within. The whole of Asa's reign is marked by a time of true revival as the nation turns back to the Lord. Today we want to begin our consideration by looking at the divine visitor and his message.

📖 Read 2 Chronicles 15:1–7. What do you learn about the messenger (v. 1)?

_____

What is the heart of the message (v. 2)?

_____

What does the prophet remind Asa of (vv. 3, 5)?

_____
_____
_____
_____

Where did the victory lie (vv. 4, 6)?

_____

The first, and perhaps the most important observation we need to make about this incident, is that it is the Lord who takes the initiative. The Spirit comes on Azariah, and sends him to Asa. The lesson to Asa in the message, and to us as well, is that *"the LORD is with you when you are with Him."* The prophet reminds Asa and the people of their recent history. The nation suffered because they did not seek the Lord or give Him their hearts. God wants to be sure everyone understands why He allowed them to defeat the Ethiopians.

📖 Now look at verse 8. What two things did Asa immediately do in response to the direction from God?

_____
_____

Asa immediately did two things in response to Azariah's prophecy. First, it gave him the encouragement he needed to remove *"the abominable idols from*

> **Siding with the Lord is more than mere profession, more than lip service. It is wholehearted surrender to the Lord—His Word and His way. When we surrender, the Lord is free to act on our behalf.**

all the land of Judah and Benjamin and from the cities which he had captured in the hill country of Ephraim." The little phrase, "took courage" suggests that this was something he had already been thinking about, but was afraid to do. The second thing Asa did was to restore (renovate) the altar of the Lord.

APPLY All idols are sin, and all sin is an idol. In other words, anything that comes before God and His will in our lives is sin and an idol. What idols have been in your life that God is encouraging you to remove?

_____

_____

_____

When we set out to tear down the idols in our lives, we need to be careful that we don't simply replace them with other idols. When Asa removed the idols, he also restored the altar of God. It is all too easy to get rid of the bad things in our lives and replace them with seemingly good things. But if our focus is on anything but God Himself—even serving Him, we are idolatrous. God wants us to turn away from sin and *to* Him—the only true Victor over sin.

📖 Read through 2 Chronicles 15:9–15. What did Asa do then (v. 9)?

_____

_____

Why were these men of other tribes in Judah (v. 9)?

_____

What did they do when they had assembled (vv. 11–14)?

_____

_____

_____

_____

What was the condition of their heart in doing this (v. 15)?

_____

And what was the result (v. 15)?

_____

_____

Asa gathered together all Judah and Benjamin (the two tribes of the Southern Kingdom known as Judah), as well as people from three of the tribes of the Northern Kingdom (Israel). The explanation given here is significant— *". . . for many defected to him from Israel when they saw that the LORD his God was with him."* Asa sealed this new era of following God with a special sacrifice of seven hundred oxen and seven thousand sheep from the spoils of the battle, and together with the people, makes a covenant with God to seek Him with all their hearts and souls. Asa's example is followed by the people and a great revival and time of peace results.

> ## "Little children, guard yourselves from idols."
>
> ## I John 5:21

THE HEART OF WORSHIP IS SURRENDER.

"I urge you therefore, brethren, by the mercies of God, to present your bodies a living and holy sacrifice, acceptable to God, which is your spiritual service of worship." Romans 12:1

📖 Finally, read 2 Chronicles 15:16–18 and record what additional actions Asa takes in this revival he is leading.

_____

_____

_____

_____

_____

In Asa we see a breath of fresh air as the wind of the Spirit blows through Judah and rekindles the flame of faith.

In his pursuit of holy obedience, Asa removes Maacah from the position of queen mother because of the terrible idol she built and worshiped. In Oriental culture, honoring family elders was almost demanded. For Asa to go against this shows his wholehearted devotion to the Lord as the preeminent authority in his life. Not only did he demote the queen mother, but he personally cut down her horrible idol, broke it to pieces and then burned it. Verse 17 tells us that the high places were not removed from Israel, indicating that as wonderful as this revival was, it didn't reunify the nation or deal with the wrong worship of Israel (the northern ten tribes who were under a different king). Yet in Asa we see a breath of fresh air as the wind of the Spirit blows through Judah and rekindles the flame of faith.

Asa **DAY FOUR**

FAILING TO TRUST AND REPENT

Asa was a godly king, and for the early part of his reign, he led the people as no one had since David. But unfortunately he didn't finish as he started. In the thirty-sixth year of Asa's reign, his devotion and trust was again tested, and this time he didn't fare so well.

The stage was set—what would Asa do? His decisions at this point mark the second period of his reign and form a sad chapter in an otherwise noble biography. Yet at the end of his reign, he is honored by the people with uncharacteristic fanfare reflecting the fact that the memory of Asa's good years far outweighed his mistaken choices in the end. Today we will look at the circumstance that reveals Asa's turning away from trusting the Lord.

📖 Read 2 Chronicles 16:1–6. What situation was Asa faced with (v. 1)?

_____

_____

_____

_____

Baasha, the wicked king of the northern ten tribes of Israel took over Ramah, a city that served as a gateway of sorts between the two kingdoms. Most likely, Baasha tried to stem the tide of defections from Israel to Judah that Asa's good and godly reign had produced. Since the high road to and from Jerusalem passed through Ramah, he made this frontier town a military station, as the text says, *"in order to prevent anyone from going out or coming in to Asa king of Judah."*

How did Asa respond (vv. 2–6)?

_____

_____

_____

_____

_____

_____

Asa, instead of seeking the Lord or trusting Him to deliver, made a hasty, ill-advised treaty with the pagan king of Aram, Ben-hadad, using the temple treasures as payment. Ben-hadad accepted the payoff and attacked Israel forcing Baasha to leave Ramah to defend his territories, and in the short run Asa's plan appeared successful. The pressure was removed.

📖 Now, read 2 Chronicles 16:7–9. What was God's message to Asa through Hanani, the prophet of God?

_____

_____

_____

_____

Why should Asa have known better (v. 8)?

_____

_____

Hanani was a _"seer"_ (one who had visions from God) and was sent by the Lord to rebuke Asa. His message was a simple one: "Because you have trusted Ben-hadad instead of the Lord, you have missed out on the blessing God wanted to give you, and instead, have brought trouble on yourself." He reminds Asa of the victory God gave early in his reign, because _"you relied on the LORD."_ The implication is that if Asa had trusted the Lord, God would have delivered both Baasha and Ben-hadad into his hands and two of his enemies would be gone. Now, instead of removing Ben-hadad as an enemy, Asa has strengthened him with the wealth of Judah—a mistake that would come back to haunt him. Hanani closes his rebuke with a powerful reminder of God's heart toward His people: _"The eyes of the LORD move to and fro throughout the earth that He may strongly support those whose heart is completely His."_ What a powerful promise this is! And yet, for Asa it was a haunting reminder of why he had missed a blessing: his heart was no longer completely the Lord's. God had promised Asa and all Israel, _"The LORD is with you when you are with Him. And if you seek Him, He will let you find Him; but if you forsake Him, He will forsake you"_ (2 Chronicles 15:2). If Asa had sought the Lord, he would have had God's direction. More importantly, if his heart had been completely the Lord's, he would have enjoyed the strong support of God. What blessings we miss when we place our trust anywhere but in the Lord!

📖 Read 2 Chronicles 16:10. How did Asa respond to Hanani's rebuke?

_____

_____

> **"The eyes of the Lord move to and fro throughout the earth that He may strongly support those whose heart is completely His." 2 Chronicles 16:9**

What does that say to you about Asa's heart?

_____

_____

_____

Instead of receiving this rebuke from God with a humble, penitent heart, Asa allowed his kingly pride to be offended, and in his anger he threw this messenger of the Lord into prison. God alone knows what the outcome would have been if Asa had repented in humility and asked the Lord's forgiveness. Instead, he bowed his back and refused to be instructed.

It would seem from the text that it is worse from God's perspective to fail to repent than to fail to trust. Asa became enraged. There is such a thing as righteous anger, yet most human anger is far from righteous: it is the fleshly opposite of humility and repentance. Not only did Asa vent his anger on Hanani the seer, but apparently he also took it out on the people as well. The text tells us he *"oppressed some of the people at the same time."* We are not told what form this oppression took. Most likely it was either persecution of others giving him the same message of concern over the foolish treaty, or of any who would dare take sides with Hanani.

APPLY How do you tend to respond when God confronts you with your sin?

_____ I avoid thinking about it.
_____ I get angry with the messenger.
_____ I avoid God, church, godly friends and the Bible.
_____ It breaks my heart, and I turn to God for help.
_____ I'm upset with myself and determine to try harder.
_____ I compare myself to others and decide I'm not all that bad.

What was your typical response a year ago?

_____

How we consistently respond to sin is one of the best indicators of our spiritual growth. It is evidence of God's work in our lives and our response to Him. The temptation to avoid truly dealing with sin can be a subtle snare.

Sin always has consequences, but it would seem from the teaching of Scripture, that the greatest consequences in our lives are not for acts of sin, but for the failure to repent when we are directly confronted by the Lord with our sin. That is certainly the case with Asa. God is mindful that we are but dust. If there is any lesson to be learned from David, it is that even as sinners it is possible to have a heart after God's heart if we are willing to humbly admit our sins and repent of them. Unfortunately, Asa did not learn that lesson from his great-grandfather.

Read through 2 Chronicles 16:11–13, and identify the consequence of Asa's refusal to repent.

_____

_____

_____

Put Yourself in Their Shoes
GOD WANTS HUMBLE DISCIPLES

This is what He wanted in Asa's life; it is what He wants in our lives also.

• He shows us our sin, so He can show us His love and mercy.

• He wants to show us His forgiveness and get us back in fellowship following Him.

• He calls us to humble ourselves in repentance, turning to Him and His truth so we can walk in the light with Him.

The longsuffering of the Lord is seen in the fact that He waits three years before chastening Asa for his lack of repentance. Eventually the consequences come in the form of a disease in his feet. Most likely Asa's illness was the debilitating disease known as gout, or else some gangrenous condition. The phrase, *"his disease was severe"* is probably better translated "moved upwards in his body," which would seem to indicate the latter diagnosis.

Worse than the physical consequence of this painful disease is the spiritual consequence of a hardened heart. Tragically, even this disease did not move Asa to repentance. Instead of calling on the Lord, he called on the physicians. Most likely these were the Egyptian physicians who were in vogue at the time, pretending to expel diseases by means of charms, incantations, and mystic arts. The greatest tragedy is what might have been if only Asa had returned to the Lord with a whole heart.

Though the end of Asa's life was not what one would hope, he was for the most part, a good and godly king, beloved by the people. They remembered him not for his mistakes, but for his victories and for the revival he brought to Judah.

📖 Take a moment to read carefully through 2 Chronicles 16:14, and write the details of how the people handled his death.

_____

_____

_____

Even though Asa failed, he was fondly remembered. The details given here of his funeral—buried in a carved tomb, surrounded with perfumes and spices, the *"great fire"* made for him—make it clear that the people had not forgotten his goodness, nor the blessings they enjoyed throughout most of his reign. The fact that we are given no such details of special funeral arrangements for any of the kings before him speaks of the special place Asa had in the hearts of his subjects. There is much to learn from his right choices as well as his mistakes.

> *"The Lord is not slow about His promise, as some count slowness, but is patient toward you, not wishing for any to perish but for all to come to repentance."*
> 2 Peter 3:9

FOR ME TO FOLLOW GOD

Asa DAY FIVE

What a powerful promise the words of Azariah are to us today: *"The Lord is with you when you are with Him."* Yet it is not without a stern warning, for Asa was also told, *"if you forsake Him, He will forsake you."* This does not mean that if we stumble the Lord will abandon us, or that if we sin we will go to hell. All of us "have sinned and fall short of the glory of God," and not all of those sins were committed before we met the Lord.

What God seems to be saying to Asa (and to us as well) is that if we abandon Him in the crisis circumstances of our lives, He will sometimes give us over to those circumstances as a tutor to lead us back to Him. Thank goodness there is mercy with the Lord and He doesn't always give us what we deserve. But sometimes in His sovereign wisdom, the Lord sees that the best way He can help us is not to help us. Rather, He forsakes us to the consequences of our choices to forsake Him.

Although the main lesson of Asa's life is not the family he came from, one thing that speaks loudly is the fact that he turned from their wicked ways, and did not use their failures as an excuse for his own. Perhaps you grew up in a godless home as Asa did. Maybe you didn't have the benefit of godly parents or a stable home life.

 As you look at your own walk with God, identify how your family affects you today. (Check all that apply.)

☐ My upbringing prods me to make godly choices.
☐ My home life tempts me toward wrong choices.
☐ I blame my parents for my mistakes and failures.
☐ I use my upbringing to excuse my sinful choices.
☐ I learn from the mistakes of my family.

We are not so much the product of our environment as we are the product of our choices. We cannot control our family's relationship with God. We can only control our own relationship with Him and through the grace we receive from Him, how we respond to our family.

In a crisis we will either trust the Lord, or we will trust something else. In Asa's life we see both illustrated. When he trusted God with the impossible situation of the Ethiopian invasion, he was able to experience seeing God do what only He could do. But when he was faced with a lesser crisis—the invasion by Baasha of the Northern Kingdom—he looked elsewhere for deliverance, and he failed. Proverbs 30:5 tells us, *"Every word of God is tested; He is a shield to those who take refuge in Him."* God is our shield, but just as an umbrella doesn't keep you dry if you don't stand under it, our shield only works when we take refuge there.

God is with us when we are with Him. In a very tangible sense, to be "with God" is to make Him our trust and to place Him first rather than trusting ourselves and putting our desires before His.

 Consider the different areas of your life, and grade how you think you are doing in trusting God with that area and putting Him first. When you face problems in each of the following areas of your life, who do you tend to turn to fix it? (Place an "X" in the appropriate location on the line).

Me	Hopes and Dreams	God
Me	Career	God
Me	Finances	God
Me	Closest Relationships	God

📖 Read Proverbs 3:5–6. What do these verses tell you about what trusting God means?

_____

_____

_____

> # We are not so much the product of our environment as we are the product of our choices.

Trusting God with all our hearts means that we're not holding on to any dependence on ourselves—we're not waiting in the wings with a backup plan. It also means not trusting our own understanding of circumstances: God knows the big picture. It means giving Him His place in every part of our lives; there's nothing we can keep back for ourselves and our agenda. And it means He will lead us. We can count on it because He promised it.

 If someone you knew was struggling with trusting God in one of these areas, what would you tell them to do?

_____

_____

_____

_____

Second Chronicles 16:9 tells us, *"The eyes of the Lord move to and fro throughout the earth that He may strongly support those whose heart is completely His."* The most revealing truth about you right now is not what you are going through, but where your heart is as you are going through it. So once again, how do we keep our hearts with the Lord?

- ✓ Listen daily to what He tells us in His Word.

- ✓ Seek Him in prayer every day.

- ✓ Look at the circumstances of our lives from the perspective that God is God and we are not.

You may be going through a time of great blessing right now, but if your heart is not completely His, that blessing could be a curse in your life. You may be going through a time of great adversity, but you can know that if your heart is completely His, you will enjoy His strong support, and the adversity will one day turn into blessing.

One of the reasons Asa lost the strong support of the Lord was not just because he didn't trust God in the battle with Baasha, but that he didn't repent when confronted with his wrong choice.

Are there any wrong choices in your life that the Lord has convicted you of through this study? Perhaps God wants to use this lesson at this particular time in your life to warn you and to call you back to trusting Him. The key question is "Will you listen?"

 Write down the things the Lord seems to be touching in your heart—perhaps He is convicting you of areas where your heart is not completely His. Or maybe He is identifying trials in your life where you are trusting yourself or others instead of trusting God to be your deliverance. Whatever comes to mind, write it down as a confession to Him.

_____

_____

_____

_____

> *The most revealing truth about you right now is not what you are going through, but where your heart is as you are going through it.*

As I surrender to the Lord Jesus and His Word, I enter into the victory of His Life.

Now, take this opportunity to align yourself with the Lord. Remember, the most important word in the Christian life is not "commitment" but "surrender." Victory is not us overcoming anything, but rather, Jesus overcoming us. As you close this lesson out, take a few moments to open up your life in prayer to the Lord right now.

O Lord, forgive me for my failures to rely completely on You. My life is Yours, and I want to trust You, my Provider, rather than Your provisions of family, friends, or abilities. Train my heart to turn first to You in every circumstance. I want to be sensitive to anything I put before You in my life. Open my eyes to everything that would distract my heart from You. I want to be wholly with You throughout all the days of my life. Thank You for wanting to be with me. In Jesus' name, Amen.

Write out your own prayer of surrender, making your heart completely His. You may not be used to writing out prayers, but you will find that putting them down on paper makes it harder to say something you really don't mean.

_____

_____

_____

_____

_____

_____

_____

_____

_____

_____

_____

Notes

Notes

Ahab

THE SINS OF SERVING SELF

Solomon replaced David as king, and began well. Yet, in his latter years his wives turned his heart away from God and he *"did what was evil in the sight of the LORD, and did not follow the LORD fully, as David his father had done"* (1 Kings 11:6). As a result Israel was split into two kingdoms. Many of the kings of the Southern Kingdom (the two southern tribes) followed the Lord, though their godliness can be traced to the ministry of the prophets God placed around them. It is not surprising that the kingdom of Judah lasted nearly 150 years longer than the Northern Kingdom.

The northern ten tribes followed Jeroboam, Solomon's slave master, and were led into false worship complete with idols, pagan altars, false priests and even false feasts. Israel (the Northern Kingdom) went from Jeroboam to his son Nadab who followed in his sinful footsteps (1 Kings 15:26), and then to Baasha who did likewise (15:34). Baasha was followed by the drunken king, Elah, who was assassinated by Zimri, his commander. Zimri's reign lasted only seven days, but was characterized as walking in the sinful ways of Jeroboam (16:19). When the people displaced him he committed suicide. He was replaced by Omri, the commander of the army, who was the most wicked king yet (16:25–26). Omri's reign lasted twelve years and then he was replaced by his son, Ahab, who took evil ruling to new depths of depravity. Ahab was probably the most wicked king ever to rule over God's people. In his life we see a clear picture of what happens when a leader serves himself instead of others.

Ahab ruled over the Northern Kingdom of Israel from 874 to 853 BC. He began to reign at the conclusion of Asa's reign in Judah and during most of the reign of Jehoshaphat (873–848 BC). He followed his wicked father Omri and was followed by his son Ahaziah. Elijah and Micaiah prophesied in Israel during his reign.

Ahab's life is a clear picture of what happens when a leader serves himself.

WHEN DID HE REIGN?

1050	1000	950	900	850
SAMUEL GAD			SHEMAIAH IDDO Hanani the Seer	OBADIAH JOEL
Judge and Prophet	NATHAN		ODED	Jahaziel the Levite
			AZARIAH	
			Rehoboam Asa	Jehoshaphat Jehoram Ahaziah Joash
			931–913 911–870	873–848 (Joram) 841 835–796
Saul	David	Solomon	Abijam	853–841 Athaliah
1051–1011	1011–971	971–931	913–911	841–835
			Jeroboam I Nadab Elah Zimri	Ahaziah Jehu
			931–910 910–909 886–885 885	853–852 841–814
Ishbosheth ruled over Israel			Baasha Tibni Ahab	Jehoram
1011–1004	960—Temple finished		909–886 885–880 874–853	(Joram)
			Omri	852–841
David ruled over Judah from Hebron			885–874	
1011–1004			AHIJAH the Shilonite	
			"A man of God from Judah"	JEHU, son of Hanani
	David ruled over all Israel and Judah from Jerusalem		A prophet from Samaria in Bethel	MICAIAH
	1004–971		ELIJAH	ELISHA
	Hiram I of Tyre		Benhadad I of Syria	Benhadad II of Syria
	981–947		900–860	860–841

SELFISHNESS IN WORSHIP

What kind of king was Ahab? Evil and wicked do not seem to be strong enough terms to describe his perverse reign. First Kings 16:30 tells us, *"And Ahab the son of Omri did evil in the sight of the LORD more than all who were before him."* What an overwhelming statement! There were some incredibly evil kings before Ahab: Jeroboam brought false worship to Israel; Elah spent most of his reign in a drunken stupor; Omri, Ahab's father, was called the most wicked king yet. But Ahab surpassed them all. Sadly, when a leader is wicked everyone is stained.

Some may have argued, "Ahab is evil, but he does a good job leading the country." After all, he was an effective military leader. "Maybe Ahab's personal life should not matter as long as the country is prospering." Yet it is impossible to separate a leader's performance from his character. The character and behavior of a leader sets the standards for the nation. Ahab's sins made it easy for all of Israel to take their own personal sins lightly.

Perhaps nowhere does Ahab's selfishness show itself more clearly than in worship. Israel's forefathers had established the pattern of worship given to them from the Lord. From Abraham to Moses to David, God had not only defined *who* to worship, but also *how* He was to be worshiped. But Ahab wanted to worship his own way. As some have pointed out, the middle letter in "sin" and the middle letter in "pride" are the same—"I."

> *The character and behavior of a leader set the standards for the nation.*

📖 Read 1 Kings 16:29–33. What three things did Ahab do to begin and set the tone of his reign?

_____

_____

_____

What clues about Ahab's reign do you see in his marriage (v. 31)?

_____

_____

_____

How did his reign compare with that of previous kings (vv. 30–31, 33)?

_____

_____

_____

> *Ahab led the people not only away from the Lord but also against the Lord.*

The idea of verse 31 is that the wickedness of Jeroboam was nothing compared to Ahab. In hindsight we can appreciate more what a terrible influence his wife, Jezebel would be. Since her father is identified as *"Ethbaal king of the Sidonians,"* we can draw a few conclusions.

First, since his name includes "baal" we can assume that he held a lifelong observance of this pagan religion with all of its wicked practices including infant sacrifice. Second, we know from history that the Sidonians were among the idolatrous tribes that made up the Canaanites. Remember, it was because of the sins of the Canaanites that God removed them from the land. Third, since Jezebel was the daughter of a king, most likely their marriage was intended to form a political alliance.

Apparently it is through Jezebel's influence that Ahab makes his push to drag Israel into the worship of Baal as well as the Asherah. Asherah was a female deity worshiped as the mother of some seventy gods including Baal. Sidon was the center of that particular form of idolatry. What an incredible commentary on Ahab's life that he *". . . did more to provoke the LORD God of Israel than all the kings of Israel who were before."* The implication of this comment is not just that he was more wicked than any of the kings before him, but that he was more wicked than *all* of them put together!

📖 Now look at 1 Kings 16:34, compare it with Joshua 6:26. What does this incident tell you about Ahab's reign?

_____

_____

_____

God had made it clear in Joshua's day that Jericho was never to be rebuilt. Joshua 6:26 tells us, *"Cursed before the Lord is the man who rises up and builds this city Jericho; with the loss of his first-born he shall lay its foundation, and with the loss of his youngest son he shall set up its gates."* Not only does 1 Kings 6:34 show us that God fulfilled His promise against the man who attempted to rebuild Jericho, but it is significant that the attempt occurred during Ahab's reign.

Scripture does not tell us if anyone had attempted to rebuild Jericho before this man, Hiel the Bethelite. Perhaps others also had this idea. But in previous reigns the salt and light of a God-fearing nation and God-fearing kings prevented this. That Ahab allowed this blatant violation of the revealed will of God shows his personal disregard for the Lord and His dictates. Following God was unimportant to him. The wickedness of Ahab's reign is reflected not only in the fact that *he* allowed this to be done, but that apparently none of the people attempted to stop this sinful act either.

📖 Look at 1 Kings 18:4, 13, 19 and 22. What else does Ahab allow to happen during his reign?

_____

_____

_____

_____

What does it say about his selfishness in worship?

_____

_____

_____

Although we are given no details of when, or exactly why, apparently Ahab's evil wife, Jezebel had every prophet of the Lord she could lay her

Ahab disregarded the LORD and defied His Word.

With Ahab, ethics were supplanted by expedience.

hands on put to death. Jezebel was not a Jew, but Ahab was. Yet he allowed this atrocity to take place during his reign. This shows how little value he placed on the worship of the Lord and his failure to take Jehovah seriously.

Not only does he allow Jezebel to put the prophets of the Lord to death, but he also allows her to put 450 prophets of Baal and 400 prophets of the Asherah on her personal payroll (eating at her table). There is no indication in any of this that Ahab was a devout worshiper of any god but himself. Apparently it is Jezebel who is serious about Baal worship, but by allowing it Ahab places his wife above the God of Israel and shows how he has devalued Jehovah. Ethics are supplanted by expedience.

Perhaps no story that involves Ahab is more familiar than the encounter with Elijah and the prophets of Baal on Mount Carmel. We'll look at that story more thoroughly in another volume when we study Elijah, but there are a few significant points to highlight here. As you probably remember, the encounter at Carmel (1 Kings 18) came at the end of a three-year drought sent from the Lord. Elijah challenged the prophets of Baal to a contest: they would call to their god, and he would call to his. The god who answers with fire is the god Israel will worship.

Of course Baal did not answer since he was a god invented by men. When it was Elijah's turn, he prayed to the one true God, Jehovah, and was answered by fire from heaven which consumed his sacrifice. Israel repented of their Baal worship and put to death all 850 pagan prophets. Now let's look at Ahab's role in all of this.

📖 Read 1 Kings 18:41—19:2, and list everything Ahab did.

_____
_____
_____
_____
_____

What things would you have expected him to do that he didn't?

_____
_____
_____

Did You Know?

WHO WAS REALLY TO BLAME?

Ahab blamed Elijah for the drought and resulting famine in Israel. He even sent his representatives to the surrounding nations to find Elijah, making the people swear an oath if they said that Elijah was not there (1 Kings 18:10, 17–18). A man controlled by selfishness always looks for someone to blame for his problems.

"If the LORD is God, follow Him." 1 Kings 18:21

Ahab's immediate response to the encounter at Carmel is a bit surprising. He offered no rebuke to Elijah, and even seems to be following his instructions. If Ahab were truly devoted to Baal one would expect some form of grieving or even revenge. Instead there seems to be a sense of complacency. We must realize however that the people affirmed that the Lord (Jehovah) is God (Elohim). Ahab's silence was probably motivated more by fear of the people than by fear of Jehovah. This seems evident since he immediately ran home to inform Jezebel who then vowed revenge.

All of this seems to suggest that Ahab had no religious convictions in either direction. His worship was simply pointed in whichever direction was expedient at the time. Truly, he was only devoted to himself. He was the object of his worship.

SELFISHNESS IN BATTLE

Once the choice is made to enthrone self, it quickly stains every area of our lives. As Ahab becomes the object of his own worship, his own will and way become more important than truth or right. The difference between the kings of Judah and these northern kings began in the first days of their reign. The first act of a king of Judah, like their forefathers, David and Solomon, was to write a personal copy of the Law which they were responsible to read regularly (Deuteronomy 17:18–20).

Ahab had made no such copy, and with most of the priests and prophets either dead or banished, he had no regular reminders of God's will. His will was all that mattered to him. He was accountable only to himself. As the famous wisdom of Lord Acton states, "Power corrupts, and absolute power corrupts absolutely." When any of us lose sight of our accountability to God, self begins to dominate. One of the most important tasks a king was responsible for was leading the nation militarily. Although Ahab was an effective military commander, because he wasn't submitted to God personally, his military leadership was stained by his selfishness.

📖 Read 1 Kings 20:1–12. Summarize the circumstances in which Ahab finds himself.

_____

_____

_____

How did Ahab respond (vv. 4, 7–9)?

_____

_____

_____

We always looks for the easiest way out personally, regardless of what it costs those around us.

Not only did Ben-hadad king of Aram (Damascus) come against Ahab, but with him came thirty-two other kings. In those days, each city usually had its own king, so this represented a formidable opponent for Ahab. Yet his quick capitulation to Ben-hadad's demands is surprising. Not only was he willing to forfeit his wealth for the sake of peace, but he was willing to put his wives and children in harm's way to protect himself. But that was not enough to satisfy Ben-hadad. His next demand was that his servants be allowed to tour the palace and cart off everything desirable. On advice of his counselors, Ahab drew a line in the sand and refused to concede anything else.

Had Ahab been a king of godly character, he would have sought the Lord first of all. And he would have chosen death with honor over such a dishonorable peace. But we always look for the easiest way out personally, regardless of what it costs those around us.

📖 Read 1 Kings 20:13–21. Identify what the Lord did for Ahab.

_____

_____

Why did the Lord do this (v. 13)?

_____

Is there any evidence of gratitude on Ahab's part?

_____

Even though Ahab did not seek the Lord, for the sake of His people, God graciously sent word through a prophet that He was going to bring deliverance. God gave Ahab the wisdom needed, telling him by whose hand He would deliver him, but that he should attack first. Most importantly, God gave Ben-hadad into his hands and allowed the much smaller army to vanquish this marauding multitude.

The reason for God's dealings here, according to verse 13, was so that Ahab would know that He is the Lord. Conspicuously absent from this narrative is any evidence of thankfulness or gratitude. There is no acknowledgment of God at all. Ahab followed the Lord's instructions for his own sake, but he never sought the Lord, and gave no thanks or glory to the Lord for his deliverance.

📖 Read 1 Kings 20:22–30. What else did the Lord do for Ahab?

_____

_____

_____

What two reasons does He give this time (v. 28)?

_____

_____

A second time God sent word through a prophet warning Ahab of an upcoming attack and giving wisdom on what to do about it. He warned that at the turn of the year, Ben-hadad will return, and that he must be ready. In verse 28 we see two reasons given for God's defeating Ben-hadad: **a)** to judge the blaspheming of the Arameans, and **b)** to show Ahab that He is the Lord.

Yet again, there is no acknowledgement by Ahab of the Lord or expression of gratitude, nor is there any evidence of repentance from his evil deeds. Few of us have had such opportunities to witness God's power and deliverance, but there is no indication that any of this changed Ahab's view toward God.

📖 Read 1 Kings 20:31–43. What did God want Ahab to do?

_____

_____

_____

What did he do instead?

_____

_____

_____

It is God's nature to give—to provide and protect. Ahab failed to see this over and over again. He was too focused on himself to show gratitude for all the Lord was doing.

God wants people to know that He is indeed the LORD (JEHOVAH or YAHWEH), and then to respond in reverence, love, and obedience (1 Kings 20:13, 28).

God had given Ben-hadad into Ahab's hands. The phrase *"I had devoted to destruction"* (v. 42) indicates God had placed Ben-hadad "under the ban," meaning there were to be no prisoners taken and no peace treaties signed. Everyone was to be killed because of God's judgment (Deuteronomy 7:2; 20:16–18). Since they were under the ban, God must have communicated this to Ahab in advance. Through the personal circumstances of the prophet, God illustrates that He desired Ahab to strike Ben-hadad. Instead, Ahab let his enemy escape for the promise of future benefit.

He made the same mistake as Saul, and like Saul, would lose his kingdom because of it. Ahab was more concerned about his own glory and profit than the will of the Lord. There is no gratitude for deliverance, no acknowledgment of the Lord, no seeking of God's will. Ahab was only concerned with saving himself. Instead of being repentant and humbling himself before the Lord, he went home and had a pity party (my own translation of *". . . sullen and vexed"* [v. 43]). What a tragic thing it is, when those positioned to serve God by leading, end up serving themselves.

It is amazing grace that God would do so much for such a wicked king—that God would go to such pains to make himself known to Ahab, the most wicked king Israel had ever known. Yet God continually placed around Ahab evidences of Himself. Leadership is God's idea. In fact, Romans 13 calls governing authorities a *"minister"* of God. Yet no one can truly lead who has not learned to follow God. Sadly, though the recipient of such grace, Ahab chose to follow himself instead of God, and instead of serving the people, he served only himself.

> **Ahab was more concerned about his own glory and profit than the will of the Lord.**

SELFISHNESS IN POSSESSIONS

DAY THREE

One of the greatest reflections of David's heart was his view of his possessions (and of the things he did not possess). When Saul possessed the throne after he had been rejected as king, David refused to take it by force, but waited on the Lord to give it to him. When Ornan the Jebusite offered to give him the threshing floor where Abraham had sacrificed Isaac, he refused to take it without payment, being unwilling to worship God with that which cost him nothing. When his mighty men were moved by his longing to drink from the well in Jerusalem and risked their lives to fetch water for him, instead of guzzling it down, he pours it out as an offering to the Lord in recognition of their sacrifice. When preparations were being made to build the temple, it was David who took the lead, starting the project with a gift of 100,000 talents of gold and 1,000,000 talents of silver as well as innumerable quantities of bronze and iron, timber and stone (1 Chronicles 22:14). Then in addition, he gave a second offering of 3,000 talents of gold and 7,000 talents of silver (1 Chronicles 29:2–5).

Obviously, David was not possessed by his possessions. In his prayer for the temple he revealed his heart: *". . . who am I and who are my people that we should be able to offer as generously as this? For all things come from Thee, and from Thy hand we have given Thee"* (1 Chronicles 29:14). What a contrast is this example of Ahab! Like David, his view of possessions reflected his heart, and what a different heart it was. Today we will see what is revealed there.

Did You Know?

PROPERTY RIGHTS IN ISRAEL

Naboth would not part with his land because it was "the inheritance of my fathers" (1 Kings 21:3) and as such was not to be sold or traded out of his tribe. Numbers 36:7–9 clearly stated that land was not to be transferred from one tribe to another. Each tribe was to hold on to their inheritance. The law in Leviticus 25:23 also said the land could not be sold permanently. Naboth saw Ahab's proposal as against the Lord ("the LORD forbid") and His Word, a sin against Him.

📖 Read 1 Kings 21:1–4. What do you learn there about Ahab's desires?

_____

_____

_____

How did he respond when he didn't get his way (v. 4)?

_____

_____

_____

Ahab looked out his window one day and decided he wanted the vineyard of his neighbor, Naboth. Ahab did nothing wrong in making a request of the land. The price he offered was a fair one. But because of the family ties to the land Naboth was unwilling to sell. The phrase, _"the LORD forbid"_ indicates that Naboth viewed selling the land as a violation of the law and disobedience to God.

Ahab went into a tailspin, throwing another pity party followed by a king-sized tantrum. Although he lived in luxury in the ivory palace he had built for himself (1 Kings 22:39), he could not be satisfied staring at something he could not have, and hid himself in his room for a royal pout, refusing even to eat. Without contentment the selfish heart cannot be satisfied even in abundance.

📖 Read 1 Kings 21:5–16. How did Jezebel go about getting the vineyard over which Ahab was pining?

_____

_____

_____

_____

When Jezebel saw Ahab's pouting, she took matters into her own hands and arranged to get Naboth out of the way. Through a conspiracy with the elders of the city she trumped up false charges of cursing God and the king, and had Naboth stoned to death.

Although the elders were participants in this evil act, that does not mean they supported it. By using the royal seal on the instructions, Jezebel made them a royal mandate. Disobedience to a royal mandate from the king (she did it in Ahab's name) would probably result in death. Ahab showed no regret for this action of treachery. As soon as the dirty deed was completed, he made haste to take possession of the object of his desire. A selfish heart does not care who gets hurt so long as it gets what it wants.

📖 Read 1 Kings 21:17–26. What rebuke did Elijah give to Ahab (vv. 19, 25–26)?

_____

_____

_____

Without contentment the selfish heart cannot be satisfied even in abundance.

A person who has rejected righteousness, hates those who are righteous.

How did Ahab view this messenger from God (v. 20)?

_____

_____

God revealed to Elijah the wicked thing that Ahab had done and called Elijah to confront him with his sin. God pronounced judgment: Ahab would die, and the dogs would lick up his blood in the same place where Naboth died. It was a harsh but fitting punishment.

Ahab's heart is revealed in how he received the messenger from God. His first response was to call Elijah his "enemy." A person who has rejected righteousness hates those who are righteous. To be confronted with his sin was a good thing for Ahab, but he did not receive it as such. What a sad commentary on his wicked life is found in verses 25–26: *"Surely there was no one like Ahab who sold himself to do evil in the sight of the Lord, because Jezebel his wife incited him. And he acted very abominably in following idols, according to all that the Amorites had done, whom the Lord cast out before the sons of Israel."*

📖 Read the conclusion of the story in 1 Kings 21:27–29. What was Ahab's response?

_____

_____

What did the Lord do (v. 29)?

_____

_____

Ahab's response here is surprising. For the first time we see evidence of repentance and humility. Instead of pouting over this bad news, he tore his clothes, put on sackcloth, and fasted—accepted signs of a godly repentance. It is difficult to determine what is more amazing here, that the wicked king Ahab would ever repent, or that God would relent of His judgment because of it. Although there were still to be consequences, they are delayed until after Ahab's death.

What an amazing thing that even a wicked king like Ahab can repent and find mercy with the Lord. Remember, *"there was no one like Ahab who sold himself to do evil."* No prodigal is beyond the reach of the Lord's lovingkindness if he is willing to humble himself.

> *It is difficult to determine what is more amazing here, that the wicked king Ahab would ever repent, or that God would relent of His judgment because of it.*

Selfishness in Counsel

Ahab DAY FOUR

One of the lessons we have seen over and over again is that God's wisdom is always available to those who seek it. God graciously makes His will known in ways we can understand. We will find Him if we will seek Him. And even when we do not seek Him, His grace is sometimes manifested in His seeking us and placing people around us to point us back to Him. God wants us to follow Him, and as the Good Shepherd, He seeks after His wandering sheep.

As we will see today, God faithfully placed around Ahab people who would point him the right way. But God would not force His will on him. Ahab had to choose if he would follow God or follow self. That same choice is placed before each of us. Perhaps we can learn from Ahab's mistakes.

📖 Take a few minutes to skim back through the story of Elijah and the prophets of Baal in 1 Kings 18:20—19:2. How did Ahab respond to God's powerful proving of Himself (vv. 41–42, 45; 19:1)?

_____

_____

As with the battles against Ben-hadad, Ahab was given every possible reason to believe in God, yet there was no acknowledgment, no repentance, no seeking of the Lord. I have never seen fire fall from heaven. I have never witnessed a three-and-a-half year drought or its end as a result of specific prayer. I have never seen a whole nation turn to God in revival. Yet as Ahab shows, if I am not willing to be dethroned by One greater than myself, even these things will not make me believe. Ahab reigned during the ministry of one of the greatest prophets of the Old Testament, Elijah, yet he paid no heed to his message.

📖 Read 1 Kings 16:31. What happened when Ahab married Jezebel?

_____

_____

We are told that as a result of marrying Jezebel, Ahab *"went to serve Baal and worshiped him."* As we saw yesterday, Ahab embraced the plan of Jezebel to have Naboth put to death.

From what you have learned of Ahab so far, why do you think he was willing to listen to the counsel of Jezebel?

_____

_____

_____

First Kings 16:31 links Ahab's marriage with Jezebel to the extreme nature of Ahab's evils. That she was the daughter of Ethbaal is significant, for not only was he the king of the Sidonians, but he was also their high priest in Baal worship. Ahab knew this and allowed Jezebel to draw both him and the Northern Kingdom into Baal worship.

In this case, as with the murder of Naboth, Ahab listened to Jezebel because she was saying what he already wanted to hear. Even though he did not know about her plans for Naboth until after the fact, he embraced them and showed no regret. A self-focused person not only listens to those who tell them what they want to hear, but also surrounds themselves with those kind of people.

📖 Read 1 Kings 22:1–12. What is wrong with the message of the four hundred prophets (vv. 1–6)?

_____

_____

_____

A self-focused person not only listens to those who tell him what he wants to hear, but surrounds himself with those kind of people.

"The way of a fool is right in his own eyes, but a wise man is he who listens to counsel."

Proverbs 12:15

To appreciate what the majority counsel was, we must understand who these men were. They were not true prophets of the Lord. They worshiped at Bethel in a pagan way established by Jeroboam that included a golden calf (1 Kings 12:28–29). They were also on Ahab's payroll. They did not rebuke his evil acts but overlooked his Baal worship (probably they participated in it) and only spoke good prophecies to him (v.8). Ahab had surrounded himself with "yes" men. A self-focused leader wants to be told he is right even when he is not.

What, according to verse 8, was Ahab's view of Micaiah, and why?

_____

_____

_____

_____

Ahab hated Micaiah (whose name means "who is like the Lord?") because as Ahab puts it, *". . . he does not prophesy good concerning me."* God had placed around Ahab a brave prophet who was willing to tell him what he needed to hear, instead of tickling his ears, as the others had done. But Ahab was not teachable. He didn't care if Micaiah was right or not. His only consideration was if he liked what the prophet had to say. Proverbs 12:15 tells us, *"The way of a fool is right in his own eyes, But a wise man is he who listens to counsel."*

📖 Read 1 Kings 22:13–29. How did Ahab respond to Micaiah's prophesy (vv. 18, 26–27, 29)?

> There is no escaping God's judgment when we choose to follow our own way in rebellion against Him.

_____

_____

_____

_____

Ahab's response to Micaiah is two-fold. First, he had Micaiah imprisoned and fed sparingly (22:26–27). Second, and more telling though less obvious, he ignored the truth Micaiah brought him from the Lord. He went up against Ramoth-gilead even though Micaiah had told him it would cost him his life.

One of the greatest ways God's wrath is manifested to the hardened heart is to let it have its way. By grace God made known to Ahab the outcome of this ill-fated venture, but Ahab only valued the opinion of those who told him what he wanted to hear.

📖 Read 1 Kings 22:30–40. What happened to Ahab (vv. 34–35, 37–38)?

_____

_____

_____

Ahab's life ended in tragedy as he received the consequences of following self instead of God. Even his trickery with Jehoshaphat did not prosper. What a powerful illustration of the sovereign hand of God that he died by an arrow drawn at random (aimed at no one) that happened to strike him in the only place his armor would allow a fatal wound. There is no escaping God's judgment when we choose to follow our own way in rebellion against Him.

FOR ME TO FOLLOW GOD

We can learn some valuable lessons from Ahab. Wisdom purchased from the mistakes of others is much less costly.

Ahab is the antithesis of one who follows God. First Kings 16:30 tells us, *"And Ahab the son of Omri did evil in the sight of the LORD more than all who were before him."* His reign was ruinous for Israel, and was characterized in a consistent selfishness. He never really left the nursery, and throughout his life we see a striving to accumulate toys, and juvenile tantrums when he didn't get what he wanted. Though it is doubtful anyone of similar wickedness would have any interest in a Bible study such as this one, there are important lessons even the most godly can learn from this negative example. If we are wise, we will learn from his mistakes and not let them become our own. Wisdom purchased from the mistakes of others is much less costly.

Selfishness stained all that Ahab did, and one of the first things we observed in Ahab was how selfishness stained his worship. Hopefully none of us have erected altars to Baal, but, to some degree, all of us from time to time allow our worship to be stained by self-centered values. For example, I have often wondered what would happen to charitable giving if we no longer got a tax deduction for it. It might make offerings smaller, but it would sure purify motives. Now, I am not saying that it is wrong to accept a legal tax advantage, but hopefully that is not the reason we give.

While other gods may not show up in the rituals of our religious activity, they may lurk in our priorities and practices the rest of the week. John identifies our temptations in 1 John 2:16 as, *". . . the lust of the flesh and the lust of the eyes and the boastful pride of life."* The lust of the flesh would include gods of a sensual nature, such as sex and food. The lust of the eyes points toward our possessions—a lust for material things such as cars, boats, houses, etc. Even these things can become our gods if we worship and serve them. The boastful pride of life speaks for itself—it is the enthronement of self above God, the lust for accomplishments and awards to tell us how great we are compared to others.

While all of us are tempted in each of these areas from time to time, there is probably one of the three that we fall into more than others. As you look honestly at your own life, rate these temptations as to how difficult each one is for you (with "1" being the hardest to resist).

_____The lust of the flesh
_____The lust of the eyes
_____The boastful pride of life

Realize that self is at the root of each of these. Paul warned Timothy that in the last days *". . . men will be lovers of self, lovers of money . . . lovers of pleasure rather than lovers of God"* (2 Timothy 3:2,4). How does God view a selfish life?

Ahab is a biblical model of the enthronement of self. First Kings 21:25 tells us that he *". . . sold himself to do evil in the sight of the Lord."* The wording makes him sound like a harlot. Not only did selfishness stain his worship, it also stained his leadership which was usually self-serving. God wants each of us to serve others and to trust Him to meet our needs. In fact, when we stop striving to meet our own needs and reach out to meet those of someone else it is one of the purest acts of faith in God. Though we are not Ahabs, we have the same disease of self lurking in our hearts. As painful as it may be, if we really want to follow God, we have to be willing to examine our hearts to see what is there. David instructed Solomon, *"watch your heart with all diligence,"* for out of the heart flow the springs of our life. If we see selfishness flowing from our hearts, it is able to stain even the good things that we do and make them of no account to God. The right thing, done from wrong motives, is only the "form of godliness." The Pharisees did "good deeds" but man-centered righteousness is "filthy rags" to the Lord.

Consider these areas of your life, and take a few moments to evaluate any stains of selfishness you see there.

Worship

Giving

Personal benefits/ ← 1 2 3 4 5 6 7 8 9 10 → Pleasing God/
(Recognition, tax credit)   (as unto the Lord)

Service

Personal pride/ ← 1 2 3 4 5 6 7 8 9 10 → Pleasing God
Attention of others   Meet others' needs

Business/Family

Ethics

Benefit self ← 1 2 3 4 5 6 7 8 9 10 → Do the right thing

Relationships

Be right ← 1 2 3 4 5 6 7 8 9 10 → Put others first

Possessions

Attitude

It belongs to me ← 1 2 3 4 5 6 7 8 9 10 → It belongs to God

Sharing What I Have

What does it ← 1 2 3 4 5 6 7 8 9 10 → What needs can
cost me?   I meet?

Advice of Others

Seeking Advice from Others

Tell me what I ← 1 2 3 4 5 6 7 8 9 10 → Tell me what I
want to hear   need to hear

Accepting Rebuke

Take offense ← 1 2 3 4 5 6 7 8 9 10 → Look for truth

One of the hardest things about looking honestly into your own heart is realizing that selfishness has left so many stains. For example, in my home, do I discipline my children for their good or for my own convenience? In an argument with my wife, am I more concerned about proving myself right, or loving my mate and hearing her heart? I see so many stains of selfishness when I look honestly at my own life. Confession may be good for the soul, but it is bad for the reputation. Truth is, I fall so far short of the man I want to be (and the man I want others to think that I am). I am a sinner in need of the Savior. I am not what I ought to be, but by His grace I am not what I used to be, and by His working and my surrender, I am not what I am going to be.

As painful as it may be, if we really want to follow God, we have to be willing to examine our hearts to see what is there.

I am not what I used to be, I am not now what I ought to be, and I am not what I am going to be.

As you evaluate the stains of selfishness revealed in the areas listed, write down any actions you need to make in surrendering an area back to the Lord.

_____

_____

_____

_____

"Do nothing from selfishness or empty conceit . . ."
Philippians 2:3

In Philippians 2:3–4 the apostle Paul admonishes us, _"Do nothing from selfishness or empty conceit, but with humility of mind let each of you regard one another as more important than himself; do not merely look out for your own personal interests, but also for the interests of others."_ One of the ways we can gauge the "selfishness quotient" of our hearts is by looking at whose interests we place as most important. The great Chicago Bears football player, Gale Sayers wrote a book entitled, "I Am Third." The unusual title was actually his philosophy of life. He felt that the right priorities required that in any situation, "God must be first, my friends second, and I am third." Of course, that slogan is easier to say than to live, but we see that lived out consistently by the Lord Jesus.

In the categories listed below, mark an "E" for "easy" beside each area where you find it easy to put God and others first, and an "H" for "hard" beside each area where you find it difficult to put God and others first.

_____ Work   _____ Friendships
_____ Mate   _____ Church
_____ Community   _____ Home
_____ Other_____

Another area where selfishness is clearly seen in Ahab's life was his tendency to surround himself with people who told him what he wanted to hear. Are there any ways this is true in your life?

_____

_____

_____

_____

If you are like me, the truths of this lesson have surfaced much selfishness in your heart. How do we deal with that? The same way we deal with all sin.

Confession
Dealing with sin begins with true confession, agreeing with God about our sins. Confession is not simply saying "I'm sorry." That could mean only that we regret the consequences of our action. True confession means coming to the place where in our hearts we are ready to agree with God that what we did was wrong.

Are there any sins God has brought to your mind? Have you confessed them?

_____

_____

_____

Repentance

True confession always involves repentance, a turning away from the action or attitude. If we say that something is sin, but we are not willing to turn from it, then we haven't really agreed with God that it is wrong. Is there anything God has surfaced this week for which you need to repent?

_____

_____

_____

_____

Romans 13:14 tells us, "*. . . make no provision for the flesh in regard to its lusts.*" This means "don't make it easy for yourself to sin." Is there anything you need to do to stop making provision for your flesh in this/these area(s)?

_____

_____

_____

_____

Restitution

The next step in dealing with sin is restitution. This means doing whatever is in our power to make what is wrong right. It may mean asking for forgiveness from someone we have wronged. It may mean money—paying to replace something or making it up to someone we have defrauded. It may mean willingly accepting the consequences of our sinful action. Or it may mean a sacrificial act of love to someone who has been robbed by our selfishness. Whatever it is, restitution involves doing what is in our power to make things right. Are there any acts of restitution you sense the Lord calling you to?

_____

_____

_____

_____

Surrender

The most important realization we must come to is that if we could please God in our own strength and energy, we wouldn't need a Savior. To deal with sin rightly we must surrender that area back to the Lord's control. We must acknowledge our need for His empowerment in that area, and we must make active choices to trust Him situation by situation. What do you need to surrender?

_____

_____

_____

_____

Growth

Finally, if we are to become the kind of people we really want to be, the kind of people who follow God faithfully instead of living our lives as "lovers of

Repentance is an action.

"To deal with sin rightly, we must surrender that area back to the Lord's control."

self," we must grow. We must study God's Word in the areas of our weaknesses, and we must apply that Word to our lives.

If there is any one point we need to close with in our study of Ahab, it is this single, amazing fact: Even the most wicked king can repent and get mercy from God. As you close your study, write out a prayer that includes what you need to say to God in the areas of confession, repentance, restitution, surrender and growth along with gratefulness for all of God's mercies.

_____
_____
_____
_____
_____
_____
_____
_____
_____
_____
_____
_____

Notes

Notes

Jehoshaphat

UNEQUALLY YOKED

Jehoshaphat reigned over Judah from 873 to 848 BC. Jahaziel spoke the word of the Lord in his day. Three kings ruled in Israel at that time, Ahab, Ahaziah, and Jehoram (Joram), and Micaiah prophesied to Ahab and Jehoshaphat.

*I*n 2 Corinthians 6:14 the apostle Paul warns us, *"Do not be bound together with unbelievers; for what partnership have righteousness and lawlessness, or what fellowship has light with darkness? Or what harmony has Christ with Belial, or what has a believer in common with an unbeliever? Or what agreement has the temple of God with idols?"* The phrase, *"do not be bound together . . ."* is literally "do not be <u>unequally yoked</u>." The picture is of a team of oxen where one is strong and the other is weak. The strong ox cannot force the weak one to pull at his speed, so he must slow down and go at the pace of the weaker ox. In the strongest of terms, Paul makes it clear that the believer is not to make unhealthy ties to the world, whether through marriage, or business or anything else, for the only things the two will have in common are the things of the world. Though Jehoshaphat was a righteous man and faithful leader, he was not as effective as he could have been because he linked himself with unbelievers. Jehoshaphat did not realize the far-reaching consequences on generations to come that resulted from allowing himself to be unequally yoked with unbelievers.

WHEN DID HE REIGN?

1050	1000	950	900	850
SAMUEL GAD Judge and Prophet NATHAN			SHEMAIAH IDDO Hanani the Seer ODED AZARIAH	OBADIAH JOEL Jahaziel the Levite
			Rehoboam Asa 931–913 911–870 Abijam 913–911	Jehoshaphat Jehoram Ahaziah Joash 873–848 (Joram) 841 835–796 853–841 Athaliah 841–835
Saul David Solomon 1051–1011 1011–971 971–931				
Ishbosheth ruled over Israel 1011–1004 960—Temple finished			Jeroboam I Nadab Elah Zimri 931–910 910–909 886–885 885 Baasha Tibni Ahab 909–886 885–880 874–853 Omri 885–874	Ahaziah Jehu 853–852 841–814 Jehoram (Joram) 852–841
David ruled over Judah from Hebron 1011–1004				
David ruled over all Israel and Judah from Jerusalem 1004–971			AHIJAH the Shilonite "A man of God from Judah" A prophet from Samaria in Bethel	JEHU, son of Hanani MICAIAH
				ELIJAH ELISHA
Hiram I of Tyre 981–947			Benhadad I of Syria 900–860	Benhadad II of Syria 860–841

WHEN HE STANDS ALONE, HE STANDS TALL

It is written of Jehoshaphat, "His heart took delight in the ways of the LORD."

2 Chronicles 17:6 (NKJV)

Jehoshaphat was one of the godliest kings Judah ever had. He loved the Lord and trusted him when trials came. We are told in 2 Chronicles 20:32 that *". . . he walked in the way of his father Asa and did not depart from it, doing right in the sight of the LORD."* He had grown up in a believing home and as a child witnessed the revival of his father's reign. He had first-hand knowledge of the mighty way the Lord delivered his father Asa and the armies of Judah from the attacking Ethiopians. He witnessed the positive changes in society as the pagan gods were put away and the worship of the Lord again dominated the land. He learned at his papa's knee the importance of seeking the Lord and listening to His prophets. He even saw the other side of the coin, watching with despair when his father's rejection of the prophecy of Hanani led to his downfall—the declining last five years of Asa's reign. Today we want to begin looking at Jehoshaphat's heart for God and righteous choices.

📖 Read 2 Chronicles 17:1–6. What did Jehoshaphat do when he became king (vv. 1–2)?

_____

_____

_____

What was his relationship with God like (vv. 3–4)?

_____

_____

_____

What were the results of that relationship (vv. 5–6)?

_____

_____

_____

Did You Know?
THE HIGH PLACES

In Numbers 33:50–53, the Lord told Moses to instruct the people to remove the High Places, hills upon which the Canaanites offered incense and practiced their worship of the Baals. Israel used many of these places as a place dedicated to the Lord. Under Solomon there were places where many offered incense to the Lord, but the Lord made it clear that He had a specific place (the Temple) and a specific way (the offerings through His chosen priests) that He wanted His people to offer sacrifices and worship Him. This was to help insure the purity of their worship for their good and the good of the nation. As He knew, the compromises of leaving the High Places would eventually corrupt the worship of God and lead to the practice of idolatry, just as it did in Solomon's life. Jehoshaphat removed the High Places and the detestable idols associated with them.

Our first introduction to Jehoshaphat highlights his wisdom as he stationed troops in strategic places to secure the safety of the kingdom. He enjoyed the blessing of God because he followed the pattern set forth under David, and turned away from Baal worship. He not only sought God, but followed His commandments, and turned from the wicked example of Israel (the northern ten tribes). He was loved and honored by the people, evidence of what kind of leader he must have been. Verse 6 tells us, *". . . he took great pride in the ways of the LORD and again removed the high places and Asherim from Judah."* He apparently reaffirmed the ban on the high places and Asherim (wooden images of a Phoenician goddess), instituted under his father. Apparently such divergent worship may have crept back into Judah during the declining years of Asa's reign.

📖 Looking at 2 Chronicles 17:7–9, identify the reforms Jehoshaphat instituted in the third year of his reign.

_____

_____

_____

What do you think his motives were for doing this?

_____

_____

Amazing as it may seem, Jehoshaphat was the first of Israel or Judah's kings to institute a system of religious instruction for the people. He obviously had the wisdom and insight to realize the need for people to *think* rightly if they were to *live* rightly. This was not a new value in Israel, but he was the first king to actually devise a workable system to make sure that religious education was being conducted throughout the kingdom. The group he appointed—five princes, two priests, and nine Levites—likely did not do all of the instruction themselves, but oversaw the program and insured that it was not neglected.

📖 Read 2 Chronicles 17:10–19 and list the results mentioned of Jehoshaphat's godly reign.

_____

_____

_____

_____

_____

Put Yourself in Their Shoes
PUTTING OFF AND PUTTING ON

Jehoshaphat illustrates one of the foundational truths of walking with God, that we need not only to put off the old things, but also to put on the new.

Putting Off:

• He rid the land of the high places and idols.

Putting On:

• He sent out men to teach the people the Word of God.

• He sent out Levites and priests to instruct the people in proper worship and to perform sacrifices.

One tangible result of Jehoshaphat's following of the Lord, was that the other nations respected both God and him. As a result, they were not willing to make war against Judah. Instead, they brought gifts of appeasement, strengthening the kingdom. As you add up the numbers in the armies of Judah listed here, the total, amazingly, is more than 1.1 million troops. Because this is double what the army numbered under Asa, some have suggested that this was not a numbering of actual troops, but rather, of all the males in Judah available for military duty. It must be remembered though, that because the Lord had been with both Asa and Jehoshaphat, a steady stream of immigrants from Israel to the north had been making their way to Judah. It is quite possible this is the reason for such a large increase in so short a time.

Although we are skipping ahead in Jehoshaphat's reign, it will be helpful to move forward to 2 Chronicles 19 to see yet another of his positive reforms in Judah during the years of his reign.

📖 Read through 2 Chronicles 19:4–11. What did Jehoshaphat himself do (v. 4)?

_____

_____

What did he appoint others to do (v. 5)?

_____

_____

Summarize his instructions to these men (vv. 6–11).

_____

_____

_____

_____

_____

_____

Though Jehoshaphat lived in Jerusalem, he wouldn't allow himself to lose touch with the people and their needs. The statement that he *"went out again among the people . . . and brought them back to the Lord, the God of their fathers"* seems to suggest a second phase of his religious education initiative.

This second wave of emphasis was not only on religious reform, but also on establishing the justice such a righteous stand demands. Through political appointments of Levites, priests, and patriarchs (v. 8) as judges, we see that judicial fairness was important to Jehoshaphat. His warning to these appointees that they were accountable to God for the standards they used to judge went a long way toward establishing a vision for fairness and justice. No wonder he was loved by the people.

Jehoshaphat **DAY TWO**

Did You Know?
THE ENEMIES OF ISRAEL

The Moabites and Ammonites were descendants of Lot and his daughters as a result of their incest after the destruction of Sodom and Gomorrah (Genesis 19:30–38). Those of Mount Seir were the Edomites (descendants of Esau, Jacob's brother), who, like the Israelites, were given their land by the Lord. When Israel came out of Egypt, the Lord instructed Moses that He had given each of them their land and not to take it from them (Deuteronomy 2:4–5, 9, 19). Israel had honored that command. Now they faced these people as enemies and God dealt with them.

WHEN HE STANDS WITH GOD, HE STANDS STRONG

Jehoshaphat is perhaps most remembered for trusting God in battle with the Moabites and Ammonites, and for the mighty deliverance he saw as a result. It was the brightest spot in his reign as king. But it probably happened as a result of lessons learned at the knee of his father. Asa had seen God's power manifested when Judah was attacked by the Ethiopians. No doubt the glory and wonder of God's rescue was remembered fondly as he recounted the details. Perhaps it was young Jehoshaphat's favorite bedtime story. One can almost hear the child calling, "Dad, tell me again about the Ethiopians!"

What we know for certain is that the lesson, probably indelibly written on his heart during the impressionable years of his youth, was not lost on Jehoshaphat. When he was faced with the greatest military crisis of his reign, without hesitation Jehoshaphat called upon the Lord. And like his father before him, he saw God do the things that only God can do. Today we will begin investigating Judah's victory over Moab and Ammon.

📖 Read 2 Chronicles 20:1–2. Summarize the circumstances that surrounded Jehoshaphat.

_____

_____

_____

In verse one we are told that a military coalition of the Moabites and Ammonites, along with some Meunites, has come against Judah. Normally the Moabites and Ammonites were enemies, yet in the climate of the day alliances were formed and broken all the time. No doubt a fragile alliance was formed based on a common enemy—Judah. The report reached Jehoshaphat that this *"great multitude"* was at Engedi and on its way.

Although the New American Standard reads that they came *"out of Aram"* some manuscripts read "Edom" which makes much more sense geographically and historically. This would mean they came around the southern tip of the Dead Sea, the only direct route to Judah that would take them through Engedi. This southern route would allow the invaders to hide their movements by shadowing the mountain chain, which would explain how they were able to make it to Engedi before reports of the invasion could be sent to the king. No doubt the surprise of the attack made the outnumbering army appear even more fearsome.

📖 How, according to verse 3, does Jehoshaphat respond when confronted with the invasion of the enemy?

_____

_____

It is significant first of all that Jehoshaphat was afraid. Fear is a very real, human emotion, and emotions are not sin. What is key is what he did with his fear. The text tells us he *"turned his attention to seek the LORD."* As an act of his will, Jehoshaphat turned his focus away from the object of his fears and turned it to the Lord. Emotions are not sin, but they can turn into sin if we indulge them and do not take them to the Lord.

(APPLY) Think back to the last crisis you faced. Which of the following best describes your response?

_____ Fearful and sought the Lord for His strength.

_____ Fearful and sought answers in my own ability to fix it.

_____ Other:_____

Not only did Jehoshaphat turn his attention to the Lord, but he also turned the attention of the nation to the Lord. By proclaiming a national fast, including the women and even the children (v. 13), he led the people to trust the Lord with the crisis facing them.

📖 Now read 2 Chronicles 20:4–13. What else does Jehoshaphat do?

_____

_____

_____

"O our God . . . We are powerless against this great multitude who are coming against us; nor do we know what to do, but our eyes are on Thee."
2 Chronicles 20:12

Summarize five main points Jehoshaphat makes in his prayer:

_____

_____

_____

_____

_____

After calling the fast, Jehoshaphat gathered the nation and personally led them in corporate prayer. Jehoshaphat's prayer had several key components: **a)** he gave their situation to the Lord and affirmed that only He could save them, **b)** he reminded the Lord of their covenant relationship with Him, **c)** he recognized God's sovereignty over the situation, **d)** he acknowledged their powerlessness and that they didn't know what to do, and **e)** he professed complete dependence on God for their deliverance. Verse 13 shows that the prayer was followed by *"standing before the Lord."* They were waiting on God to answer. All too often we neglect this important aspect of prayer.

📖 Read 2 Chronicles 20:14–19. What does God say in response?

_____

_____

_____

How does He say it?

_____

_____

_____

It should be noted first of all that God spoke, and that when He spoke, He did so by way of a prophet. God always answers the prayers of His people, and one of the ways He speaks to us today is by giving us the wisdom we need in the form of anointed counsel from others.

God speaks through Jahaziel, who being a descendant of Asaph, the leader of praise appointed by David, may have been one of the choir directors. Through Jahaziel, God gives **1)** encouragement (*"do not fear . . . for the battle is not yours but God's"*); **2)** information (*". . . they will come up by the ascent of Ziz . . ."*); and **3)** instruction (*"stand and see the salvation of the Lord"*). Jehoshaphat again led by example, and the people followed him in worshiping the Lord and praising Him.

Jehoshaphat and the people of Judah were obedient to the Lord, and rather than engaging the enemy, they stood before the Lord and sang praises. The army was there—they were prepared for further instructions—but they were waiting on God to do what only He could do.

📖 Read 2 Chronicles 20:22–25. What happened the next day?

_____

_____

_____

Once Judah demonstrated their total dependence upon Him by their praise, the Lord set ambushes against their enemies. Verse 23 indicates that the Moabites and Ammonites destroyed one another. Perhaps the Lord used their long-standing animosity with one another to shatter the fragile coalition they had formed to attack Judah. In any case, by the time Judah investigates, all they find are corpses and *"much spoil."* The term "spoil" was used of the plunder one could carry away in a victorious battle, and there was so much for Judah to gather that it took three days to collect it all, and in the end they were unable to carry it all (v. 25).

📖 Read verses 26 through 30. How did the people respond to the victory (vv. 26–28)?

_____

_____

_____

What was the effect on the nations around Judah (vv. 29–30)?

_____

_____

On the fourth day, Judah gathered and blessed the Lord (v. 26) and then headed back to their homes. As a result of Jehoshaphat and the people of Judah trusting the Lord and the Lord intervening in such a powerful way, verse 29 tells us that *"the dread of God was on all the kingdoms of the lands when they heard that the LORD had fought against the enemies of Israel."* The end result was a period of peace.

The world is not at all impressed with the "good deeds" we do for God. Other religions do good deeds. Even secular society has humanitarian organizations devoted to good deeds. But when God intervenes and does the things that only He can do—then the world stops and takes notice. What the church needs today is people who are willing to trust God and join Him in those things that only He can do.

> **"Then the realm of Jehoshaphat was quiet, for his God gave him rest all around."**
> **2 Chronicles 20:30 (NKJV)**

WHEN HE STANDS WITH AHAB, HE STUMBLES

 **DAY THREE**

W̲e have not looked at the details of Jehoshaphat's reign in a completely chronological fashion, but rather have tried to isolate the positives of his rule first. Yet, we must recognize that the main life principle we can draw from him is not a positive one. Though he was a good and godly king, his willingness to ally himself with those who were not good and godly stained his life and his legacy. Though Jehoshaphat was a righteous man and faithful leader, he was not as effective as he could have been because he unequally yoked himself with unbelievers. In fact, the greatest consequences of his foolish alliances would not be seen until after he was dead and gone.

> *Jehoshaphat's willingness to ally himself with those who were not good and godly stained his life and his legacy.*

Scripture does not tell us why Jehoshaphat sought an alliance with Israel and their wicked king, Ahab, but most likely part of his motive was seeking unity. No one liked the chasm that civil war had formed between the twelve tribes. Yet even the alliances he forged didn't produce unity. They may have given some measure of uniformity, but there can never be true unity between those devoted to God and those who pursue wickedness or other gods. Uniformity with such people only comes as a result of sacrificing truth. In Jehoshaphat's life and reign we see a warning against being unequally yoked with unbelievers.

Having looked at all the positive aspects of the reign of Jehoshaphat, we now need to back up and identify the mistakes he made to see what we can learn.

📖 Read 2 Chronicles 18:1. Record the first example of his life being unequally yoked.

_____

_____

What do you think may have motivated him to do this?

_____

_____

_____

It is important in answering this question that we do not try to look at it through the eyeglasses of our own culture. The text tells us, *". . . he allied himself by marriage with Ahab."* The marriage was between his son Jehoram and Ahab's daughter (21:6), but it was Jehoshaphat who made the choice. Unlike our culture, in those days parents normally made the marital choices, and here the arrangements were made between Jehoshaphat and Ahab. Quite often royal marriages were arranged specifically to form alliances with other nations. Most likely it was Ahab (or his conniving wife, Jezebel) who initiated things.

Jehoshaphat's power and wealth made him an attractive target for the mercenary Ahab, who according to 1 Kings 16:30 did more evil than any of the kings before him. Probably part of Jehoshaphat's reasoning was a desire to see Israel and Judah reunited. Perhaps it was his hope that when his son took the throne, there would no longer be two nations, but one. Sadly, he sought unity by compromising truth and allying himself with a worshiper of Baal. And out of the marriage alliance with Ahab grew other alliances.

📖 Read 2 Chronicles 18:2–3, and identify the second alliance and how it was initiated.

_____

_____

It is while Jehoshaphat visited that Ahab buttered him up with a huge party to entice him to form a military alliance. Ahab wanted Jehoshaphat to fight with him in recapturing Ramoth-gilead, a city of Israel that Ben-hadad captured when Baasha was king of Israel. Jehoshaphat's response is very telling: *"I am as you are, and my people as your people, and we will be with you in the*

Compromising the truth does not lead to unity nor does it build relationships. It is the first step in creating disunity and in destroying relationships.

battle." While this statement was clearly his desire, it was not truth. Although Israel and Judah were all descendants of Abraham, Isaac and Jacob, they were not the same. The people of Judah were worshipers of the one true God, but the people of Israel were devout followers of Baal. Jehoshaphat sacrificed truth for the sake of unity, and would endanger his own life in the process.

But Jehoshaphat did not make an alliance with Ahab without first seeking the Lord.

📖 Read 2 Chronicles 18:4–28. Who desired to seek the Lord (vv. 4–6)?

_____

_____

How did they go about seeking the Lord (vv. 7–11)?

_____

_____

What is the basic message from the Lord (vv. 14–22)?

_____

_____

_____

_____

What did Ahab and Jehoshaphat do with the information received from the only true prophet (vv. 25–28)?

_____

_____

_____

It was Jehoshaphat's idea to seek the Lord, but he entrusted the task to Ahab who assembled four hundred false prophets. Most likely these were not prophets of Baal, but rather, prophets of the Lord on Ahab's payroll who were hired to be "yes" men and give favorable messages. Micaiah's answer initially was the same as these "yes" men of Ahab, but apparently his tone of voice and gestures made it clear he was speaking sarcastically, for Ahab recognized he does not mean what he said. The rest of the story is that Micaiah speaks the truth from the Lord, and sadly, though Jehoshaphat inquired of the Lord, when God spoke, he didn't listen. It does no good for us to seek God if we will not follow Him. As Jesus said in Luke 6:46, *"Why do you call me 'Lord, Lord' and do not do what I say?"*

 Which of the following best describes you and your trust in God and His direction in your life?

_____ I don't seek Him because I'm afraid of what He may say.

_____ I seek Him because I know I'm supposed to, but the decision is mine.

_____ Lord, I love You. Whatever you want for me is good, acceptable, and perfect. My answer is yes no matter what the question may be.

When you seek God's will, do you want to know it so that you can then decide if you will do it? Many times that is our attitude. And often, that may be an

> ## "Yes, Lord" should be the answer whatever the Lord may ask.

important part of why we struggle so to know God's will. God desires that we say yes to Him up front, and then trust Him to hold us to that choice when we are faced with difficulties. When God lays a path out before us, the choice has already been made. Surrender is at the heart of all those who follow God.

📖 Read 2 Chronicles 18:28–30. What danger did Jehoshaphat place himself in because he didn't listen to the Lord?

_____

_____

_____

Ahab was playing Jehoshaphat for a fool. Not only had he enticed Jehoshaphat into battle with him, but he convinced the trusting king to impersonate him, wearing the kingly robes while Ahab traveled in disguise. Little did Jehoshaphat know that he had stepped into the middle of the enemy's battle plan and placed himself in harm's way. By wearing the royal robes into battle while Ahab traveled in disguise, Jehoshaphat almost got himself killed.

📖 Now look at 2 Chronicles 18:31—19:3. How did Jehoshaphat handle the crisis in which he found himself (v. 31)?

_____

_____

What was the outcome of Jehoshaphat's plan?

_____

_____

_____

What was the outcome of Ahab's plan and will?

_____

_____

What did God have to say to Jehoshaphat when he returned to Jerusalem?

_____

_____

When the armies of Aram saw Jehoshaphat, they mistook him for Ahab (just as Ahab intended), and that became the rallying point of the battle. Wisely Jehoshaphat cried out to the Lord and was delivered. Ahab on the other hand, did not fare so well. His conniving did not protect him from the sovereign hand of God. Only the Lord could have engineered it so that a random arrow found an unrecognized target and delivered the only fatal wound his armor would have allowed, severing a major artery and causing Ahab to bleed to death. Though Jehoshaphat escaped with his life, he was rebuked by the Lord through Jehu the prophet for his choice to *"help the wicked."*

It is significant that Jehu, the prophet who delivered the Lord's reprimand, was none other than the son of Hanani, who had delivered a similar rebuke to Jehoshaphat's father, Asa—a rebuke which was rejected and led to his decline. No doubt Jehoshaphat remembered this and apparently took the reprimand to heart, for it was on the heels of this confrontation that he

"Should you help the wicked and love those who hate the LORD?"
2 Chronicles 19:2

expanded his educational reforms and initiated his judicial reforms as well. Sadly, though, the ill-fated alliance with Ahab was not the last mistake Jehoshaphat made in this area of being unequally yoked with unbelievers.

WHEN HE STANDS WITH AHAZIAH, HE FAILS

We have seen that, for the most part, Jehoshaphat was a commendable king, bringing much good to Judah. But he sometimes chose expedience over truth, and was careless with his partnerships. Perhaps this character flaw flowed out of a timid unwillingness to confront the wrong in others. Or possibly it was rooted in the pride of his inability to admit that he could be captivated and succumb to the temptations being unequally yoked placed in his path. Maybe he was so good-hearted that he naively ignored the flaws of others. Or perhaps he just wanted so badly to see Judah and Israel reconciled, that he was willing to sacrifice truth for harmony.

Whatever his reasons for initiating them, Jehoshaphat's continual attempts to join with backslidden Israel were abject failures. In the same way today, we must recognize that there is no unity between those who follow God and those who don't. Unless we are willing to compromise our distinctiveness, we will have to limit our relationships with unbelievers to calling them to repentance and faith in Christ.

Today we will begin looking at the failed business association Jehoshaphat fashions with Ahab's son, Ahaziah. After Ahab's death, his son Ahaziah took the throne for a brief two-year stint. It was during this brief window of time, immediately following the disastrous military coalition with Ahab, that Jehoshaphat forged an economic alliance with Ahaziah.

📖 To fully appreciate the circumstances of the joint business venture between Jehoshaphat and Ahaziah, it will be helpful to read both accounts from Scripture. Read 2 Chronicles 20:35–36 and 1 Kings 22:44, 48, and then list the details you find by comparing the two accounts.

_____

_____

_____

_____

_____

_____

In 2 Chronicles 20:35–36 we see a clear commentary not only on what Jehoshaphat did but on how God viewed it. We are told that he *"allied"* himself with Ahaziah, and from God's perspective, he *". . . acted wickedly in so doing."* Verse 36 makes it clear that the objective of the affiliation was a shipping venture. In 1 Kings 22:44 we are told that one of the indictments

> **Did You Know?**
> ### GETTING THE NAMES STRAIGHT
> Ahaziah, son of Ahab, ruled in Israel (853–852) while Jehoshaphat and Jehoram ruled as co-regents in Judah. Eleven years later Jehoshaphat's grandson named Ahaziah, son of Jehoram and Athaliah, ruled in Judah for one year (841). By the marriage of Jehoram and Athaliah, Ahaziah their son was the nephew of Ahaziah of Israel.

An alliance of wickedness will not prosper.

against Jehoshaphat's reign was that he made peace with the king of Israel. In verse 48 we see that the goal of this joint shipping venture was the renewal of the gold trade with Ophir begun in the days of Solomon (1 Kings 9:28).

📖 Read 2 Chronicles 20:37. What happened as a result of the business venture?

_____

_____

Why did it end this way?

_____

_____

The rebuking words of the prophet Eliezer indicate the business failed for supernatural reasons. Somehow the Lord caused the ships that had been built to be broken and unseaworthy. There were perhaps a thousand things that could have gone wrong in such a venture, and the most important thing to notice is not what went wrong but why it went wrong. The Lord would not allow it to succeed. Perhaps in heaven we will look back on failures in our lives and recognize that it was the sovereign working of God that caused them. God loved Jehoshaphat too much to allow him to prosper in such a mistaken alliance.

What was the motive for this economic alliance? Most likely it was motivated by greed. Solomon amassed great wealth through this gold trade with Ophir. At today's prices, he imported two hundred million dollars in gold. Greed is often the author of compromise, as it seems to have been with Jehoshaphat.

📖 Read 1 Kings 22:49. What do you learn there about the events that follow the initial failure of the business venture?

_____

_____

_____

What does that say to you about Jehoshaphat?

_____

_____

> ## "We will never find what we are looking for in life outside the will of God. He loves us too much to allow our wandering plans to succeed."

After the initial business failure, 1 Kings 22:49 indicates that Ahaziah tries to give it another go, but Jehoshaphat is unwilling. Perhaps he has finally learned his lesson. He listened to the counsel the prophet Eliezer brings him from the Lord, and apparently realizes that this project is not God's will. We will never find what we are looking for in life outside the will of God. He loves us too much to allow our wandering plans to succeed.

Overall, Jehoshaphat was a good and godly king, bringing blessing to Judah. In 2 Chronicles 20:30–34 we see that his reign brought peace to Judah and that it was characterized by *"doing right in the sight of the Lord."* Although his attempts to have the people do away with the "high places" were not completely successful, we are told in 1 Kings 22:46 that those sodomites who remained after Asa's reign, he expelled from the land. Jehoshaphat instituted a systematic program of religious education. He reformed the judicial system of the nation. He led them to trust God in their war with Moab and Ammon. But sadly his long-term legacy fell far short of what it could have been. Let's close out today by looking at some of the long-term consequences of his besetting problem of allowing himself to be unequally yoked.

Jehoshaphat forged an alliance with Ahab, the wicked king of Israel, by marrying his son to Ahab's daughter. Not until both kings were dead and gone was the full cost of this mistake realized.

📖 First, read 2 Chronicles 21:1–6. Long after Jehoshaphat died, the consequences of his alliance with Ahab were still being felt. List all of those consequences you can find from this passage.

_____

_____

_____

One of the first acts Jehoram performed as king was to put to death any rivals who might lay claim to his throne. We are not told in the text, but as we will see later, there is the suggestion that his wife was behind this wicked deed. We are told that through her evil influence, Jehoram followed in the way of Israel's corrupt kings instead of following God as his father did.

📖 Now read 2 Chronicles 22:1–12, and identify what other wickedness came out of the foolish marriage of Jehoshaphat's son with the daughter of Ahab and Jezebel.

_____

_____

_____

_____

_____

_____

Athaliah, the depraved daughter of the evil king Ahab and his wicked wife, Jezebel, became the chief counselor to the king when her son Ahaziah (apparently named after Ahab's son and successor as king) replaced Jehoram on the throne. She guided him toward wickedness and brought in others of the house of Ahab to influence him. Ahaziah renewed the joint military venture begun by Ahab and Jehoshaphat to recapture Ramoth-gilead and got himself killed in the process. As a result, Athaliah seized the throne and put to death every rival she could lay her hands on. It was only God's protection that rescued Joash and prevented the line of David from being extinguished before the Messiah had come.

Jehoshaphat's foolish alliances, becoming unequally yoked, resulted in a resurgence of Baal worship in Judah, the decline of the nation, and almost resulted in the end of the line of David. Like Jehoshaphat, we may not be around long enough to see the full weight of consequence that comes from fleshly choices we make. This should drive us to make certain never to succumb to Jehoshaphat's weakness of being unequally yoked.

Did You Know?
THE CONTINUING CONSEQUENCES OF BEING UNEQUALLY YOKED

Jehoshaphat's alliance with Ahab led Jehoram, Jehoshaphat's son, to marry Athaliah, Ahab's daughter. Jehoram killed all his brothers and led Judah into further idolatry. Therefore God judged him—the Philistines and the Arabians invaded Judah, took all his possessions, his sons (except Jehoahaz, his youngest son), and his wives. He was struck with a painful and deadly intestinal disease and within two years died in severe pain, without honor and *"to no one's sorrow"* (2 Chronicles 21:20, NKJV).

GOD IS IN CONTROL

"I know that Thou canst do all things, And that no purpose of Thine can be thwarted." Job 42:2

FOR ME TO FOLLOW GOD

No one is an island. The whole of our life is spent in weaving together different relationships—some forced upon us by circumstance, and some of our own choosing. We have no say in who our parents are, or our neighbors. We may have no input into who becomes our boss or our governmental leaders. We may not get to pick all of our teachers. In areas beyond our control, we trust the sovereignty of God. But in the relationships we choose, we must choose wisely how those relationships are defined. Strictly speaking, being "unequally yoked" is not just being in a relationship, but choosing a "binding" relationship such as marriage, business partnerships, etc. Scripture makes it clear that we are never to choose to be bound together with unbelievers.

The life lesson we see in Jehoshaphat is the tragedy of how being unequally yoked can wreck a godly legacy. For all of his good points, and personal godliness, this one flaw neutralized much of his effectiveness. He stands in Scripture as a beacon light of warning to us all.

📖 Look at the following passages, and identify how exactly Jehoshaphat became unequally yoked with unbelievers.

2 Chronicles 18:1 _____

_____

_____

2 Chronicles 18:2–3_____

_____

_____

2 Chronicles 20:35–36_____

_____

_____

In these three incidents we see three different kinds of relationships where the principle of being unequally yoked with unbelievers is violated. With Jehoshaphat's son, it is the arena of intimacy and romance—the marriage relationship—where a bond is formed. With Jehoshaphat and Ahab, the unequally yoked relationship is a military and political one. When Jehoshaphat links himself with Ahaziah, the partnership is an economic alliance. In these three we see plenty of common ground to the areas we are prone to make mistakes: romance, politics, and business.

As you reflect on Jehoshaphat's alliance with Israel and their wicked king, Ahab, what do you think may have been his motives for this alliance?

_____

_____

_____

_____

> **Scripture makes it clear that we are never to choose to be bound together with unbelievers.**

Scripture does not give us the answer to this question, and we have already conjectured as to Jehoshaphat's motives. Whether he was moved by a nostalgic longing for unity, or the hope of restoring Israel to her former glory, Jehoshaphat sought after unity with the Northern Kingdom. Yet there is a big difference between "unity" and "uniformity." We can have uniformity with those who do not follow God, but we can never have unity. Even such uniformity can only come by sacrificing truth and ignoring wickedness.

APPLY What are the areas where you are tempted to compromise with unequal yoking?

- ☐ Business partnerships
- ☐ Romance (dating/marriage)
- ☐ Politics
- ☐ Friendships
- ☐ Living Arrangements
- ☐ Other _____

What motives make such binding relationships attractive?

_____

_____

_____

Can you think of any examples in your own life or in the lives of friends where unity was sought wrongly and at the expense of truth?

_____

_____

_____

_____

What consequences came from this?

_____

_____

_____

_____

We must realize that God has painted for us a very human, a very accurate (and sometimes unflattering) portrait of Jehoshaphat, so that through him we might look at our own lives. Integrity demands that we not only study Jehoshaphat's life, but our own lives as well. As you have looked at the lessons from this king of bygone years, God is pricking your own heart and conscience to evaluation and application.

Honestly ask yourself if the truth you have seen this week demands any changes in your present relationships, and write those changes below:

_____

_____

_____

_____

We can have uniformity with those who do not follow God, but we can never have unity.

Along with this, are there any issues in the past that you can't change but you can repent of and make any restoration necessary?

_____

_____

_____

Are there any temptations on the horizon you need to say "no" to because of what you have learned this week?

_____

_____

_____

_____

_____

Guard yourself from wavering on this by making yourself accountable to a trusted, godly friend. Share with them your commitment to not becoming unequally yoked, and ask them to pray for you.

Spend some time in prayer with the Lord right now.

Father, I want you to be Lord of all the kingdoms of my heart. Give me the courage to place my relationship with You first—before my pleasure, before my possessions, before my pride. Guard me from my own weaknesses. Place others in my life to remind me of Your will. Do not lead me into temptation, but deliver me from the stains of evil partnerships. Help me to trust that doing things Your way is really the best way and the way of blessings without regrets. In Jesus' name, Amen.

Write out your own prayer. Remind yourself that your alliance with Him is the most important alliance in your life.

_____

_____

_____

_____

_____

_____

_____

_____

_____

_____

_____

Notes

Notes

Hezekiah

FOLLOWING GOD IN THE CRISES OF LIFE

Hezekiah took the throne in 715 BC and reigned for twenty-nine years. He was one of the greatest kings Judah had known and the last bright spot in a dark period of their history. As a teenager he witnessed the captivity of Israel (the northern ten tribes) in 722 BC. Their land was repopulated with ungodly foreigners from Babylon and other places who flooded it with their false religions and intermarried with what remained of Israel, creating the mixed race known as the Samaritans.

Hezekiah's father was one of the worst kings of Judah, yet led by such advisors as Isaiah, Hosea and Micah, Hezekiah stands as a king who followed God. His reign was marked by tremendous spiritual reforms. Pagan altars, temples and idols were destroyed. Even the bronze serpent Moses had made in the wilderness, which had become an idol to the people, was not spared. Unfortunately, his reforms were short-lived, and were not reproduced by his son, Manasseh. The Scripture has this commentary on his life: *"He trusted in the LORD, the God of Israel; so that after him there was none like him among all the kings of Judah, nor among those who were before him. For he clung to the LORD; he did not depart from following Him, but kept His commandments. . . . And the LORD was with him; wherever he went he prospered"* (2 Kings 18:5–7). The crises that marked Hezekiah's life revealed his character and showed him to be a man who was willing to follow God.

It is likely that Hezekiah first served alongside his father, Ahaz as co-regent from 729 to 715. Hezekiah then ruled as king in Judah from 715 (age 25) to 686 BC. He likely shared a co-regency with his son Manasseh from 695 until his death in 686. During Hezekiah's reign, the prophets Isaiah, Micah, and Hosea prophesied.

WHEN DID HE REIGN?

800	750	700	650	600
"A Prophet" (sent to Amaziah)	ISAIAH MICAH		NAHUM ZEPHANIAH HABAKKUK HULDAH (a prophetess) JEREMIAH	Jehoiachin
Amaziah 796–767	Jotham 750–735 Ahaz 735–715	Manasseh 697–642	Amon 642–640 Jehoahaz (Jeconiah) 609 598–597	
Azariah (Uzziah) 790–739	Hezekiah 715–686		Josiah 640–609 Jehoiakim Zedekiah 609–598 597–586	
Jehoahaz 814–798 Joash (Jehoash) 798–782	Zechariah Menahem Hoshea 753–752 752–742 732–722			605—1st Captivity DANIEL Hananiah
Jeroboam II 793–753	Shallum Pekahiah 752 742–740 Pekah 752–732	There are no more kings or prophets in the Northern Kingdom. Foreign peoples are resettled into the land.		Mishael Azariah 597—2d Captivity
JONAH	AMOS ODED HOSEA			EZEKIEL Nebuchadnezzar 605–562
	Tiglath-pileser I 745–727 Shalmaneser V 727–722	722—Assyria takes Israel into captivity Sennacherib 705–681		612—Fall of Nineveh

SUCCEEDING IN THE CRISIS OF CHOICE

Ultimately, when all is said and done, our lives are a reflection of the choices we make. In fact, life is an unending sequence of choices. Yet often we fail to realize their far-reaching consequences. Hezekiah succeeded in most of the choices that faced him during his reign. As an act of the will, he consistently pursued that which was *"good, right, and true before the LORD his God. And every work which he began in the service of the house of God in law and in commandment, seeking his God, he did with all his heart and prospered"* (2 Chronicles 31:20–21). But the choices that shaped Hezekiah's life did not begin when he took the throne. His choices had been determining the kind of king he would be, long before he began to reign. Perhaps the most important choice of his early life was choosing not to follow his father's example.

📖 Read through 2 Chronicles 28:1–4, 22–27, and record all that you learn there about the kind of king Hezekiah's father proved to be.

_____

_____

_____

_____

_____

_____

Perhaps the most important choice of Hezekiah's early life was his decision not to follow the example of his father, Ahaz.

In 2 Chronicles 28:1–4 we see that instead of following the godly example David had set for the kings, Ahaz followed the negative pattern established by the self-appointed kings of Israel (the Northern Kingdom). He made molten images (idols) for Baal worship. He burnt incense in the Valley of the Son of Hinnom, adopting the pagan practices of his northern neighbors. This valley was also known as "the place of burning" where Molech worship, including infant sacrifice, was practiced. He even went so far as to sacrifice one of his sons as a burnt offering to Molech, an Ammonite deity (2 Kings 16:3), thus resurrecting the pagan practices of the Canaanites who dwelled in the land before Israel. Every form of pagan ritual was brought back during the reign of Hezekiah's father. We do not know which of Hezekiah's brothers was sacrificed to Molech, or if Hezekiah was old enough to remember it, or was even alive at the time—but no doubt his family told him of it. Most likely, it was the first-born son of Ahaz that died by his evil apostasy.

In 2 Chronicles 28:22–27 we see that after the kings of Aram (Syria) had defeated Ahaz in battle, he began worshiping the pagan gods of Damascus. He also closed up the temple, destroying temple artifacts and using their precious metals to pay tribute to other gods. So abhorrent was the reign of Ahaz, that when he died he was not even given a king's burial. It says much of Hezekiah's character that growing up in such a dysfunctional home, he was able to choose instead to follow the Lord.

📖 Look over 2 Chronicles 29:1–19. What does Hezekiah say is to blame for their present state (vv. 6–9)?

_____

_____

_____

_____

What did he propose (vv. 5, 10–11)?

_____

_____

_____

How did the Levites respond (vv. 15–19)?

_____

_____

_____

_____

The Levites, chosen of God to serve in the Temple, had been kept from their sacred duties by the evil choices of King Ahaz (28:24). Here we see that not only did Hezekiah resurrect the priesthood and charge the Levites with reopening the temple, but he had the insight to recognize that it was because of Judah's unfaithfulness during the reign of his father that hard times had come (29:7–9). He reinfused the priesthood with a vision for their God-given responsibilities (29:10–11) and placed Levite leaders in charge of the collections and preparations for cleansing the temple (29:12–14). It is significant that the cleansing work began on the first day of the first month (talk about New Year's resolutions!) and took sixteen days to complete. The priests and Levites began with the outer court of the temple and worked their way inward, once again treating the house of the Lord as holy.

📖 Now read 2 Chronicles 29:20–36. How did Hezekiah know what needed to be done to appropriately reinstitute Temple worship (v. 25)?

_____

_____

How did the priests and Levites respond (v. 30)?

_____

_____

How did the people respond (vv. 31, 36)?

_____

_____

_____

Hezekiah apparently had both a written and oral history of the earlier kings at his disposal. Having studied these and having concluded that it was Judah's abandonment of the Lord that had brought them to the low place they now experienced, he chose to return the nation's worship to the pattern established by David (29:25). It is also obvious by the statement _". . . for the_

Did You Know?
WORSHIP AT THE TEMPLE

After the Temple was cleansed and in order, Hezekiah led the people in a great celebration of worship. As the sacrifices were offered, the Levites played the instruments David had provided, the priests played the trumpets, and the Levitical singers sang the song of the Lord, offering praise and thanksgiving with gladness. Hezekiah also ordered the Levites to sing _"the words of David and Asaph the seer,"_ most likely including some of the Psalms written by David (75 or more) and Asaph (12), (See 2 Chronicles 29:25–30).

command was from the LORD through his prophets," that Hezekiah was receptive to the spiritual leadership of Isaiah, Hosea and Micah, the prophets ministering when he took the throne. God is always faithful to give us the wisdom we lack if we set our hearts to seek Him.

This leadership by the new king became a catalyst for great rejoicing both in the priesthood (29:30) and in the nation (29:36), and the suddenness of the change gives evidence that God had visited His people with revival.

📖 Read 2 Chronicles 30:1–27. What celebration did Hezekiah promptly reinstate?

_____

_____

What were some of the things that were necessary in order for this to happen (vv. 3, 5, 14, 17)?

_____

_____

_____

_____

Did they get everything exactly right (vv. 2–4, 18)?

_____

_____

How did God respond (vv. 12, 18–20)?

_____

_____

How did the people of Israel respond (vv. 21–23, 26)?

_____

_____

_____

Put Yourself in Their Shoes

THE MARKS OF A SPIRITUAL AWAKENING

• Hezekiah led the people to seek the Lord with all their hearts.

• The Lord gave them oneness of heart to obey and follow the king and the Word of the Lord.

• They worshiped with great joy.

When God delivered His people from Egypt through His plagues, their faithful observance of the Passover protected their first-born sons from the angel of death. This observance was meant to be an annual reminder of how God delivered His people. How ironic that Hezekiah's father had not only abandoned this important religious observance, but even sacrificed his infant son to pagan idols.

The detailed preparations both in cleansing the temple and in reinstating the feast make it clear that this revival was no impulsive, emotional whim, but an abiding change of heart. In this important passage we see that even though all the rituals were not fully observed (they were a month late, and many had neglected the ceremonial details of purification—30:13, 17), Hezekiah prays that God would *"pardon everyone who prepares his heart to seek God . . . though not according to the purification rules of the sanctuary"* (30:18–19). God's acceptance of the people shows that a purposed and prepared heart is far more important than religious ritual.

So great was the revival of those days that the Passover observance was held over for a second week (30:23). Perhaps the greatest commentary on this revival is found in 30:26, *"So there was great joy in Jerusalem, because there was nothing like this in Jerusalem since the days of Solomon the son of David. . . ."*

The final evidence that Hezekiah succeeded in the crisis of choice is seen in his removal of the idols in the land.

📖 Read 2 Chronicles 31:1–2, and identify all that Hezekiah destroyed.

_____

_____

_____

_____

The intense emotions associated with the two week revival eventually would subside. But the true measure of revival is not in the emotions that accompany it, but in the resolve that is acted on after it. Hezekiah and the people translate the emotion to action by breaking the pillars into pieces (pillars were associated with Baal worship) and cutting down the Asherim (wooden images of Asherah, the supposed mother of seventy pagan gods, including Baal). Even the high places and altars which worshiped the right God in the wrong place, were torn down. True revival always leads to a purer life. Truly, Hezekiah's reign began with a mighty movement of God.

APPLY Describe the last time you had a spiritual "mountaintop" experience.

_____

_____

_____

How long did it last?

_____

How can you see its effects in your life today?

_____

_____

My great-uncle and aunt were part of the Asbury revival of 1970. They often spoke of the mighty movement of God's Spirit in those days. What started as a brief time of sharing at the normal chapel service ignited into a flame of revival as person after person would get up and share of things God had wrought in their hearts. Classes were canceled at tiny Asbury College in Wilmore, Kentucky where Uncle Henry taught Biology. At noon that first day he called Aunt Irene and said, "You had better get down to the college, revival has broken out and the chapel service is still going on."

Aunt Irene once told me that none of the video documentaries or books written about the revival have come close to capturing the sense of awe, the tangible presence of the Lord, she felt as she walked up the steps of the

True revival always leads to a purer life.

When revival comes the idols of the heart that are torn down stay down.

chapel before she even went inside. Classes were canceled, and chapel continued unabated through the night. One student who was unaware of what was going on showed up for class to find it empty and feared the rapture had come and he had missed it.

The atmosphere was electric at these chapel services where student after student would come to the podium confessing sins, making wrong relationships right, and giving praise to God. Chapel continued day after day into weeks. Pockets of revival began to break out in other places as students returned to their home churches and shared of the moving of God on their campus. But eventually the emotion subsided and the "twenty-four hour chapels" stopped.

I asked my Aunt and Uncle if they were sad to see the revival come to an end. Their answer was that it didn't. The intense emotion of the revival went away, but the decisions of surrender did not. The idols of the heart that were torn down stayed down. The results of the revival were played out in pulpits and missionary endeavors, and in jobs and homes all over the world. The results of the Asbury revival of 1970 still continue today.

Hezekiah **DAY TWO**

SUCCEEDING IN THE CRISIS OF INVASION

The nation of Israel in Hezekiah's day was but a shadow of its former grandeur. All that remained was Judah (the two southern tribes). And though the glories of Solomon's day were gone, Jerusalem was significant enough that it captured the attention of Sennacherib king of Assyria. Assyria was the dominant world power of the day. They already had conquered Israel and taken them into captivity. Now their sights are on Judah.

📖 Read 2 Chronicles 32:1–8. What situation faced Hezekiah (v. 1)?

_____

What did Hezekiah do (vv. 3, 5–6)?

_____

_____

_____

How did he reassure the people (vv. 7–8)?

_____

_____

"With him is only an arm of flesh, but with us is the LORD our God to help us and to fight our battles."
2 Chronicles 32:8

—Hezekiah to the people of Jerusalem, ca. 701 BC

It was after the initial revival of Hezekiah's reign that he faced one of his greatest tests. Sennacherib laid siege to Jerusalem. In this type of warfare the idea was to surround a fortified city and simply cut it off from supplies, waiting for the enemy to surrender, rather than trying to break through its defenses. Hezekiah wisely decided to cut off the water flowing out of the city to make it harder for Sennacherib. He also repaired the fortifications, prepared implements for war, and organized his troops.

Perhaps the most important thing Hezekiah did though was to encourage the people to trust the Lord in the war. His battle call, *"Be strong and courageous,"* was the same employed by Joshua years before when Israel trusted God to conquer this land. By saying, *"With him is only an arm of flesh, but with us is the LORD our God to help us and to fight our battles,"* he is drawing their focus off of Assyria and back to the Lord. The people *"relied on the words of Hezekiah king of Judah."*

📖 Now take a few minutes to read 2 Kings 18:13–37. Paying special attention to verse 36, identify how Hezekiah prepared the people for their encounter with the messenger from the king of Assyria.

_____

_____

Hezekiah recognized that the biggest battle would be one of faith. He knew that if Assyria could draw the people's focus away from the Lord, their fears would keep them from trusting God. He couldn't prevent Assyria from speaking to the people (though he tried by his men asking the dialog to be carried out in Aramaic instead of Judean [Hebrew] so the people wouldn't be exposed to their threats). He wisely prepared the people by instructing them not to give an answer to anything that was said. Hezekiah was more concerned that they talk to the Lord about Assyria than that they talk to Assyria.

📖 Read through 2 Kings 19:1–5. How did Hezekiah respond personally to the crisis (v. 1)?

_____

_____

_____

What message did he send (vv. 2–4)?

_____

_____

_____

When King Hezekiah heard that the invasion had become a reality, he did three things: he tore his clothes, covered himself with sackcloth (both a sign of mourning and humility), and entered the house of the Lord (evidence of his desire to seek God).

Next he sent Eliakim (also covered with sackcloth) to Isaiah the prophet. It may seem too obvious to mention, but notice that everything Hezekiah did revolved around seeking the Lord, not preparing for Sennacherib. Second Kings 19:14 also tells us that Hezekiah took the letter written to him from Sennacherib and spread it out before the Lord—a physical manifestation of his laying the problem before the Lord. He wisely recognized too, that the words of Assyria were an offense to God, not just to Judah.

📖 Read 2 Kings 19:6–7, and identify the word of the Lord through Isaiah.

_____

_____

Did You Know?

HEZEKIAH'S TUNNEL

In preparation for siege, Hezekiah ordered the digging of a tunnel through solid rock under the city of Jerusalem from the Gihon Spring outside the walls to the Pool of Siloam inside the walls. This tunnel, large enough to walk through and 1700 feet long, assured the inhabitants of Jerusalem that an abundant water supply would be available and protected (2 Chronicles 32:30).

"Nothing restrains the Lord from saving by many or by few."

1 Samuel 14:6

Now read 2 Kings 19:35–37. What actually happened?

_____

_____

_____

The word of the Lord through Isaiah was, *"Do not be afraid because of the words that you have heard, with which the servants of the king of Assyria have blasphemed Me. Behold, I will put a spirit in him so that he shall hear a rumor and return to his own land. And I will make him fall by the sword in his own land."* It is faith-building to recognize that God is able to circumvent the wicked with their own devices. In 2 Kings 19:35–37 we see that what God promised, He delivered.

Hezekiah DAY THREE

SUCCEEDING IN THE CRISIS OF SICKNESS

Crisis has the ability to reveal our true character. When we face a crisis, it squeezes out of us what we really are. Today we want to look at a third crisis in the life of King Hezekiah. How would he handle this crisis? Would he pass the test, or would he fail? Often when we face crises, we want to blame them for our response. Yet in reality, trials do not make us respond a certain way—they merely reveal our character. Much like a tube of toothpaste, when we are put under pressure, what is inside gets squeezed out. Our character is revealed by our crises. This time Hezekiah's crisis was a personal one, but as we have seen in all the others, he trusted the Lord.

Trials do not make us respond in a certain way, they merely reveal our character.

Read 2 Kings 20:1, and identify as much information as you can about this third crisis in Hezekiah's life.

_____

_____

_____

When it rains, it pours. As if the impending invasion by Assyria wasn't enough trial for Hezekiah, at about the same time he had to face another crisis of a more personal nature. He became mortally ill. The text doesn't tell us, but most likely Hezekiah sought the counsel of his friend and advisor, Isaiah. The report was not good. Isaiah informed him that his disease would be fatal. He went directly from the frying pan of Assyrian invasion to the fire of failing health.

Now read verses 2 and 3, and record what you learn there about how Hezekiah responded to the gloomy report from Isaiah.

_____

_____

_____

When crisis appears suddenly there is no time to plan a response. That is why crisis has the ability to reveal what our character truly is. Our initial response is one of reflex—it flows out of who we are. Hezekiah's knee-jerk reaction was to immediately seek the Lord. The meaning of his turning his face to the wall is unclear. It may mean that he turned away from the messenger and his unwanted message. In any case, it seems clear that he was positioning himself to fully focus on the Lord. In his prayer he reminds the Lord of his past faithfulness, but more importantly, he bears his heart. Verse 3 tells us that his prayer includes weeping bitterly before the Lord. What a comfort it is to know that the Lord receives our honest entreaties. We can tell him what we really feel.

📖 Look at 2 Kings 20:4–7, and list the details of the outcome of Hezekiah's prayer.

_____

_____

_____

_____

The Lord's response to Hezekiah's prayer was immediate. While Isaiah walked away, the Lord told him to return to the king with a new message: he would be healed. It is significant that not only did the Lord listen to Hezekiah's prayers, He saw his tears. Not only did the Lord communicate healing and how long it would take (three days), but He also told Hezekiah how long the healing would last (fifteen years). The principle here is noteworthy—we can appeal to the Lord and He will hear us. He may or may not answer just as we'd like, but He always hears.

📖 Now read 2 Kings 20:8–11, and record the details of how the Lord confirmed Hezekiah's healing.

_____

_____

_____

_____

How do you think this affected Hezekiah?

_____

_____

_____

The first point that should be made is that the sign was Hezekiah's request—it flowed from his desire for assurance from the Lord. The miraculous sign of the shadow reversing its course was an affirmation that the Lord would fulfill His promise of healing. Notice, this miracle had no affect at all on the outcome of the event. Hezekiah would have been healed with or without the sign. What the sign accomplished was to free Hezekiah from three days of anxious uncertainty.

The principle here is a powerful one. Even after God has spoken, He understands our struggle with trusting Him for the miraculous. He is willing to go the extra mile to insure that He communicates His will in a way that we can understand and trust. He is mindful that we are but dust. I am greatly encouraged by the lengths to which the Lord went to assure Hezekiah's doubting heart.

What a comfort it is to know that the LORD receives our honest entreaties. We can bear our hearts to Him.

Did You Know?
HEZEKIAH'S SIGN

What occurred in this sign of the shadow of the sun retreating ten degrees? Some believe it refers to the shadow on an actual staircase in Jerusalem. Others see here some sort of instrument that belonged to Ahaz which had a series of steps ("degrees") to measure time by the movement of the sun. Regardless of where the shadow fell, on a staircase or an instrument, it is evident God gave Hezekiah a miraculous sign to comfort and assure him in the midst of this trial.

Did You Know?
HEZEKIAH'S SICKNESS AND HIS SONGS

Some consider Psalm 130 one of the "songs" Hezekiah composed (Isaiah 38:20) in his gratitude and praise to God for his healing. It is certain that Hezekiah wrote Isaiah 38:9–20 out of the experience of his illness and healing.

STUMBLING IN THE CRISIS OF PROSPERITY

Of all the adversities man must navigate in life, none is so challenging as prosperity. Having walked through *"the valley of the shadow of death,"* I find the prosperous hills a more difficult path—a harder place to follow God. Hezekiah had done well in life. He had succeeded in the crisis of choice, faithfully following God instead of the negative examples around him. He had succeeded in the crisis of invasion, trusting God instead of trying to come up with his own solution. He had succeeded in the crisis of sickness, trusting God on his deathbed and experiencing a mighty deliverance. But as we will see today, he stumbled in the crisis of prosperity. It is easier to follow God in adversity than in prosperity. Nothing tests us like blessing.

Although not the most significant, Hezekiah's healing was the most personal of his blessings.

📖 Read the summary report of his healing in 2 Chronicles 32:24–26, and write what you learn there about Hezekiah's response to his healing.

_____

_____

_____

_____

Why do you think he initially responded as he did?

_____

_____

_____

Why do you think he changed?

_____

_____

Perhaps no attitude is more disappointing in a follower of God than to see him wrongly believe that the mercies of the Lord are deserved. Although Hezekiah experienced a rare and undeserved blessing in the form of healing and extension of life, verse 25 tells us he *"gave no return for the benefit he received."*

The reason for Hezekiah's ingratitude was his own proud heart. Apparently he somehow convinced himself that his blessing was something he deserved. Perhaps because of his position as king he had begun to see himself as indispensable to the Lord's plan. The highest leader in God's economy is still just a servant. Or perhaps he thought that his past faithfulness meant that the Lord somehow owed him blessing. We must remember that when we are faithful we are only doing what we should. This doesn't mean that God owes us. Because of his prideful response, wrath came on him and on Judah and Jerusalem. Fortunately he realized his error and repented, and the wrath was delayed for a time.

WE ARE ALL SERVANTS

"Does he [his master] thank that servant because he did the things that were commanded him? I think not. So likewise you, when you have done all those things which you are commanded, say, 'We are unprofitable servants. We have done what was our duty to do.'" Luke 17:9–10 (NKJV)

📖 Take a minute to read 2 Kings 20:12–15, and identify the foolish choice Hezekiah made.

_____

_____

_____

What do you think might be behind such a choice?

_____

_____

_____

As word got out about Hezekiah's illness, the son of the king of Babylon brought letters and gifts to Hezekiah as condolence. Hezekiah should have been wary. People from Babylon were among those who had resettled the territories of Israel after the fall of the Northern Kingdom. Yet perhaps driven by a love of attention, he not only welcomed the visitor into his home, but in a tour of the royal palace, Hezekiah foolishly showed off all the treasures of the kingdom. Again we see a stumbling rooted in pride. Hezekiah should have known the wise words of his ancestor Solomon: _"Pride goes before destruction, And a haughty spirit before stumbling"_ (Proverbs 16:18). Rightly did Isaiah confront his foolishness.

📖 Read through Isaiah's rebuke in 2 Kings 20:14–19. What warnings did Isaiah give?

_____

_____

_____

_____

The first questions from Isaiah's mouth are "where are these men from?" and "what have they seen?" Obviously Isaiah understood the mistake that had been made. Until Hezekiah had shown them the treasury, Babylon probably thought little of Judah and Jerusalem. It was a small, fragile, fractured kingdom whose glory days were long gone. But now, the expansionist lusts of Babylon had been awakened. All the wealth of Jerusalem was now known. Isaiah prophesied that the day was coming when Babylon would overrun Judah and take away all the treasure as well as the descendants of Hezekiah. His pride would bring calamity. Nothing good ever comes from bragging.

📖 How, according to verse 19, did Hezekiah respond to the dire prophesy of Isaiah?

_____

_____

What attitude do you see in his response?

_____

It is curious that Hezekiah would call Isaiah's prophecy good. It would seem that Hezekiah doesn't adequately grieve because the consequences would come after his death. It may be that Hezekiah called the prophecy good in

> _"The fear of the LORD is to hate evil; Pride and arrogance and the evil way, And the perverted mouth, I hate."_
>
> **Proverbs 8:13**

acknowledgment that Isaiah had always served as a faithful messenger of God, and he received this rebuke as from the Lord. Or perhaps he only viewed the consequences selfishly and was glad that they would be delayed. It could be, however, that Hezekiah had already resigned himself to the fact that like the Northern Kingdom, Judah was headed to captivity, and he was glad at this bright spot that it would be delayed. Even in this "best case" scenario however, it is disappointing that he did not seek God's mercy as he had done regarding his own death.

📖 Second Chronicles 32:31 gives additional insight into the incident of the visiting envoys. In this passage we have commentary on why God allowed this situation. Read the verse, and write what you learn of God's plan.

_____

_____

The context of this verse is sandwiched between the triumphs and glories of Hezekiah's reign. While we can learn from Hezekiah's mistake here, we should not allow his humanness to stain our view of the many good things that took place during his reign. The verse begins by saying, *"And even in the matter of . . ."* showing us that although it was a failure, it shouldn't be viewed as the only commentary on his life.

We learn here that God *"left him alone."* This phrase suggests that, unlike many of the other crises of his reign, in this one God did not forewarn him through the godly counsel of Isaiah and others around him. God allowed this circumstance as a test to see all that was in his heart. In a tangible sense, we can conclude that the results of this test were recorded for our benefit. God lets us see this human frailty of Hezekiah so that we can recognize that even in the most godly leaders there will be cause for repentance. As James puts it, *"we all stumble in many ways"* (James 3:2).

There are two errors we can make in looking at Hezekiah: we can ignore his one failure and think too highly of him, or we can focus only on that failure and miss the godliness that marked most of his reign. Perhaps the single most important application from the life of Hezekiah is that no matter how godly we become, we are never beyond stumbling, and we never outgrow our need for God's grace and help. *"Let him who thinks he stands take heed lest he fall"* (1 Corinthians 10:12). The greatest protection against stumbling is the willingness to admit we could.

Hezekiah **DAY FIVE**

FOR ME TO FOLLOW GOD

The greatest commentary we can give on Hezekiah's life is that he responded to God. God placed wisdom around him, and he followed. His life is replete with examples of seeking God and of listening to the prophets the Lord had placed around him. When Hezekiah took the throne at age twenty-five, Isaiah was probably in his 50's or 60's and was a faithful counselor to him. The prophet Micah also spoke faithfully to the king on the Lord's behalf, and this king obviously listened. God is faithful to place around us the wisdom we need to follow Him. If any of us lacks wisdom He is quick to harken to our cry and send the direction we need (see James 1:5). Sometimes

God speaks wisdom to us through a timely sermon. On other occasions it is the godly counsel of a faithful friend, or a book we stumble upon. Most often it is through a studied passage of Scripture which comes alive to our situation or a truthful text which the Spirit brings to mind in our time of need. However God chooses to speak, He is faithful to give His wisdom generously and without reproach. God is faithful to us in all of our crises to make available the needed wisdom. Are we looking to Him for that wisdom?

Hezekiah did. He was quick to seek God. He allowed the crises of his life to drive him to the Lord. When in humility he sought God's wisdom, he received it and was quick to act on it. When he sought direction and followed the Lord, he prospered in all that he did. Second Chronicles 31:21 tells us, *"And every work which he began in the service of the house of his God in law and in commandment,* **seeking his God***, he did with all his heart* **and prospered"** [emphasis added]. In fact, the only negative we see in his life is when he foolishly showed the temple treasures without inquiring of the Lord, but even then he was quick to repent. He allowed every difficulty he faced to drive him to the Lord. Do we allow the difficulties of life to drive us to the Lord, or do we search for another solution?

As you look at your own life, identify the order in which the actions below usually occur when you encounter a crisis. (Number each from "1" upward in the order they usually appear, leaving blank any that do not apply).

_____Try to resolve the situation through your own efforts
_____Cry out to the Lord for wisdom
_____Fear and panic
_____Grumbling and complaining
_____Looking to others to rescue you
_____Trust and faith
_____Despair and depression
_____Recognize your need for wisdom

Someone has wisely recognized that it seems we are always either **a)** going into a trial, **b)** in the middle of a trial, or **c)** heading out of a trial. Our trials also seem to consistently show up in one of three areas: **1)** our health, **2)** our relationships, or **3)** our finances.

Is there a crisis in one of these areas of your life right now?

_____

_____

If so, what has your response been so far?

_____

_____

_____

What do you sense the Lord is saying to you from the example of Hezekiah?

_____

_____

_____

_____

> ## "The way of a fool is right in his own eyes, But a wise man is he who listens to counsel." Proverbs 12:15

One of the main reasons Hezekiah's reign was so positive was because he was faithful to listen to the godly counsel around him. The Lord surrounded him with men such as Isaiah, Micah and Hosea to meet his need for wisdom. Proverbs 12:15 reminds us, *"The way of a fool is right in his own eyes, But a wise man is he who listens to counsel."* Think about this. True wisdom is not reflected in how much we know, but in how willing we are to learn. Everyone is foolish in some area, but if we are teachable, and willing to be instructed by others, we are wise. Conversely, if we are arrogant and unteachable, clinging to our own opinions and unwilling to be instructed by others who know more than we do in a particular area, we are living our lives as fools. Do you tend to seek out and listen to the godly counsel of mature believers around you, or do you ignore it and lean on your own understanding? (Identify where you fit on the scale below).

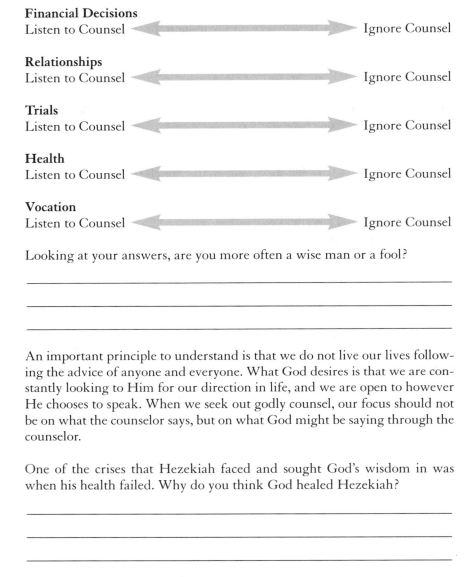

Financial Decisions
Listen to Counsel ⟷ Ignore Counsel

Relationships
Listen to Counsel ⟷ Ignore Counsel

Trials
Listen to Counsel ⟷ Ignore Counsel

Health
Listen to Counsel ⟷ Ignore Counsel

Vocation
Listen to Counsel ⟷ Ignore Counsel

Looking at your answers, are you more often a wise man or a fool?

_____

_____

_____

An important principle to understand is that we do not live our lives following the advice of anyone and everyone. What God desires is that we are constantly looking to Him for our direction in life, and we are open to however He chooses to speak. When we seek out godly counsel, our focus should not be on what the counselor says, but on what God might be saying through the counselor.

One of the crises that Hezekiah faced and sought God's wisdom in was when his health failed. Why do you think God healed Hezekiah?

_____

_____

_____

It would seem that nothing good came of the fifteen years added to Hezekiah's life. There were no more great victories of faith. Perhaps Hezekiah's sin began with his unwillingness to go to heaven when God sent for him. The only tangible product of the extension of his life was an heir—Manasseh—who turned out to be a wicked, dismal failure as king, and a bane on Judah, leading them back into false worship. Yet we know that no purpose of God can be thwarted. God intended judgment to fall on Judah, and though Manasseh was wicked, he did continue the line of David from which the Messiah ultimately would come. God had the final say, and we cannot sit in judgment on what He chose to do.

As far as Scripture records, God healed Hezekiah because he asked, even though he didn't necessarily manage this blessing as he should have. Second Chronicles 32:25 tells us, *"But Hezekiah gave no return for the benefit he received, because his heart was proud."* God honored his entreaty. There is no rebuke from the Lord for his asking. Even if God says "no" to our request, He still welcomes our asking.

Philippians 4:6–7 tells us the right way to approach God in our need: *"Be anxious for nothing, but in everything by prayer and supplication with thanksgiving let your requests be made known to God. And the peace of God, which surpasses all comprehension, shall guard your hearts and your minds in Christ Jesus."* God lays out what we should do and the order in which we should do it.

- ✓ We must choose to lay aside our anxieties. We cannot keep ourselves from feeling anxious, but we can choose not to dwell on those feelings or fears.

- ✓ In every situation we are to seek God **with thanksgiving**. God knows that we need the reminder of past blessings both for a balanced perspective and for encouragement to trust.

- ✓ We can let our requests be made known to God. In other words, it is okay to let God know what we really want—to be completely honest with Him.

- ✓ God does not promise to give us our requests, but He does promise something greater—to guard our hearts with peace. When we have followed God's process, we have the peace of knowing that He has heard us, and that the only reason He will not give us what we ask for is if His will is better.

As you reflect on your own crises, why not close out this week's lesson by following these steps in a written prayer. As you do, be sure to include the essential element of thanksgiving, for there is always something to be thankful for if we look long enough.

_____

_____

_____

_____

_____

_____

_____

_____

_____

_____

Notes

THE IMPACT OF FOLLOWING THE WORD OF GOD

Josiah reigned in Judah from 640 to 609 BC. The prophet Jeremiah began his ministry during Josiah's reign. Zephaniah, Huldah, Habakkuk, and possibly Nahum prophesied during this time as well.

The story of Josiah is a testimony to the impact that can be realized by those who choose to follow God and His Word. First, influenced by others, then influencing many throughout Judah and Israel, Josiah's life is set before us as an example of the dynamic impact the choice to follow God can make, regardless of what others say or do.

Josiah was born in 648 BC to the family of a young sixteen-year-old Amon, son of Manasseh, king of Judah. Amon was both young and wicked. He died eight years later after reigning two years as king, and his son Josiah became king at the age of eight. In a land saturated with the influences of idolatry, Josiah stands as one who chose to seek the Lord as David had—to follow the Lord and His Word fully, regardless of what others did. In the Scriptural account of the life of Josiah, we find many others who were willing to follow God in the midst of a society that followed its own desires. We can learn many lessons from the life and times and choices of Josiah, lessons that will serve us well in a time much like his.

WHEN DID HE REIGN?

800	750	700	650	600
"A Prophet" (sent to Amaziah)	ISAIAH MICAH		NAHUM ZEPHANIAH HABAKKUK	
			HULDAH (a prophetess)	
			Amon 642–640	JEREMIAH Jehoiachin (Jeconiah)
Amaziah 796–767	Jotham 750–735 Ahaz 735–715	Manasseh 697–642		Jehoahaz 609 598–597
Azariah (Uzziah) 790–739		Hezekiah 715–686	Josiah 640–609	Jehoiakim Zedekiah 609–598 597–586
Jehoahaz 814–798 Joash (Jehoash) 798–782	Zechariah Menahem Hoshea 753–752 752–742 732–722			605—1st Captivity DANIEL
Jeroboam II 793–753	Shallum Pekahiah 752 742–740			Hananiah
	Pekah 752–732			Mishael Azariah
JONAH		*There are no more kings or prophets in the Northern Kingdom. Foreign peoples are resettled into the land.*		597—2d Captivity EZEKIEL
	AMOS ODED HOSEA			Nebuchadnezzar 605–562
	Tiglath-pileser I 745–727	722—Assyria takes Israel into captivity		
	Shalmaneser V 727–722	Sennacherib 705–681		612—Fall of Nineveh

THE IMPACT OF OTHER PEOPLE

Josiah was born in the land of Judah during the waning years of a nation saturated in idolatry. The Word of God had been forsaken. Many prophets warned the nation of God's judgment of their unfaithfulness to their covenant with God. Many kings of Judah sought to bring the nation to follow the Lord and His Word with a whole heart. Other kings pursued the evil desires of their wicked hearts. Manasseh (Josiah's grandfather) was one of those wicked kings, the fourteenth king of Judah after Solomon.

📖 Read 2 Kings 21:1–18. What characterized Manasseh's reign (vv. 3–7, 16)?

_____

_____

_____

_____

_____

What is his reign likened to (vv. 2, 9, 11)?

_____

_____

_____

How did God respond to him (vv. 12–15)?

_____

_____

_____

When we go head-strong after what God has forbidden, God has ways of getting our attention to turn us back to Him and His Word—for our good and the good of those around us. He did this with Manasseh.

Manasseh began his reign at the age of twelve and reigned for fifty-five years. He did not follow the righteous path of his father Hezekiah. Instead, he followed a wicked course of idolatry, rebuilding the high places his father had destroyed, erecting altars to Baal, setting up an Asherah, and worshiping the stars, moon, and sun: *"the host of heaven."* Not only that, Manasseh practiced witchcraft and other occult activities, even sacrificing some of his sons in the fires of the pagan altar in the Valley of the Son of Hinnom. He took Judah into a level of evil deeper than even that of the nations that were in Canaan when Joshua first brought Israel into the land.

The Lord sent many prophets to proclaim judgment on Jerusalem and Judah. Manasseh ignored them and, adding to the evil of his idolatry, shed much innocent blood including that of some of the prophets. According to tradition it was Manasseh who executed the prophet Isaiah by having him sawn in two (Hebrews 11:37).

📖 Read 2 Chronicles 33:10–17. What happened to Manasseh toward the end of his reign (vv. 10–12)?

_____

_____

_____

What was the result (vv. 13–17)?

_____

_____

_____

_____

_____

Manasseh paid no attention to the Lord's warnings, so the Lord brought the Assyrian army to Jerusalem. They captured Manasseh and took him to Babylon in chains. Manasseh turned to the Lord in the midst of this ordeal, humbled himself, repented of his idolatry, and called on God.

God restored Manasseh to the throne in Jerusalem, and Manasseh sought to restore worship of the one true God. He destroyed the idols he had set up and began worshiping the Lord God only and called on the people to do likewise. During these years of Manasseh's reform Josiah was born and grew as a young child.

What kind of impact do you think Manasseh would have had on the young Josiah (a four to six-year-old child)?

_____

_____

_____

One of the things to consider in looking at the life of Josiah, is the change that would have become evident during the reform years of Manasseh. Manasseh began removing foreign gods and idolatrous altars and focused his attention on the Lord. He also called the people to worship and serve the Lord God of Israel only. As a child, Josiah doubtless saw this and probably heard much from the lips of his grandfather Manasseh, as well as from the people surrounding him in Jerusalem. The impact would soon be seen in his reign.

When Josiah was six years of age (642 BC), his grandfather Manasseh died, and his father Amon came to power at the age of twenty-two.

📖 Read 2 Chronicles 33:21–25. What kind of reign did Amon have?

_____

_____

_____

_____

Amon walked in the old idolatrous ways of Manasseh, sacrificing to the carved images in the land. He did not follow in Manasseh's call to serve the Lord of Israel only. Instead, he walked in pride and did much evil in the sight of the Lord, multiplying his sin and guilt. His palace servants conspired to kill him, and Amon's two-year reign ended at their hands. The people of the land executed those responsible for Amon's death and placed Josiah as king over Judah.

> _"...And let him return to the LORD, And He will have compassion on him; And to our God, For He will abundantly pardon."_
>
> **Isaiah 55:7**

How do you think the reign of his father Amon and the events surrounding his death might have impacted young Josiah?

_____

_____

_____

_____

Josiah would have seen a great contrast between his grandfather Manasseh and his father Amon. There must have also been a great contrast in the minds of many of the palace servants who eventually killed Amon. Josiah had the opportunity to see true worship in action alongside the idolatrous practices of his father. The difference would have had a great impression on Josiah at the ages of seven and eight, and this too would affect his reign in the years to come.

Josiah came to the throne at the age of eight. The people who were behind him wanted a king who would rule with order, not anarchy and rebellion (they had executed the servants who killed Amon). Obviously, the men who counseled Josiah had a great impact on him and on the nation itself. Consider these men whom God had raised up.

We are introduced to Shaphan the scribe in 2 Kings 22:3. This loyal servant followed the desires of Josiah throughout his reign. We learn from Jeremiah 36:10, 19, 25 that his son Gemariah was a protector of Jeremiah and sought to protect the scroll of the Word of God. Another son of Shaphan and servant of Josiah, Ahikam (2 Kings 22:12, 14), served the king well. Jeremiah 26:24 speaks of Ahikam protecting Jeremiah from those who wanted to harm him. Ahikam's son Gedaliah served as a good governor of Judah for a time after the Babylonians conquered the land (2 Kings 25:22–25; Jeremiah 40:7—41:4). Achbor (2 Kings 22:12, 14), another servant of Josiah, had a son Elnathan, who also sought to protect the scroll of the Word of God that Jeremiah had penned through his servant Baruch (Jeremiah 36:12, 25). Each of these servant-leaders, Shaphan, Ahikam, and Achbor give us a picture of those surrounding Josiah and reveal a true desire to follow the Lord God of Israel and obey His Word.

What kind of influence do you think these men would have had on the young king Josiah?

_____

_____

_____

Josiah was blessed with the companionship of those who wanted what was right. They were loyal to Josiah and doubtless had an impact for godliness in the young child's life.

Zephaniah prophesied most likely in the early years of Josiah's reign, when Josiah was around the ages of eight to eighteen (Zephaniah 1:1). The conditions he mentions remind one of the ways of Manasseh or Amon. They were certainly conditions which were at hand before Josiah instituted any reforms. At that time the prophet Zephaniah proclaimed the soon-coming judgment of God on Judah for its failure to follow the one true God. He also spoke of the future Day of the Lord when the whole earth would know His judgment.

In the land of Judah, Josiah heard the cry of Zephaniah, "Seek the LORD, all you meek of the earth, Who have upheld His justice. Seek righteousness, seek humility. . . ."

Zephaniah 2:4 (NKJV)

📖 Read Zephaniah 1:4–13, noting the condition of the nation (vv. 4b–6, 8b–9).

_____

_____

_____

_____

How was the Lord going to deal with it (vv. 4a, 8, 10–13)?

_____

_____

_____

What impact would this prophesy have made on Josiah?

_____

_____

Zephaniah warned of God's judgment on all those who had gone after the Baals and worshiped the host of heaven (astrology) as well as other detestable gods. They were turning *"back from following the LORD"* and refusing to seek the Lord or call on Him (v. 6). Their sin had multiplied, and God would deal with it specifically and fully. Josiah had seen and heard all his grandfather Manasseh had said. He had seen the ways of his father Amon and he knew how the people were living. Zephaniah's prophecy came shining into the midst of the darkness of the land, and it appears that Josiah was listening.

One of the truths we begin to see in the life of Josiah is that if one is going to follow God, it is best to walk with those who follow God. The influence of others on our lives is unmistakable and can mean the difference in our choices to follow God or walk away from Him. First Corinthians 15:33 says, *"Do not be deceived: 'Bad company corrupts good morals.'"*

> **If one is going to follow God, it is best to walk with those who follow God.**

🛑 **APPLY** What about you? What kind of company are you keeping? Are they helping you follow God, or are they helping you turn back to any one of a thousand idols?

_____

_____

_____

_____

THE IMPACT OF SEEKING THE LORD

Josiah | DAY TWO

We have seen that Josiah reigned at a time when the Lord was still speaking to His people through prophets like Zephaniah. God is ever faithful to His covenant people. But what do we find in the Scripture record about how well Josiah was listening?

> **As a sixteen-year-old youth, it was said of Josiah, "he began to seek the God of his father David."**
>
> **2 Chronicles 34:3**

📖 Read 2 Kings 22:2 and 2 Chronicles 34:3a. What do you learn about the young Josiah?

_____

_____

_____

_____

In the eighth year of Josiah's reign he began to seek the Lord. He was a teenager—sixteen years old—and the Scriptures paint a picture of a young man seeking the Lord as David had. First, he sought **the God** of his father David, and second, he did so by following **the ways** of David. He did what was right in God's sight. He was not like so many in Israel and Judah who had reverted to the days of the Judges, when _"everyone did what was right in his own eyes"_ (Judges 21:25), depending on their own limited wisdom: not seeking the wisdom of God, but seeking only the desires of their own heart.

For Josiah, this seeking was a whole-hearted pursuit. He did not want to be distracted in the least. Second Kings 22:2 says _"he did not turn aside to the right hand or to the left"_ (NKJV). Josiah was focused on the Lord. He wanted to walk with Him the way David had. The influence of those who followed God made an impact on Josiah. What impact would Josiah make on the nation?

📖 We have looked at the first half of 2 Chronicles 34:3. Read the remainder of that verse. How did Josiah's heart for God work out in his life and in his reign?

_____

_____

_____

Did You Know?
THE HIGH PLACES

Though Jehoshaphat had removed the High Places in his reign over 200 years before, other kings such as Ahaz allowed them to be established once again. Hezekiah removed them after Ahaz's reign, but after him Manasseh and Amon promoted their use and the corrupt worship practiced there. In seeking the Lord and His ways, Josiah once again removed the High Places and their idols.

In the twelfth year of his reign (age twenty), Josiah set about to purge the land of idolatry. He began by purging Judah and Jerusalem of the high places and ridding them of the Asherim (Asherah poles), carved images, and molten images. Verses later in the chapter give a further summary of all Josiah did during his reign to rid the land of every trace of idolatry, but we will look at that on Days Three and Four.

📖 Read Jeremiah 1:2. How does Jeremiah fit into what we've seen so far of Josiah's reign?

_____

_____

In the thirteenth year of the reign of Josiah (age twenty-one), and one year after he began purging the land of the many idols, the young prophet Jeremiah began to prophesy. In a land filled with the past influences of many wicked kings and much idolatry, paganism, and superstition, the Lord had a ministry and message to speak through Jeremiah. That ministry would last through the coming Babylonian sieges and the captivity of the people of Judah. For the present, he had a ministry in the reign of Josiah, a ministry impacted by the godly example of Josiah, and a ministry that, in turn, impacted the young king's life and reign.

Jeremiah spoke of the works of Josiah that resulted from him seeking the Lord and contrasted them with the reign of Josiah's son Jehoiakim who reigned from 609 to 598 BC (Jeremiah 22:13–18).

📖 Read Jeremiah 22:15–16. What does he tell us about Josiah?

_____

_____

_____

It was evident to Jeremiah that Josiah truly knew the Lord. He showed it in a reign marked by justice and righteousness. Josiah sought to serve all the people, making sure he cared for the poor and needy. Things went well in the land when Josiah reigned because he reigned with the heart of a God-centered servant, as David had done.

In the eighteenth year of his reign, at the age of twenty-six, Josiah ordered the cleansing and repair of the Temple, the center of worship of the one true God.

📖 Read 2 Chronicles 34:8–13. What do you learn about . . .

Josiah? _____

_____

_____

the Temple and its support? _____

_____

_____

the workmen? _____

_____

_____

> "Iron sharpens iron, So one man sharpens another."
>
> **Proverbs 27:17**

In his purging of the land, Josiah desired to see the people worship the Lord in truth. Therefore, **Josiah** sent Shaphan, Maaseiah, and Joah to repair the house of the Lord, the place God had appointed for all to seek Him with a whole heart. Verse 8 notes that this was the house of *"his God"*—Josiah's God. He had set his course and sought to honor and serve the Lord according to all He knew in God's Word.

Exodus 30:12–16 reveals how the Lord had designed the offerings of the people to support the work of the **Temple** (see also 2 Chronicles 24:4–11). Second Chronicles 34:9 notes that the Levites had collected money not only from those in Jerusalem, Judah and Benjamin, but also from many in the territories of Manasseh, Ephraim, and from the remnant throughout the land of Israel. This took care of the repair needs, just as God had designed.

The **workmen** were given what they needed to do the job and they faithfully carried out the repairs, an example of faithfulness to what God had called them to do.

Josiah first began ridding the land of idolatry and then set about to restore the Temple and its worship to its proper place and order. Here is a good example of bringing everything into a right relationship with the Lord. Along with cleansing the land of the abomination of idolatry, Josiah continued to seek the Lord by making sure the Temple was in order so that all the people could seek the Lord as He had taught them to.

APPLY Is everything in your life in order so that you are not distracted from seeking God with a whole heart? What are some areas in your life that need cleaning out?

_____

_____

_____

_____

_____

Start dealing with the first thing God shows you, and then go to the next thing. This is all part of following God—of seeking Him with a whole heart.

Josiah **DAY THREE**

Did You Know?

? **A COPY OF THE BOOK OF THE LAW**

Some believe that the copy of the Book of the Law of the LORD found by Hilkiah may actually have been written by Moses. Second Chronicles 34:14 says it was *"by Moses"* which some translate "at the hand of Moses" referring to him actually writing it. We do know the Lord ordered Moses to place a copy of the Book of the Law in the Tabernacle beside the Ark of the Covenant (Deuteronomy 31:24–26). Moses did this after he had finished writing all the words of the Law.

THE IMPACT OF THE WORD OF GOD

In the process of cleaning and repairing the Temple, Hilkiah the high priest found a copy of the Book of the Law (2 Chronicles 34:14). Possibly it had been hidden by a priest at one time to protect it from destruction by one of the wicked kings such as Ahaz, Manasseh, or Amon. Perhaps it had been removed when the ark was removed from the Holy of Holies by one of these kings. Second Chronicles 33:7 reports that Manasseh set up a carved image in the house of the Lord, and that could have been the occasion for removing the ark and the copy of the Book of the Law. Many believe this scroll contained the entire Pentateuch (Genesis, Exodus, Leviticus, Numbers, Deuteronomy), while others believed it was a copy of Deuteronomy.

Hilkiah gave the scroll to Shaphan who took it immediately to the king (2 Chronicles 34:15–18). He read the Book of the Law to Josiah. What did Josiah hear that day?

📖 Read Deuteronomy 28:15–68 (a long passage, but it will give you a sense of the gravity of that day in Josiah's life). Put yourself in Josiah's place. What thoughts might have come to his mind? What effect do you think this would have had on him?

_____

_____

_____

_____

_____

_____

_____

When we read Deuteronomy 28 we can readily see the seriousness of being in a covenant relationship with the Lord God of Israel. Josiah realized that Judah was due the wrath of God for not keeping the covenant—for not following the Lord and His Word.

📖 What did Josiah do when he heard the reading of the Book of the Law, according to 2 Chronicles 34:19–21?

_____

_____

_____

What do you see about his attitude toward the Word of God?

_____

_____

Josiah tore his robes in anguish over the evident sin of the people of Judah. His first action was to send his most trusted men to inquire of the Lord for him and for those in Israel and Judah. He wanted to know what the Lord would say at this time in the life of the nation. Josiah knew the absolute necessity of obeying the Word of God and he was seeking to do that with all his heart.

The men sent by Josiah went to Huldah, a prophetess who lived in the Second Quarter (a section of Jerusalem on the west side, probably built under Hezekiah's leadership). Her husband Shallum was responsible for the wardrobe either of the king or the priests (2 Kings 22:14). Huldah faithfully spoke the message God had for Josiah and the people of the land.

📖 Read 2 Kings 22:15–17. What was God's message to the people of Judah?

_____

_____

_____

_____

Why was this going to happen (v. 17)?

_____

_____

_____

The message was clear to the people of Judah. Because they had forsaken the Lord and followed other gods, the Lord's wrath was already kindled against them, and it would certainly come upon them and not be quenched. The words of Deuteronomy 28:15–68 would have come to mind as they considered the words of Huldah. God had warned them and now He was fulfilling His Word. Judah would *become a desolation and a curse* (2 Kings 22:19).

📖 Read 2 Kings 22:18–20. What was God's message to Josiah?

_____

_____

_____

> "He who despises the word will be destroyed, But he who fears the commandment will be rewarded."
>
> **Proverbs 13:13 (NKJV)**

> "He who gives attention to the word shall find good, And blessed is he who trusts in the LORD."
>
> **Proverbs 16:20**

Why was it different?

_____

_____

_____

The message to Josiah was also a fulfillment of the Word of God. Josiah had a tender heart, sensitive to what the Lord said. When he heard the Word read by Shaphan after the Book had been found, he immediately humbled himself before the Lord and His Word. He wept, and he cried out to the Lord in prayer. Because of that Josiah would die in peace without seeing the desolation the Lord would bring on Judah and its inhabitants.

📖 Read 2 Kings 23:1–3. How did Josiah immediately respond to the message from the Lord?

_____

_____

_____

What do you see about the place of the Word of God in Josiah's thoughts and actions?

_____

_____

> **The Lord longs to see prompt obedience, quick application, and a willing spirit. Josiah showed all of these in his response to the Word of God.**

The first thing Josiah did was to call the elders of Judah and Jerusalem to a meeting at the Temple. The people of Judah and Jerusalem went along with him. The priests and the prophets were there as well, which probably included Zephaniah, Jeremiah, and possibly Habakkuk and Nahum. Josiah had little to say. He simply began reading the words of the book of the covenant which could have included all the first five books of the Law. He made a personal covenant to follow the Lord and His Word. The people followed his lead and entered into that covenant. The Word of God was making an impact not only on Josiah, but under his leadership, on the nation as well.

 *Josiah* **DAY FOUR**

THE IMPACT OF FOLLOWING GOD ONLY

God only. It has been said that partial obedience is total disobedience. The same is true of following God. Partial following is like being partially married. Partial following actually means forsaking, and that is spiritual adultery. Josiah understood that, as we will see in his application of the Word of God to the ways of the nation. But let's start today from a bit of a different angle.

Thinking back over what we've looked at the last few days, what do you think Josiah understood about following the Lord?

_____

_____

_____

APPLY What does an honest look at your own life tell you about how you define following God in a practical way?

_____

_____

_____

_____

_____

📖 According to 2 Kings 23:3 and 2 Chronicles 34:31–33 what does it mean to follow the Lord?

_____

_____

_____

_____

_____

Word Study
COMMANDMENTS, STATUTES, AND TESTIMONIES

Mitsvah ("commandment")—It refers to God's orders, the direction in which to go or not to go. Proverbs 6:23 says it is a lamp giving light to the eyes—so we can see where to walk or not walk.

Chuqqah ("statutes")—It refers to a fixed pattern or a boundary line cut in or set in place. Within God's boundary lines there is true freedom.

Eduth ("testimonies")—It speaks of God's witness about something, His perfect view or viewpoint on something, how He sees things.

For Josiah, following the Lord meant keeping His commandments (His directions), His statutes (His boundary lines), and His testimonies (His viewpoint on any matter) with all one's heart and soul. That also meant getting rid of anything contrary to the Word of God, anything displeasing to Him. To follow God means to obey His Word.

📖 As you consider the place of the Word of God in Josiah's thoughts and actions in 2 Kings 23:2–3, also note that the next verse, verse 4, is connected to the actions of the previous verses. What do you discover in that connection?

_____

_____

_____

_____

In the meeting at the house of the Lord, Josiah placed a priority on reading the Word of God. Once it was read and understood, he made it clear that he would faithfully keep God's Word with all his heart and soul. He set his heart to fulfill the requirements of the covenant with God as found in the Book of the Covenant.

From all that Josiah had read in the Word of God, he knew that many of the kings of Judah had sinned grievously against the Lord, and the people had followed them. He began purging the land of idolatry in the twelfth year of his reign (2 Chronicles 34:3). Now it was the eighteenth year of his reign. As a young man of twenty-six, his zeal was greater than ever, and his understanding of the Word was clearer. Second Kings 23:4 begins to reveal more of his purge of idolatry.

📖 Read 2 Kings 23:4–14 and 2 Chronicles 34:4–5. What actions did Josiah take in response to his fuller knowledge of the Word of God and in fulfillment of this covenant to follow the Lord and His Word? (Make a summary list of each action and where it took place.)

ACTION	LOCATION
_____	_____
_____	_____
_____	_____
_____	_____
_____	_____
_____	_____
_____	_____
_____	_____
_____	_____
_____	_____
_____	_____

It was clear that the land needed cleansing of all the abomination of idolatry. Josiah began with the **Temple** and cleared out the vessels and everything that related to the worship of other gods—Baal, Asherah and all that related to the astrology so widely practiced. He burned all the idols in the Kidron valley and later took the ashes to Jeroboam's altar at Bethel in order to defile it. In his purge he destroyed carved images, wooden images, and molten images. The wooden image taken out of the Temple was burned at the brook Kidron and the ashes thrown on the graves of those who had worshiped these false gods (see 2 Chronicles 34:4). Josiah also tore down the places of the cult prostitutes in the Temple area.

Jerusalem contained many other places of idolatry. Included in this purge were the high places in and around Jerusalem. He defiled the area known as Topheth in the Valley of the Son of Hinnom outside the city where child sacrifices had occurred (New Testament Greek, *Gehenna*, Matthew 5:22, 29; Mark 9:48; James 3:6). There were horses and chariots dedicated to the worship of the sun. They were removed from their quarters near the entrance of the Temple, and the chariots were burned with fire. The rooftop altars of Ahaz and Manasseh in the Temple courts were torn down. The high places Solomon built for Ashtoreth, Chemosh, and Milcom, Josiah defiled with human bones and destroyed the pillars and images there.

In all the cities of **Judah**, Josiah removed the priests that offered incense to Baal, to the constellations, and to the sun and moon at the high places around Judah. From Geba, the northernmost part of Judah to Beersheba, the southernmost part, Josiah purged the land of its many abomination.

📖 Read 2 Kings 23:15–18 along with 1 Kings 13:1–3. What happened at Bethel? [You may want to review the entire account of what happened in Jeroboam's day. It is in 1 Kings 13:4–32.]

_____

_____

_____

_____

What does this show you about following God only?

_____

_____

_____

Josiah traveled to Bethel about ten miles north of Jerusalem. He took the ashes from the burning in Jerusalem and placed them on the altar at Bethel to defile it. He also burned a wooden image that had been placed there, took the bones of the worshipers out of their graves and burned them on the altar, then tore down the altar. This was a fulfillment of the prophecy "the man of God from Judah" had made about three hundred years before (1 Kings 13:1–3). He had chosen to follow God only and God used him to speak against Jeroboam I and his altar. Josiah also honored the tombs of the man of God as well as the prophet of Bethel (1 Kings 13:30–32). But Josiah did not stop when he completed his work at Bethel.

📖 Read 2 Kings 23:19–20 with 2 Chronicles 34:6–7. What did he do next?

_____

_____

Josiah also traveled to the cities of Samaria, destroying the high places. He executed the false priests who served there and who led the people in forsaking the Lord. He went throughout the territories of Manasseh, Ephraim, Simeon, and as far north as Naphtali (the region of Galilee), then he returned to Jerusalem. Israel (the Northern Kingdom) had been conquered and dispersed in 722 BC, and many of the people now there were open to his leadership and followed him in this purge of idolatry.

📖 Read 2 Chronicles 34:33 with 35:1; then read 2 Kings 23:20–21. What do you think about Josiah's timing in calling the people to celebrate the Passover?

_____

_____

_____

Josiah had led the people in a renewed determination to follow the Lord and His Word. They had applied God's Word to the matter of idolatry and sought to rid the land of that uncleanness. The Book of the Law made it clear that they were to celebrate the various feasts and as the month Nisan approached, the Passover and Feast of Unleavened Bread were due to be celebrated. Having read the Word of God and in his continuing quest to honor that Word and follow God alone, Josiah called for a full celebration of the Passover.

Passover was the unique feast at the heart of the nation of Israel. It was the first of the feasts of Israel and the feast that most clearly defined them as a nation. This feast was first celebrated while they prepared to leave Egypt. It was then they were _passed over_ by the Death Angel, while the Egyptians experienced the judgment of death on their firstborn children and livestock (Exodus 12—13). The Passover, along with the Feast of Unleavened Bread that accompanied it (for the seven days after Passover), was a time to recall the truth and significance of their relationship to God as their God, their only God, and themselves as His chosen people.

In dealing with uncleanness, Josiah was following the Lord. For us, following God means dealing with sin.

📖 Read the full account of the celebration in 2 Chronicles 35:1–19. What was Josiah primarily concerned with (vv. 4, 6)?

_____

_____

_____

What stands out as unique in this celebration of the Passover (vv. 7–9)?

_____

_____

_____

Following God means obeying what He says and all He says, in the way He says it.

Josiah was seeking to follow God in His Word, and he sought to make sure the Passover was celebrated in accordance with all the Word of God. That included the order for the priests and Levites that had been set forth by David and Solomon (1 Chronicles 15, 23–26; 2 Chronicles 8:14–15), as well as the original instructions written by Moses (Exodus 12:1–30, 43–50; 13:3–10; Deuteronomy 16:1–8). Josiah was so committed to doing things right, that he and those who served alongside him gave bountifully so that all could join in the celebration in Jerusalem. Each of the priests and Levites were able to serve at their respective posts and all the people joined in the celebration—not only the Temple officials and the inhabitants of Jerusalem but also those from Judah and Israel (2 Chronicles 35:18).

Josiah ordered a full celebration of the Passover according to the pattern the Lord had revealed in His Word to Moses and then further to David and Solomon. Here is another example of following God by following His Word. That means obeying what He says and all He says, in the way He says it. That also means growing in knowing His Word day by day. Just as Josiah learned new truths from the Word and then applied them, so must we as we walk with the Lord in His Word. It will make following Him the greatest adventure, an adventure of learning His wisdom for every trial, experiencing His grace for all of our weaknesses, and discovering His sufficiency for all of our needs. How are you doing in knowing and following His Word?

Following God is an adventure in learning His wisdom for every trial, experiencing His grace for all of our weaknesses, and discovering His sufficiency in all of life.

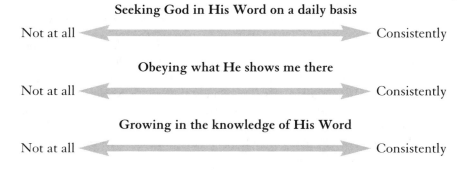

Seeking God in His Word on a daily basis

Not at all ⟸⟹ Consistently

Obeying what He shows me there

Not at all ⟸⟹ Consistently

Growing in the knowledge of His Word

Not at all ⟸⟹ Consistently

God has put His Word on earth to communicate with us, but it does us no good if we never read and study it. And reading the Bible is an empty thing if we do not allow it to change our lives. Ask the Lord to grow a hunger within you to know His Word more.

Josiah served well over the next thirteen years. It is interesting to note that during that time the prophet Daniel and his three friends Hananiah, Mishael, and Azariah (Shadrach, Meshach, and Abednego) were born and grew up as children. They would be taken as captives to Babylon at around age fourteen. There they followed God with a whole heart (Daniel 1—6). Josiah had an impact on them in their formative years—one more example of how those who follow God can influence others.

In 609 BC, Pharaoh Necho of Egypt came into Israel with his army prepared to join the Assyrians at the Euphrates River to fight against the Babylonians. Josiah did not want to see that alliance strengthened, so he intercepted them at the Valley of Megiddo as they were coming inland from the Mediterranean. Necho ordered Josiah to leave him alone since he claimed to be doing this by the will of God, but Josiah ignored his warning. In the ensuing battle Josiah was wounded and then taken back to Jerusalem where he died (2 Chronicles 35:20–24). The nation mourned greatly for this godly young king. Jeremiah even composed a lament, and many in the nation sang or spoke in lamentations over this death for many years to come (2 Chronicles 35:25).

FOR ME TO FOLLOW GOD

What an incredible thing it is to think of Josiah taking the throne of Judah at the age of eight. What an awesome responsibility placed on such small shoulders! Yet in retrospect, he turns out to be one of the greatest kings Judah ever had. Many things wove together to shape the man he would become. Certainly he was impacted by the repentance of his grandfather, Manasseh. Even apart from his personal memories would be the constant reminders from the people of the change in this initially wicked king. We can assume that another major influence was the prophet Zephaniah, whose ministry began a year before Josiah took the throne and continued until he was about seventeen years old. Zephaniah's message of soon-coming judgment from the Lord may have been the catalyst for a turning point in Josiah at age sixteen, when we are told that he *". . . began to seek the God of his father David"* (2 Chronicles 34:3). Another turning point in his life is recorded as being the twelfth year of his reign (when he was about twenty years old), when he began purging Judah and Jerusalem of idols and wrong worship. It may be that Jeremiah, whose ministry began about this time, was an influencer in Josiah's zeal. But no single event seems to have shaped Josiah more than the discovery of the Book of the Law, when at age 26, he initiated the repair of the temple. He took great joy in the book of God. The humility with which he greeted his first exposure to the Word of God would seem to be much like that expressed by John Wesley, founder of the Methodist Church:

> *I am a creature of a day, passing through life as an arrow through the air. I am a spirit coming from God and returning to God, hovering over the great gulf. A few months hence I am no more seen. I drop into an unchangeable eternity.*
>
> *I want to know one thing—if God Himself has condescended to teach the way. He hath written it down in a book . . . Oh, give me that book! At any price give me the book of God!*

Because Josiah followed the Word of God so carefully, many in the land of Israel were strengthened to do the same. When captivity came, they remembered his example and manifested a strong determination to follow the Word in the land of their captivity. Daniel and his three friends, Shadrach,

We never know how far our influence will travel or how deeply the impact of our lives will be felt.

Meshach, and Abednego, are among those whose lives bear witness of the fruit of Josiah's rediscovery of the Word of God. This conviction about the priority of the Word of God also encouraged and strengthened the people of Israel for their return to the land of Israel in 536 BC. That Word, which included many prophecies about the coming Messiah and His kingdom, continued to call them to trust the Lord in the four hundred "silent years" between the last Old Testament prophet, Malachi, and the coming of the Messiah, Jesus. We never know how far our influence will travel or how deeply the impact of our lives will be felt.

For ten years Josiah sought the God of the Word, before he saw the Word of God. The Book of the Law had been there all along, but it sat hidden, tucked out of the way, gathering dust. His "discovery" of the Word of God profoundly impacted his life. He would never be the same. As he read the words written there, he saw sins to be repented of and godly priorities to be pursued. It was his repentance and obedience to the Word of God that delayed God's judgment on Judah. Have you "discovered" the Word of God? Or is it sitting idly, tucked out of the way, gathering dust somewhere in your home?

Reflect on your Christian life, and write down when the Word of God became a force to be reckoned with in your life. Record the changes you saw as a result.

_____

_____

_____

_____

_____

_____

Have you "discovered" the Word of God? Or is it sitting idly, tucked out of the way, gathering dust somewhere in your home?

At present, how often do you spend time in the word of God?
___ every day   ___ almost every day   ___ once a week
___ once a month   ___ seldom   ___ never

What approach do you use to spend time with the Bible?
___ systematic reading ___ random reading   ___ tapes
___ Bible study guides ___ group study   ___ radio
___ church   ___ commentaries   ___ other_____

Josiah's reign was good not simply because he found the Word of God, but because he chose to obey it. In 2 Chronicles 34:27 we are told that Josiah's heart was "tender" and that he "humbled" himself before the Lord when he heard the Scriptures. As a result, he enjoyed God's favor. How would you evaluate your heart attitude toward the Word of God?

Tender ⟵————————————————⟶ Callous

As a result of what he read in the Bible, Josiah saw that change needed to be made. In 2 Chronicles 34:33 we are told that as a result of seeing the Word, "...Josiah removed all the abomination from all the lands belonging to the sons of Israel." As you look at your life in light of what you have seen so far in this or other studies, what "high places" and altars of wrong worship have you torn down in your life because of the Word?

_____

_____

_____

_____

Are there things yet in your life that out of obedience need to be torn down?

_____

_____

_____

_____

What about in your community/society?

_____

_____

_____

On a personal note, I am proud to live in a community that has been impacted by the Word of God. For as long as I have lived here, believers have fought the spread of adult book stores and topless bars, succeeding in closing most of them. As I was reading of Josiah's purging in the land, my heart was deeply moved when I realized that one of the things he rid the land of was the hideous practices that went with the worship of the Canaanite god, Molech. In 2 Kings 23:10 we are told that he ". . . _defiled Topheth_, [which means, "the place of burning"] _which is in the valley of the son of Hinnom, that no man might make his son or his daughter pass through the fire for Molech._" This speaks of the perverse form of pagan worship that involved human sacrifices of infant children being burned to death. Today there are no altars to Molech in our land, yet in almost every major city there are altars to the worship of self, of convenience, of pleasure, where unborn children are sacrificed to the god of "choice." In Chattanooga, Tennessee, several years ago concerned Christians bought and then closed the local abortion clinic, bringing to an end years of tragic sacrifices. In its place the building now houses a crisis pregnancy center and the National Memorial to the Unborn. The Word of God demands not only that we rid our lives of abomination, but we must rid our land of them as well.

Not only did the rediscovery of the Word move Josiah to tear down and remove some things from his life and his community, but it also moved him to reinstate some spiritual practices that had long been neglected. Through his initiative, the Passover was reinstated and observed with a fervor not seen since Joshua's day. As we look to apply what we have studied of his life, an important question to ask is "what spiritual practices do we need to add to our lives because of the Word of God?"

> **_The Word of God shows us what to reject and what to receive._**

_____

_____

_____

_____

Josiah was one of the greatest kings Israel ever had. During his reign the nation was fragmented and only a shell of its former glory. All that was left of the whole of Israel was the Southern Kingdom (the tribes of Judah and Benjamin) and a scattered remnant of the northern ten tribes. In a few years what was left would be overrun and carted off to Babylon. Yet for this brief moment of grace, God's favor is seen in the reign of this good and godly king. We are told in 2 Kings 23:25 that *". . . before him there was no king like him who turned to the Lord with all his heart and with all his soul and with all his might,* **according to all the law of Moses***; nor did any arise after him"* (emphasis added). Think about all the good kings who had reigned before Josiah: David, Asa, Jehoshaphat, Hezekiah. Yet none of them followed the Lord according to the Word like he did.

As we close this week's lesson, let me share with you a key to Josiah's godliness. When he rediscovered the Word of God, he *"made a covenant before the* LORD, *to walk after the* LORD, *and to keep His commandments and His testimonies and His statutes with all his heart and all his soul, to carry out the words of this covenant that were written in this book.* **And all the people entered into the covenant"** (2 Kings 23:3, emphasis added). He made a formal, public commitment to keep the Word, and as a result, others were moved to make the same covenant. Have you made a covenant with the Lord?

Why not use this prayer as a way to solidify this in your heart before the Lord (and, to make it public, trust the Lord to place on your heart someone you can share this commitment with).

 Lord, I thank You for the awesome blessing that You have written down Your will, Your heart, and Your testimony for me in the Bible. Today, I want to make a formal covenant with You, first of all, to be faithful in studying Your Word, and second, to submit myself to Your Word as the authority in my life. I know that I cannot keep Your Word with a whole heart in my own strength. I ask You to take control of the throne of my heart and live Your life through me. Empower me to keep Your Word with a heart of obedience. Amen.

Now, write out your own prayer/covenant to the Lord below.

_____

_____

_____

_____

_____

_____

_____

_____

_____

_____

> Josiah "made a covenant before the LORD, to walk after the LORD, and to keep His commandments and His testimonies and His statutes with all his heart and all his soul . . ." (2 Kings 23:3).

The Life of Josiah, King of Judah

SCRIPTURE	DATE	EVENT
2 Kings 21:1–18; 2 Chronicles 33:1–20	695–642 BC	The reign of king Manasseh, grandfather of Josiah, was marked by gross idolatry and occultism. After being warned by God, Manasseh continued in sin and was taken prisoner by Assyria (ca. 648 BC). He repented, and God restored him. He sought to restore worship of the LORD God of Israel as Israel's only God (possibly around 647 BC).
2 Kings 22:1; 2 Chronicles 33:21–25;	648 BC	Josiah was born to Amon and Jedidah in Jerusalem 6 years before the close of the reign of his grandfather Manasseh. Josiah's father Amon was 16 years old when Josiah was born.
2 Chronicles 33:10–20	648–642 BC	The first six years of Josiah's life were spent under the reign of Manasseh at the time when Manasseh had humbled himself before the Lord, repented of his idolatry, and sought to restore true worship in Judah.
2 Kings 21:19–22; 2 Chronicles 33:20–23	642–640 BC	Josiah's father Amon became king at the age of 22. Josiah was 6 years old. Amon ruled in wickedness for 2 years following the idolatrous practices of his father Manasseh.
2 Kings 21:23–24; 2 Chronicles 33:24–25	640 BC	The servants of Amon formed a conspiracy and killed him. The people of the land brought justice on the conspirators and executed them.
2 Kings 21:24, 26; 2 Chronicles 33:25	640 BC	The people of the land made Josiah king over Judah, and he reigned in place of Amon.
2 Kings 22:1–2; 2 Chronicles 34:1–2	640 BC	At the age of 8, Josiah began to reign over Judah. He did what was right in the sight of the Lord as king David had done.
Zephaniah 1–3	635–625 BC	The prophet Zephaniah proclaimed the soon-coming judgment of the Lord on Judah for its idolatry and apostasy (1:4–9). He also pronounced judgment on the surrounding nations (2:4–15) and spoke of the Day of the Lord and the millennial reign of the Lord (3:14–20).
2 Chronicles 34:3a	632 BC	In the eighth year of his reign, Josiah began to seek the Lord.
2 Chronicles 34:3b	628 BC	In the twelfth year of his reign, Josiah began to purge the land of its idols and idolatry.
Jeremiah 1:2 [See also 22:15–16]	627 BC	In the thirteenth year of the reign of Josiah, Jeremiah, possibly near the age of Josiah, began his ministry which lasted until 586 BC.
2 Chronicles 34:8–9	622 BC	In the eighteenth year of the reign of Josiah, he ordered the repair and cleansing of the Temple.
2 Kings 22:3–7; 2 Chronicles 34:9–13	622 BC	Josiah sent Shaphan to instruct Hilkiah the high priest to count and disperse the money to those who would repair the Temple. The offerings came from both Israel (Manasseh, Ephraim, and the remnant of Israel) and Judah.
2 Kings 22:8–10; 2 Chronicles 34:14–18	622 BC	In cleaning and repairing the Temple, Hilkiah the high priest found the Book of the Law and sent it to Josiah. Shaphan the scribe read the Book before the king.
2 Kings 22:11; 2 Chronicles 34:19	622 BC	When Josiah heard the Law he tore his robes in repentance for the sin of the people.
2 Kings 22:12–13; 2 Chronicles 34:20–21	622 BC	Josiah ordered Hilkiah the high priest and those with him to inquire of the Lord concerning the Law for Josiah and for the people of Israel and Judah.
2 Kings 22:14–20; 2 Chronicles 34:22–28	622 BC	The men went to Huldah the prophetess, and she prophesied the judgment to come on Judah and Jerusalem and the blessing of peace for Josiah because he humbled himself before the Lord and sought the Lord's favor.
2 Kings 23:1–2; 2 Chronicles 34:29–30	622 BC	Josiah gathered the elders and people of Judah and Jerusalem to hear the words of the Book of the Covenant that had been found in the Temple.
2 Kings 23:3; 2 Chronicles 34:31–32	622 BC	Josiah led the people in making a covenant to follow the LORD and obey His Word as written in the Book of the Covenant.
2 Kings 23:4–14; 2 Chronicles 34:33	622 BC	Josiah commanded that all the implements of idolatry be brought out of the Temple and destroyed. He removed the priests of the high places and destroyed the various idols and altars.
2 Kings 23:24; 2 Chronicles 34:33	622 BC	Josiah also put away those who went to mediums and spiritists and sought to rid the land of household idols and the abomination that accompanied the idolatry of the day.
1 Kings 13:1–3; 2 Kings 23:4, 15–16	622 BC	Josiah carried the ashes of the idols to Bethel and there defiled and destroyed the altar that Jeroboam I had established. This was in fulfillment of the prophecy of the man of God from Judah (ca. 930 BC). He also burned the bones of the false priests at that place.

SCRIPTURE	DATE	EVENT
1 Kings 13:30–32; 2 Kings 23:17–18	622 BC	At Bethel, Josiah honored the tombs of "the man of God from Judah" and the prophet of Bethel.
2 Kings 23:19–20	622 BC	He destroyed the shrines in the cities of Samaria and executed the priests of those high places. Josiah then returned to Jerusalem.
2 Kings 23:21–23; 2 Chronicles 35:1–19	In the month Nisan, 622 BC	In the eighteenth year of his reign, in response to reading the Book of the Covenant, Josiah commanded the people to keep the Passover. That would have occurred in the month Nisan, 622. Josiah followed the ceremonial requirements more closely than any had since the days of the judges (2 Kings 23:22; 2 Chronicles 35:18).
Daniel 1:1–7	619–609 BC	Daniel and his three friends Hananiah, Mishael, and Azariah were born in the reign of Josiah, probably around 619 BC. Their first 11 years would have been spent under the leadership of Josiah in Judah.
2 Kings 23:29–30; 2 Chronicles 35:20–24	609	Pharaoh Necho of Egypt, on his way to aid the Assyrian armies against Babylon, marched through Israel. Ignoring the counsel of Necho, Josiah went into battle against Necho at Meggido and died from the wounds received there.
2 Chronicles 35:24–25; Zechariah 12:11	609	All Judah and Jerusalem mourned deeply the death of Josiah. Jeremiah lamented for him as did the singing men and women of Israel.
2 Chronicles 36:1–3	609	Josiah's son Jehoahaz (Joahaz) became king in Judah at the age of 23. He ruled 3 months and was deposed by the king of Egypt.
2 Chronicles 36:4–5	609–597	The king of Egypt made Eliakim, another of Josiah's sons, king over Judah. His name was changed to Jehoiakim. He was 25 years old when he became king and his eleven year reign was marked by evil in the sight of the Lord.
2 Kings 23:25; 2 Chronicles 34:33; Jeremiah 22:15–16		Josiah made a profound impact on many in Judah and Israel. In leading the people, there was no king like him who focused the people so fully on the Word of God, *"all the Law of Moses"* (23:25), and who led them so that *"all his days they did not depart from following the LORD God of their fathers"* (34:33).

Notes

Notes

Zerubbabel and Ezra

FOLLOWING GOD'S WILL

When we turn to the Old Testament books of Ezra and Nehemiah, we find the story of how God fulfills His will and His promises. Originally one book in the Hebrew Old Testament, Ezra and Nehemiah give us the events of the nation of Israel from 538 BC to around 420 BC, almost 120 years. In those years, God faithfully brought His people out of the Babylonian captivity to which He had sent them. He had warned them of judgment to come if they continued in their unfaithfulness to Him. In 605 BC the Babylonians came into Judah and captured several people from the royal family and nobles, taking them back to Babylon. Daniel and his three friends were among the first to be taken. Over the next twenty years they came twice more, finally destroying Jerusalem and the Temple. God fulfilled His warnings.

Zerubbabel served as leader of the first return to Israel in 536 BC. He was not a king but was a descendant of David and stands in the genealogy of Jesus (Matthew 1:13). He served to lead the people spiritually. Haggai and Zechariah prophesied during this time. Ezra, who was both a priest and scribe, led the people in the second return to Israel 78 years later in 458 BC. He taught the people the Word of God.

WHEN DID THEY LEAD?

550	500	450	400
		HAGGAI	MALACHI
		ZECHARIAH	
	Zerubbabel	Ezra	
	536—First Return	458—Second Return	
	536—Rebuilding the Temple	Rebuilding the people	
	516—Temple completed		
		Nehemiah	*The Jews are without a king*
		445—Third Return	*or a prophet, living under the*
586—Final Captivity		Rebuilding the walls	*dominion of foreign rulers, and*
Jerusalem and Temple destroyed		and the city of Jerusalem	AWAITING THE MESSIAH, THE TRUE KING OF ISRAEL.
	538–Decree of Cyrus to return		
	Queen Esther		
Amel-Marduk	Cyrus	Darius I	Xerxes	Artaxerxes
(Evil-Merodach)	539–530	522–486	486–464	464–423
562–560			Socrates	Plato	Aristotle
			470–399	428–348	384–322

The story of each man can teach us much about faithfulness to God, faithfulness in following Him, and faithfulness in leading others to follow Him.

Zerubbabel and Ezra   **DAY ONE**

Did You Know?

GOD RULES OVER ALL THE CONCERNS OF MEN

Through Jeremiah (627–570? BC), the Lord had decreed the return of Israel to the land—long before Cyrus issued his decree (Jeremiah 25:11; 27:22; 29:10–14)—and Isaiah had prophesied concerning Cyrus about 150 years before he ever came to the throne (Isaiah 44:48; 45:1–7). Daniel, around 539 BC, was encouraged to pray for the return and rebuilding of the Temple because of what he read in Jeremiah. The Lord's sovereign care is evident in His sovereign ways.

God also made some promises. God had promised through the prophet Jeremiah that the captivity would last seventy years (2 Chronicles 36:21–23; Jeremiah 25:12; 29:10). Daniel read that and was strengthened to pray for God to fulfill His promises of deliverance and return. It had been about sixty-eight years since he came with the first captives to Babylon. Around 539 or 538 BC Cyrus the Persian decreed that the Jews should return to the land and rebuild the Temple. That return occurred in 536 BC, exactly seventy years after the first captives were taken to Babylon.

Though these men were not kings over Israel, they served in leading the people of God, to follow the Lord and His Word. Zerubbabel led the first return and led the people in following the will and Word of God. Ezra served in leading the second return, while Nehemiah led the third return. The story of each man can teach us much about faithfulness to God, faithfulness in following Him, and faithfulness in leading others to follow Him. In this lesson we will look briefly at Zerubbabel, and then at Ezra. (For a chronology of events see "A Chronology of Ezra-Nehemiah-Haggai-Zechariah-Malachi" at the end of this lesson.) In the next lesson we will look at Nehemiah.

STEPPING OUT TO FOLLOW GOD

To begin our study this week, we want to see how God led Zerubbabel and Israel in the first return, preparing the way for Ezra and the second return. As you study, note the Lord's sovereign hand at work to fulfill His covenant promises to the people of Israel and how Zerubbabel followed God's will for his life and for the people of Israel.

The events surrounding the leadership of Zerubbabel and the rebuilding of the Temple are found in Ezra 1—6.

📖 Read Ezra 1:1–8. Who called Israel to go back to Jerusalem (vv. 2–3)?

_____

_____

Why did he do this (v. 1)?

_____

_____

The Lord stirred up the spirit of Cyrus to call for the rebuilding of the Temple in Jerusalem, and he ordered all of God's people who would to journey there and begin the work. It's important to notice that it is God who initiated this decree through Cyrus. God was working to fulfill His Word that He had spoken through Jeremiah.

According to Cyrus' order, how was the journey to be financially supported (v. 4)?

_____

_____

_____

Who all responded (v. 5)?

_____

_____

_____

What did he send with them (vv. 7–8)?

_____

_____

Cyrus also ordered all under his reign to provide for those who would take the journey—in silver, gold, cattle, and various other goods, as well as in a voluntary offering for the Temple reconstruction. Those who responded to make the journey included leaders from the tribes of Judah and Benjamin, the priests and Levites, and everyone that the Spirit of God moved to go. Cyrus also sent the captured articles from the Temple with them back to Jerusalem. It was evident that God was providing for and protecting them.

Read Ezra 2:1–2. Who is listed as the leader of those who returned to Jerusalem (v. 2)?

_____

What distinctions are made in the following verses in Ezra 2 among the people who followed to Jerusalem?

v. 2b _____

_____

v. 36 _____

_____

v. 40 _____

_____

v. 41 _____

_____

v. 42 _____

_____

v. 43 _____

_____

v. 55 _____

_____

v. 59 _____

_____

vv. 61–62_____

_____

God has always desired that we worship Him in spirit and truth—with purity, honesty and a whole heart.

Zerubbabel led around fifty thousand Israelites in that first return to the covenant land. They were from many different families and included priests, Levites, singers, gatekeepers, and temple servants. The descendants of Solomon's servants were there as well. But they were careful to distinguish those who could not verify their descent, especially in the priesthood. Their zeal to exactly follow the Word of the Lord was evident. They knew God had called them to come back to Israel and to establish the true and pure worship of the Lord God of Israel. Once they had settled back in their land, a pure priesthood serving at a holy altar in a clean Temple was foremost in their minds.

Read Ezra 3:1–7. In each of the following verses, briefly list the things the people did after they had settled.

v. 1 _____

_____

v. 2 _____

_____

Why did they do this in the way that they did?

v. 3 _____

_____

vv. 4–5 _____

_____

According to verse 6, what had they not done yet?

_____

When the returning Jews settled in the land, they gathered together in the seventh month (v. 1). This month signaled the time of the Feast of the Trumpets (the first day), the Day of Atonement (the tenth of the month), and the Feast of Tabernacles or Booths (the fifteenth to the twenty-first). Zerubbabel and the priests rebuilt the altar and all Israel gathered together to worship the Lord in daily burnt offerings.

They knew this was God's will because *"it is written in the law of Moses"* (v. 2). After celebrating the Feast of Booths exactly as the Lord prescribed in His Word, they began offering the daily burnt offerings the Lord required as well as additional offerings on the Sabbaths, on the new moons and for each of the Feasts of the Lord (vv. 4–5). But they had not yet begun construction on the Temple.

Zerubbabel and Ezra   DAY TWO

FOLLOWING GOD IN WORSHIP—REBUILDING THE TEMPLE

Read Ezra 3:8. What did Zerubbabel and the other leaders do?

_____

_____

In their second year in the land the people began rebuilding the Temple. They wanted to follow God and they gave of their wealth and possessions to see His Temple rebuilt. The Temple was the centerpiece of the worship of the one true God, the Lord God of Israel. Without the Temple their worship was incomplete, for this was the place of sacrifice for sins and the place to express their surrender to Him as their God. It was at the heart of their covenant relationship.

📖 Read Ezra 3:9–14. What were the different responses of the people as the rebuilding began (vv. 11–12)?

_____

_____

When the people saw that the foundation was completed they rejoiced with great joy. However, those who had seen Solomon's Temple over fifty years before wept as they thought back to the grandeur of that Temple in comparison with this foundation.

Why do you think they responded as they did?

_____

_____

_____

It's important to realize how distinct Israel was among all the other nations that surrounded them. Their identity as a nation was much more than a common blood and tradition. It was a covenant with the God of the universe.

📖 Read Genesis 17:6–8. What distinguished the people of Israel in this covenant?

_____

_____

_____

_____

The covenant tied Israel to God in a special way forever. As part of that relationship, God gave the land of Canaan to Israel forever. This was the land they had finally returned to after decades of exile.

📖 Read 1 Kings 9:1–9. What did God say about the Temple (v. 3)?

_____

_____

_____

What three things did God want Solomon's sons (the kingly line of Israel) and the people to do (v. 6)?

_____

_____

_____

The Temple was to be the place of pure worship—where they met with the Lord, dealt with sin, found forgiveness and cleansing, offered themselves and their gifts in praise and thanksgiving, and celebrated in fellowship with the Lord.

Did You Know?

? THE COVENANT WITH ABRAHAM

The Lord promised Abraham a Blessing (including a Nation), a Seed (ultimately fulfilled in Christ—Galatians 3:16), and a Land—forever.

God gave Solomon one of the most beautiful promises of His presence that we see in all of Scripture: *"I have consecrated this house which you have built by putting My name there forever, and My eyes and My heart will be there perpetually."* This was the place chosen by God to manifest His presence and where He promised His name would dwell. That meant they could experience His power, His protection, and His provision in fullest measure when they were following His Word. The Temple fit into God's plans for the nation and for the fulfillment of all His promises of a kingdom of peace and prosperity under the king to come, the Messiah who would rule over all the earth. But with God's presence came a responsibility to follow Him, keeping His commandments and refusing to worship other gods.

What would be the results to Israel if they failed to follow God (v. 7)?

_____

_____

What did God say would happen to the Temple (v. 8)?

_____

_____

What was the reason all the nations would know that all this had occurred (v. 9)?

_____

_____

For Israel, the consequences of disobedience would be great. They would be cut off from the land that identified them as God's covenant people. And the Temple where they worshiped God according to His instructions would be destroyed, an act that would keep them from the hypocrisy of continuing with the form of their worship of God while they were participating in the worship of other gods.

Those who stood with Zerubbabel that day and had seen Solomon's Temple had also seen all of this come to pass. They had seen Israel forfeit the very things that distinguished them from the world as the chosen people of God. I imagine that they wept for their own former foolishness, as well as for God's incredible grace and love which had restored to His wayward people both their land and the joy of pure worship.

📖 Read Ezra 4:1–2. What happened when word of the rebuilding got out?

_____

_____

_____

_____

As they began the task of rebuilding the Temple, some of the inhabitants of the land of Israel, came and wanted to join them in the rebuilding. These were the descendants of Jews and Assyrians who intermarried after the Assyrian king Esarhaddon brought Assyrians into the land of Israel around 680–670 BC. They had become a mixed race known as the Samaritans. They also had a mixed form of worship, serving the God of Israel alongside their various idols.

There has always been some form of opposition to the pure and true worship of the living God.

📖 Read Ezra 4:3. How did Zerubbabel and the leaders respond?

_____

_____

📖 Read Ezra 4:4–5. What happened because of this?

_____

_____

_____

_____

Zerubbabel and the others wanted nothing to do with the Samaritans or their idolatry. Zerubbabel had the clear Word of God on this (Deuteronomy 7:1–11) as well as the force of the decree of Cyrus. As a result of this, these enemies of Judah showed their true colors and began opposing the rebuilding of the Temple. Their efforts succeeded and the rebuilding stopped for almost sixteen years.

Ezra 4:24 picks up with the story of the people ceasing the work on the Temple until the second year of Darius (520 BC). In that year the Lord spoke through the prophets Haggai and Zechariah.

📖 Read Ezra 5:2. How did Zerubbabel respond to the word from the prophets?

_____

_____

With the support of the prophets, Zerubbabel began once more the task of rebuilding. When challenged by their enemies, who had stopped the rebuilding previously, they reminded the king that they were acting in obedience to Cyrus' original decree. Darius responded in support of their efforts.

📖 Read Ezra 6:14–22. By whose command did they complete the Temple (v. 14)?

_____

_____

What did completion of the Temple allow the people to do (vv. 20–21)?

_____

_____

_____

The people began the work anew and with the encouragement of these prophets and with the leadership of Zerubbabel they finished the task in 516 BC, as God had commanded them. The celebration of the people was one of great joy and rejoicing in all the Lord had done as well as in the promises of a greater glory to come through this Temple. After completing the Temple the people were ready to celebrate the Passover and the Feast of Unleavened Bread, and they did so with great joy. The priests and the Levites had purified themselves, and the exiles had separated themselves together from _"the impurity of the nations of the land"_ (v. 21).

Did You Know?

THE CHRONOLOGY OF EZRA

Ezra 4:6 mentions the opposition of the enemies of Judah during the reign of Ahasuerus (Xerxes—486–464 BC), while 4:7–23 records their opposition under Artaxerxes I (around 464–460 BC) when the walls and gates were once more destroyed and burned. This is the incident noted in Nehemiah 1:1–3. Ezra 4:24 covers the cessation of work on the Temple in Zerubbabel's day up to 520 BC.

**The Lord always encourages and exhorts His people to worship Him, to place Him and His Word first and above all other considerations. To do otherwise is to live in some form of idolatry.**

FOLLOWING GOD'S WILL IN THE JOURNEY

zra 7 introduces us to Ezra the priest and scribe. Ezra was a man who knew the Word of God. He is most likely the compiler of both 1 Chronicles and 2 Chronicles as well as the books of Ezra and Nehemiah. Some think he may have been the author of Psalm 119, the psalm that exalts the greatness of the Word of God.

📖 Read Ezra 7:1–10. List at least three things you learn about Ezra (vv. 1, 5, 6, 10).

_____

_____

_____

Did You Know?
THE CHRONOLOGY OF EZRA

From the completion of the Temple under Zerubbabel in 516 BC, 58 years passed to the start of the second return under the leadership of Ezra in 458 BC.

Ezra was able to trace his lineage back to Aaron the high priest (and brother of Moses). Not only was he a priest, but he was also a skilled scribe in all the Law of Moses. His first desire was to study the Law of the Lord. He had set his heart to search and know the Law of the Lord. This was more than an intellectual or ritual exercise in literature. This was the pursuit of a heart and mind that wanted to know and follow God.

When did he make the journey to Israel (vv. 7–9)?

_____

_____

Why were they successful (v. 9)?

_____

_____

_____

Why did Ezra want to travel to Israel (v. 10)?

_____

_____

_____

God's Word meant so much to Ezra, and he knew so well the joy of walking with the Lord through His Word, that he wanted that same joy and that same walk for the people of Israel.

Ezra set his heart to study and practice (obey) the Word of God. With that as his foundation, he desired to take that Law and travel back to Israel so that he could teach those statutes and ordinances to the people there. God's Word meant so much to him, and he knew so well the joy of walking with the Lord through His Word, that he wanted that same joy and that same walk for the people of Israel. That was God's destiny for them and he wanted to be a part of getting them to that destiny.

Ezra left Babylon in the first month (March/April) and traveled for four months arriving on the first of the fifth month (July/August). Several priests, Levites, and others traveled with him. Because *"the good hand"* of the Lord God was with Ezra and the Israelites, they experienced a successful journey. Ezra 7:11–28 and 8:1–36 tell the story of the preparation for and completion of this historic journey.

📖 Read the letter and decree of King Artaxerxes in Ezra 7:11–26, and note what the king did for Ezra.

_____

_____

_____

_____

The king gave his permission for Ezra to return along with all who desired to go. To make sure the needs were met for the Temple, the king also encouraged them with a freewill offering to the Lord, access to the royal treasury and to the treasuries in the provinces west of the Euphrates. Artaxerxes called on any who would to give to Ezra's mission and gave him authority to buy whatever was needed for offering to the Lord. In addition, the king exempted Ezra and the Temple personnel from taxes and gave Ezra authority to appoint judges and magistrates and to administer justice as needed in the land.

📖 Read Ezra 7:27–28. How did Ezra view the king's actions?

_____

_____

_____

📖 Read Proverbs 21:1. What do you see about God and His ways in this situation with Ezra?

_____

_____

_____

Ezra blessed the Lord for His sovereign ways in working through the king to provide all they needed for the journey and for the continued needs of the Temple. This was truly an example of how the Lord sets in place the leader He wants, and turns the heart of that leader like channels of water to see His will accomplished. He saw this as part of the mercies of God on his behalf. Because of this Ezra was encouraged and strengthened to fulfill the mission God had given him. Ezra was confident that the hand of God was upon him and because of that he was able to encourage others to join him in the journey.

APPLY How does this affect the way you respond to the "kings" (boss, government leaders, etc.) in your life?

_____

_____

_____

God is sovereign over the leaders He has placed us under—they cannot thwart His plan and purpose. In fact, He works through them, pagan and godly, to accomplish His will. As we follow God, there is no need for us to fear the responses and actions of those in authority, for our trust is not in them, but in God Himself who directs their hearts.

> "Blessed be the LORD God of our fathers, who . . . has extended mercy to me before the king and his counselors. . . ."
> Ezra 7:27–28 (NKJV)

Around eight thousand people gathered at the river near Ahava to prepare for the journey. As they met, Ezra recognized that no Levites were there. He knew the need for Levites in the Temple at Jerusalem: their service at the Temple, as well as their teaching ability, would be indispensable to the full restoration of the people of God in the land of Israel. He sought help from Iddo at Casiphia, and the Lord provided a man of wisdom and insight in Sherebiah, as well as 37 other Levites along with 220 Temple servants, a total of 258 men (8:1–20). Ezra knew the Lord had provided these for the needs of the journey and for the needs in Israel, but he also realized the necessity of the Lord's guiding hand all along the way.

📖 Read Ezra 8:21–23. What did Ezra do (v. 21)?

_____

_____

What reasons does he give?

_____

_____

_____

Because he knew the necessity of humbling themselves under the hand of God, Ezra proclaimed a time of fasting to seek God. Because he had told the king of the might of the Lord in support of those who seek Him, Ezra was ashamed to ask for military assistance. He knew he would have to look to the Lord to be their protector and provider. They sought the Lord, and the Lord heard their cry and gave them a safe journey and protection for all their goods.

📖 Read Ezra 8:24–31. How did Ezra prepare for the journey?

_____

_____

_____

_____

What does this tell you about Ezra and his character?

_____

_____

_____

Ezra was a man of integrity. He made sure that the care for all the money and valuables given for the journey and for the House of the Lord were delegated to responsible, dependable men. They had to carry around 60,000 pounds of precious metals and several vessels. With that done, the four-month journey began on the twelfth of Nisan (March/April), 458 BC. They arrived on the first of Ab (July/August) having experienced the protective hand of God. They were undisturbed by their enemies and faced none of the common ambushes by robbers on the highway. Ezra acknowledged that it was the hand of God watching over them. He was ever careful to honor the Lord for all He had done.

Prayer with fasting is a way to humble ourselves before the Lord, help us recognize our utter dependence on Him, and focus our attention more fully on Him and His answers for the need.

"For we have regard for what is honorable, not only in the sight of the Lord, but also in the sight of men."

2 Corinthians 8:21

FOLLOWING GOD'S WILL—DEALING WITH SIN

When Ezra and the exiles arrived in the land, the gifts for the Temple were given to the priests and Levites in a way that showed full accountability, accuracy, and integrity. In all things they wanted to be honorable to the Lord and responsible with the gifts that had been given them (Ezra 8:33–34).

📖 Read Ezra 8:35–36. What did the exiles do first?

_____

_____

Why was this important?

_____

_____

First the exiles worshiped. They offered burnt offerings and a sin offering to the Lord. This was an expression of their surrender and thanksgiving to Him as well as an acknowledgment of their need of His mercy and forgiveness. They wanted to walk with Him in fellowship in the land He had given them. They were born and raised in captivity and knew the promises from the Word of God read by the Levites and recited to them by their parents and grandparents.

After worshiping the Lord at the Temple, they delivered the various decrees to the king's officials, the satraps and governors of the region. These officials then offered assistance to the people and to the House of God as directed by the king's orders. This would have been a great encouragement to the people of Israel.

Beginning in the month that they arrived and over the next several months, Ezra began teaching the people the statutes and ordinances of the Lord. The desires he had in Babylon for the people of Israel were being fulfilled. About five months later, in the ninth month (Chislev, ca. November/December), the leaders of Israel came to Ezra and reported that some of the priests, Levites, and other leaders had intermarried with the people of the land. What was God's will in this matter?

📖 Read Exodus 34:10–17 and Deuteronomy 7:1–11. What was God's clear will about the matter of intermarriage with the people of the land?

_____

_____

Why was this important to the Lord and to the people of Israel?

_____

_____

Word Study
THE LAW

The word **torah**, the *teaching* or the *Law*, is founded on the root word **yara** which means to cast or shoot. It was used of someone shooting arrows. In fact, its participle form means "archer." In reference to teaching, it pictures someone casting forth words or shooting words to convey a truth to someone. Ezra was an archer of truth, aiming at the hearts of the people of Israel.

The Lord made it clear that they were not to intermarry with any of the peoples dwelling in Canaan (Hittites, Girgashites, Amorites, Canaanites, Perizzites, Hivites, Jebusites, or any other peoples dwelling there). They were not to make any agreements with them whatsoever. The Lord had seen the magnitude of their sin and had pronounced judgment on them. The land was to be rid of every one of them along with all their idols and altars. [For some examples of the practices of the people living in Canaan see Leviticus 18:1–30 and 20:1–27.] The Lord wanted a holy people faithful to Him, His Word and His will.

Ezra knew the Word of God. He knew how the Lord viewed the abominations of the people of the land. In Ezra's day, Ezra and the people had seen the results of Jews intermarrying with the Assyrians brought into Samaria.

📖 Read Ezra 9:1–4. What was Ezra's first response when he heard the report of intermarriage between the people of Israel and the people of the land?

_____

_____

📖 What was Ezra's posture in each of the following verses?

9:3 _____

_____

9:4 _____

_____

9:5 _____

_____

9:6 _____

_____

10:1 _____

_____

What does this tell you about Ezra and his concern?

_____

_____

Ezra tore his garment and his robe when he heard the sins of the people. He pulled out some of the hair of his head and beard and sat down appalled. When he arose at the time of the evening offering, he fell on his knees and lifted his hands to the Lord. He could not lift his face but cried out to the Lord in humility, confessing with weeping, even prostrating himself before the Temple. His posture was reflective of a heart broken over the sin of the people.

📖 Read Ezra's prayer in Ezra 9:5–15. How did Ezra view God, especially in light of this sin of intermarrying with foreign wives (vv. 8, 13, 15)?

_____

_____

Word Study
ABOMINATION

The Hebrew word translated "abomination" in Ezra 9:11, 14 is **to'evah** which refers to something repulsive or sickening, even nauseating. Such a thing is loathsome, detestable, to be rejected. It can include physical disease, immorality, or idolatrous practices, as well as dishonesty in business. Marriages to foreign wives were viewed this way by God because of the compromise and corruption that would certainly result in those families and communities.

What was Ezra's main concern (vv. 10, 14, 15)?

_____

_____

Ezra recognized that the Lord is righteous in all His ways. He had shown His grace and mercy to Israel in many ways and had not dealt with them as severely as their sins deserved. Ezra knew God's Word and God's will were clear on this matter. In his prayer, he summarized the revealed will of God concerning His people and how they were to live in the land. For the present, he knew the people were sinning against the direct, clear will of God, and inviting the anger and judgment of God once again, perhaps to the point of destruction even of the remnant. Ezra was grief-stricken. This was a time of great turmoil and deep concern. What should they do?

As Ezra prayed, a large assembly of men, women, and children gathered around. They wept bitterly as Ezra prayed and wept before the Temple. Shecaniah (or Shechaniah), one of the leaders, answered.

📖 Read Ezra 10:2–4. List each point of the message and call Shecaniah gave.

_____

_____

_____

_____

_____

> **To do God's will was of utmost importance for their spiritual good, for their relationship to the Lord, and for the good of the nation.**

Shecaniah agreed that the people had sinned in marrying foreign wives, but in the midst of that there was still hope. He proposed that they make a covenant agreement with God to put away the foreign wives and their children. This was to be done with the counsel of Ezra and of those *"who trembled at the commandment of our God"*—those who had a whole-hearted desire to follow God and do His will. This covenant must be in line with God's revealed will—the Word of God. Shecaniah urged Ezra to rise up and fulfill his responsibility to guide the people in the will of God. He and others of like mind would stand with Ezra and together they would act in faith on the Word of God.

Ezra confronted the people with their sin and unfaithfulness to God in marrying foreign wives. He spoke of the guilt they bore. They must confess their sin to the Lord, surrender to do God's will, separate themselves from the people of the land (in-laws, neighbors, etc.), and separate from their foreign wives (Ezra 10:5–11).

📖 Read Ezra 10:12. How did the people respond?

_____

_____

_____

The people responded acknowledging that all Ezra said was right. It was their duty to obey the Word of God. To do His will was of utmost importance for their spiritual good, for their relationship to the Lord, and for the good of the nation.

Then because of the winter rains and the numbers of people that had to be dealt with, they made an appeal to the leaders to deal with each case at an appointed time. The elders and judges of each town would join those from their town in meeting with the leaders in Jerusalem. They began to meet on the first day of the tenth month, and the investigation of all those who had foreign wives took three months.

It's easy to question this event. How did they do this? It's evident they paid careful attention to the details of this separation—that's why they investigated each man according to his individual circumstances and with judges and elders from his own town present. They wanted to make sure everything was done with justice according to the Law of God. It's likely that according to the custom of the day, the women and children would have come under the care of a guardian (a father or brother) from their own people.

Why would God lead His people to put away their wives and children, to separate from them? This was an issue rooted in the covenant between Israel and the Lord. To marry someone not in the covenant community was to be unfaithful to the covenant and to the Lord. That is exactly the issue in chapters 9 and 10—unfaithfulness to the Lord. The purity of Israel as a nation depended on keeping the Law God had given in this covenant.

The principle here is the same one found in 1 Corinthians 5:6–8 where the Corinthian believers were commanded to purge out any leaven of malice or wickedness and celebrate their relationship with Christ with the unleavened bread of sincerity and truth. The leaven of intermarriage with its accompanying idolatry would mean ruin for the nation of Israel.

📖 From what you have read in chapters 9 and 10 what do you see about Ezra's leadership in this situation?

_____

_____

_____

_____

_____

Ezra's heart was filled with the Word of God. The impact of the people's sin struck with such force because the Word of God was so ingrained into his heart and mind. He was sensitive to the heart of God. He was clear about the will of God as revealed in His Word. Therefore, he quickly recognized any breach of the commands of God.

He was able to lead the people by the Word. As he taught them, he made sure they understood exactly what the Scripture meant and how it applied to them. He showed them what practicing the Law looked like. He wanted them to understand obedience. Most likely, that is one of the reasons some of the leaders came to him with the issue of intermarriage. He had taught the Word. That issue was addressed in the Law of God and they saw the need for prompt obedience. Ezra led them to the place of full obedience.

We see Ezra once more during this time: leading the people alongside Nehemiah as construction on the wall of Jerusalem is completed. We will look at that incident next week as we study Nehemiah.

AN UNLEAVENED LIFE

"Do you not know that a little leaven leavens the whole lump of dough? Clean out the old leaven, that you may be a new lump, just as in fact you are unleavened. For Christ our Passover also has been sacrificed. Let us therefore celebrate the feast, not with old leaven, nor with the leaven of malice and wickedness. But with the unleavened bread of sincerity and truth." I Corinthians 5:6–8

For Ezra there was no greater joy than the joy of full obedience, following God and doing His will.

FOR ME TO FOLLOW GOD

George Bernard Shaw said it well: "We learn from history that we learn nothing from history." Zerubbabel and Ezra were placed by God as leaders of the people in two separate waves as they returned to the land of Israel. Though they were not kings, in many respects they functioned as such and clearly through their spiritual insights served as the moral conscience of the fledgling rebirth of Israel. Yet little time passes in the land until we see God's people slipping into the same mistakes of their forefathers. Sin leaves its stain at the highest levels of leadership. The priests and Levites, those charged with instructing the nation in the Word of God, were the ones leading the charge into intermarriage in direct violation of the Law. Intermarriage does not simply refer to a Jew marrying a non-Jew, but rather to a practicing Jew marrying someone who would not convert, and instead, practiced a false religion worshiping another god. The very lineage of Christ gives examples of those from other nations being brought into the family of God. Ruth, the Moabitess, and Rahab, the Canaanite harlot, are both examples of non-Jews who married into the people of God, but in so doing they renounced their false gods and worshiped Jehovah, the one true God. They are direct ancestors of Christ. The intermarriage condemned in the Law is not a matter of ancestral genetics, but of divided hearts. The priests and Levites, the "princes and rulers" began to intermarry with the pagan daughters of Canaan, and left unchecked, it would only be a matter of time until this would erode the faith of the nation. There is always a danger of failing to learn from the failings of our fathers. These leaders had forgotten why their forefathers had been scattered to the nations. As George Santayana said in *The Life of Reason*, "Those who cannot remember the past are condemned to repeat it."

📖 Israel returning to the land is an incredible work of God's grace. They did not deserve God's favor. Read Deuteronomy 9:1–6, and list the reasons why God drove the Canaanites out of the promised land in the first place.

_____

_____

_____

> *There is always the danger of failing to learn from past failures.*

God's "expelling" of the Canaanites from the land of Canaan was not because of Israel's righteousness, but because of the wickedness of the Canaanites. Their religions involved worship of every god imaginable except the one true God, Jehovah. Their religious perversions included everything from burning their infants on pagan altars to homosexual acts with male temple prostitutes. God executed judgment on the Canaanites when He gave their land to Israel.

📖 Israel did not enter the land because they were righteous; yet God's favor had come to be taken for granted. They saw themselves as God's people, and mistakenly thought that made them immune to the judgment shown the Canaanites. Read 2 Kings 21:9–15, and identify why God sent Israel into the Babylonian captivity.

_____

_____

_____

Sadly, though the Canaanites were expelled from the land because of their wickedness, Israel became even worse than the Canaanites. Their wickedness and abominations before the Lord were more vile and depraved. As a result, they were taken captive and shipped off to other nations.

Even in judgment, God remembers mercy. God told Israel in advance that if they rebelled against Him and went after other gods, He would scatter them to the nations. But He also told them that when that happened, if they would return to the Lord and obey His commandments, He would restore them (Deuteronomy 30). Through the leadership of Zerubbabel and Ezra, God fulfilled this promise and restored them to the land. As He spoke years before through the prophet Joel (about 825 BC), *"Then I will make up to you for the years that the swarming locus has eaten"* (Joel 2:25). What a powerful message of hope! Failure doesn't have to be final. We can return to the Lord and enjoy His forgiveness and grace. But we cannot spurn grace and use it as an excuse to go on sinning. God brought Israel back to the land. Would they remember? Would they learn from the mistakes of the past?

Failure does not have to be final.

Think of your own life. Can you remember a time when God "scattered" you or someone you know because of sinful choices?

_____

_____

Was there repentance and restoration?

_____

_____

Was there a return to the failures of the past?

_____

_____

It was through the ministry of the prophet Haggai that the rebuilding of the temple commenced again after a delay of almost sixteen years. Five times in the short book of Haggai he calls Israel to *"Consider your ways!"* His message is clear: "all is not well in your life because God is not first in your life." He reminds them that they have *". . . sown much but harvest little"* (Haggai 1:6). What was happening to them was exactly what had been prophesied by Moses before Israel ever entered the promised land. He warned them that if they were unfaithful to their covenant relationship with the Lord, they would *". . . bring out much seed to the field but . . . gather in little."* (Deuteronomy 28:38). He is calling Israel to make the connection in their minds between their disobedience and God's judgment. Even though there was a partial repentance (they recommenced work on the Temple), yet in Ezra's day we see this further straying.

Could it be that the only thing we learn from Israel's history is that they "learn nothing from history?" The important lesson to learn from Haggai's rebuke, as well as from Ezra's grieving, is that in both instances Israel was being disobedient to the clearly revealed will of God. Haggai rebuked Israel for letting the temple work lie dormant for almost sixteen years, because God had clearly called them to rebuild the temple. Ezra rebuked the nation for intermarrying because God had clearly commanded them not to do this. In these two mistakes the remnant of Israel made, we see the two types of sin:

sins of **OMISSION** and sins of **COMMISSION**. Sins of "omission" occur when we don't do what we know God wants us to do (e.g. Israel wasn't rebuilding the temple). Sins of "commission" are acts of disobedience, when we do what we know God does not want us to do (e.g. Israel intermarrying with the Canaanites).

📖 Look at Ephesians 4:30 in its context and answer the following questions:

Which type of sin is mentioned here (look at 4:29, 31)?

    ____OMISSION   ____COMMISSION

How does this kind of sin affect God according to 4:30?

_____

_____

📖 Now look at 1 Thessalonians 5:19 in its context and answer the following questions:

Which type of sin is mentioned here (look at 5:18, 20)?

    ____OMISSION   ____COMMISSION

How does this kind of sin affect God according to 5:19?

_____

_____

We see in Ephesians 4:30 that sins of commission (such as speaking unwholesome words or bitterness, wrath, etc.) "grieve" the Holy Spirit of God who dwells in us. The word implies that such sins cause pain to the Lord. Conversely, we see in 1 Thessalonians 5:19 that sins of omission (such as failing to pray, failing to give thanks, despising prophetic directives) "quench" the Spirit of God. Often in Scripture the Holy Spirit is characterized by fire. The picture here is that when we don't do what He is calling us to do, it is like dumping a bucket of water on the fire of the Spirit in our lives.

Has this lesson surfaced any sins of "commission" in your life?

_____

_____

What about sins of "omission"?

_____

_____

📖 Zerubbabel and Ezra led the people to do the will of God and faithfully pointed it out when they strayed from God's will. Romans 12:1–2 is one of the clearest statements concerning the will of God in all of Scripture. Read those verses, and write down what they tell you God's will is like.

_____

_____

_____

> *When we are not doing what God wants us to do, we are doing what we should not have done and failing to do what we should have done. We are either obeying Him and moving forwards, or we are moving backwards.*

God's will is always "good (beneficial, helpful), acceptable (well-pleasing, a delight), and perfect (well-suited, that which reaches the intended goal)." Whenever we choose our own will over God's, we are always selecting something that is less than good, less than acceptable, and less than perfect.

📖 Now take a moment and look again at Romans 12:1–2. What three things precede proving that God's will really is "good, acceptable and perfect"?

_____

_____

_____

_____

_____

The first issue in God's will is surrender. We are called to place ourselves on the altar as living sacrifices. This requires dying to our will and way and letting the Lord rule in every area of our lives. Second, we are to lay aside worldly values. We must not allow ourselves to be "conformed to this world" and its values and priorities. Third, we must be transformed by having our minds renewed. In other words, we must allow God's truth to reprogram our thinking. This will only happen as we are committed to the Word of God.

Everything that happened to Israel can teach us something. When we see God's judgment or His blessing on Israel, we need to "make the connection" to our own lives.

When Israel walked in the will of God, life went well for them. There was peace in the land, and they enjoyed abundant provision. But when they strayed from the will of God, life became difficult. In Ezra's day it was reflecting on the sins and judgments of the past that motivated a renewed covenant to follow the will of God. In 1 Corinthians 10:11–12, speaking of some of the judgments of God's people in the Old Testament, we are told, *"Now these things happened to them as an example, and they were written for our instruction, upon whom the ends of the ages have come. Therefore let him who thinks he stands take heed lest he fall."* In other words, everything that happened to Israel can teach us something. When we see God's judgment or His blessing on Israel, we have to be willing to "make the connection" to our own lives. Are we walking in the will of God? Blessing and rebellion cannot co-exist. We can learn from Israel's mistakes or be doomed to repeat them ourselves.

As you close out this week's study, why not write your own prayer of surrender using the phrases of Romans 12:1–2 as a model.

_____

_____

_____

_____

_____

_____

_____

_____

_____

_____

_____

A Chronology of Ezra-Nehemiah-Haggai-Zechariah-Malachi

SCRIPTURE	DATE	EVENT
Isaiah 44:28	688 BC 538 BC	Prophecy about Cyrus being used by God to return His people to His land Fulfillment
Jeremiah 25:12	605 BC 539 BC	Prophecy of Babylon's judgment for the destruction of Jerusalem and captivity of God's people Fulfillment
Jeremiah 29:10	594 BC 536 BC	The people of God would be ruled by Babylon for 70 years and then return to Israel. The people return after 70 years (605–536 BC).
		Some date the 70 year period from 586, when the Temple was destroyed to 516, when the people finished and dedicated the Temple. *The Temple in Jerusalem was the focal point of the nation of Israel.*
Daniel 5:17–30	539 BC	Daniel prophesied the fall of the Babylonian Empire and the victory of the Medes and Persians. The prophecy was immediately fulfilled.
2 Chronicles 36:22, 23; Ezra 1:1–3	538 BC	Cyrus' Decree
Ezra 1:4–11; 2:1–70	536 BC	FIRST RETURN led by Zerubbabel—4 month journey
Ezra 3:1–7	536 BC	Altar consecrated and Feast of Booths
Ezra 3:8–11	536 BC	Temple reconstruction begins. The foundation is completed, and there is a celebration by many.
Ezra 3:12–13	536 BC	Many grieve over comparison with First Temple (Solomon's Temple).
Ezra 4:1–5	536–530 BC	Opposition to Temple reconstruction
Ezra 4:24 Haggai 1:4	530–520 BC	No work on the Temple—People work on their own houses.
Ezra 5:1	520 BC	HAGGAI and ZECHARIAH begin prophesying.
Haggai 1:1–11	August 29, 520 BC	Haggai's FIRST Message (6th month, 1st day, 2nd year)
Ezra 5:2 Haggai 1:12–15	September 21, 520 BC	Temple construction begins (6th month, 24th day, 2nd year) Haggai's SECOND Message
Haggai 2:1–9	October 17, 520 BC	Haggai's THIRD Message (7th month, 21st day, 2nd year)
Zechariah 1:1–6	October- November, 520 BC	Zechariah begins prophesying.
Haggai 2:10–19	December 18, 520 BC	Haggai's FOURTH Message (9th month, 24th day, 2nd year)
Haggai 2:20–23	December 18, 520 BC	Haggai's FIFTH Message (9th month, 24th day, 2nd year)
Ezra 5:3–17; 6:1–14	519–518 BC	Temple work continues.
Zechariah 1:7—6:8	February 15, 519 BC	Zechariah's eight visions
Zechariah 6:9–15	February 16(?), 519 BC	Joshua's crowning as high priest
Zechariah 7–8	December 7, 518 BC	The call to hear, the promise of good
Ezra 6:15–18	March 12, 516 BC	Dedication of the Temple
Ezra 4:6	486 BC	Accusation is sent to Ahasuerus (Xerxes) against the inhabitants of Judah and Jerusalem.
Book of ESTHER	483–473 BC	
Zechariah 9—14	489 or later 480(?) BC	
Ezra 4:7–23	ca. 464–460 BC	Letter is written to Artaxerxes I, who then stops the rebuilding of the wall and city of Jerusalem.
Ezra 4:23; Nehemiah 1:2, 3	ca. 464–460 BC	The walls of Jerusalem are torn down again and the gates burned.
Ezra 7:1–10	458/457 BC	A summary of the SECOND RETURN under Ezra
Ezra 7:11–28	458 BC	The letter and decrees are given to Ezra in preparation for the journey to Israel.
Ezra 7:9; 8:1–20	Nisan 1–12, 458 BC (March/April)	Many join Ezra in preparing for the journey. Ezra calls for some Levites to join them in the journey.
Ezra 8:21–23	Nisan, 458 BC	Ezra calls for a time of fasting and seeking the Lord for His protection.

SCRIPTURE	DATE	EVENT
Ezra 8:24–30		Ezra distributes the silver, gold, and various vessels to be carried to the temple in Jerusalem.
Ezra 7:8, 9; 8:31, 32	Nisan 12–Ab 1, 458 BC	Ezra and the exiles depart for Jerusalem on the twelfth day of the first month, and arrive there on the first day of the fifth month.
Ezra 8:33–36	Ab, 458 BC	They deliver the gifts to the temple, then offer sacrifices and worship the Lord. Then they deliver the orders from King Artaxerxes to the various officials.
Ezra 9:1–15; 10:9	Chislev, 458 BC	Four months later, some of the leaders report that some in Israel have married foreign wives. Ezra begins to grieve and prays to the Lord.
Ezra 10:1–6	Chislev, 458 BC	The people gather together and Shecaniah calls for a covenant agreement to put away the foreign wives. Ezra agrees.
Ezra 10:7, 8	Chislev 17–19, 458 BC	They issue a proclamation calling for an assembly in Jerusalem in three days to deal with the problem of intermarriage with foreign wives.
Ezra 10:9–15	Chislev 20, 458 BC	The men of Judah and Benjamin gather in Jerusalem, and Ezra calls them to separate from the peoples of the land and from their foreign wives. The people agree and call for an orderly investigation into the matter.
Ezra 10:16–44	Tebeth 1, 458 BC through Nisan 1, 457 BC	Over a period of three months, Ezra and the leaders of the assembly in Jerusalem lead the investigation of each man in the presence of the elders and judges from each man's town—after which the men are called to put away their foreign wives and children.
Nehemiah 1—12	445 BC	THIRD RETURN, rebuilding of the walls, and restoration of the city under Nehemiah. He serves his first term as governor from 445 to 433 BC
Nehemiah 1:1	Month Chislev (November-December) 446 BC (20th year)	Nehemiah serving as Cupbearer to King Artaxerxes. It is in the twentieth year of the king's reign.
Nehemiah 1:2, 3		He receives a report on the distressful condition of Jerusalem from his brother Hanani.
Nehemiah 1:4–11; 2:1	Chislev, 446 BC to the month Nisan (March-April), 445 BC	Nehemiah continues to pray to the God of heaven about the situation in Jerusalem. He prays for four months.
Nehemiah 2:1–8	Nisan, 445 BC	By serving the king and queen, Nehemiah is given the opportunity to present his burden for the needs in Jerusalem.
Nehemiah 2:6–8; Daniel 9:25	Nisan, 445 BC	Some believe the decree of Artaxerxes giving Nehemiah permission and provisions to go to Jerusalem is a fulfillment of the prophecy in Daniel.
Nehemiah 2:9	Nisan-Ab, (April-July) 445 BC	Nehemiah travels with officers of the army and horsemen on a three to four month journey.
Nehemiah 2:11	Ab 1–3, 445 BC (ca. July 16–18)	Three-day wait upon arrival in Jerusalem
Nehemiah 2:12–15	Ab 3, 445 BC	Nehemiah leads a night inspection of the condition of the walls of Jerusalem.
Nehemiah 2:16–18	Ab 4, 445 BC (ca. July 19)	Nehemiah meets with the leaders and people of Jerusalem concerning the needs of the city and the rebuilding of the walls.
Nehemiah 2:19, 20		Opposition and distraction begins. Nehemiah faces them and begins the process of rebuilding.
Nehemiah 3:1–32	Ab 4, 445 BC	Nehemiah and the people begin work on the wall.
Nehemiah 4:1–6	Around the 29th day of Ab, 445 BC	In the midst of the threats and opposition of others, the wall was built to half its height. (26 days after they began—half the time it took to complete the wall.)
Nehemiah 4:7–23		The work continues in the face of threats and distractions from the enemies of the Jews.
Nehemiah 5:1–19		Nehemiah deals with problems in the Jewish community.
Nehemiah 6:1–14		Opposition continues, as does the building of the wall.
Nehemiah 6:15–19	Elul 25, 445 BC (September 10)	The wall is completed in 52 days to the praise and honor of the Lord God of Israel. (based on 30-day months)
Nehemiah 7:1–4		Nehemiah puts Hanani and Hananiah in charge of the city of Jerusalem.
Nehemiah 7:5–73		Nehemiah gathers the people and conducts a census.

SCRIPTURE	DATE	EVENT
Nehemiah 7:53; 8:1–12	Tishri 1, 445 BC (September 16)	Ezra and Nehemiah gather the people for instruction from the Law and the celebration of the Feast of Trumpets (seventh month, first day).
Nehemiah 8:13	Tishri 2, 445 BC (September 17)	Ezra leads a continuing study of the Law and finds the instructions for the upcoming Feast of Booths. The Day of Atonement (seventh month, tenth day) is probably celebrated as well.
Nehemiah 8:14–18	Tishri 15–21, 445 BC (Sept. 30-Oct. 6)	The people celebrate the Feast of Booths/Tabernacles from the fifteenth to the twenty-first of the month (seven days).
Nehemiah 8:18	Tishri 22, 445 BC (October 7)	A solemn assembly is held on the eighth day of the Feast.
Nehemiah 9:1–38; 10:1–39	Tishri 24, 445 BC (October 9)	The leaders (Ezra, Nehemiah, and others) and the people read the Law, confess their sins, worship the Lord, and establish and sign a renewal of their covenant with the Lord to walk in His law.
Nehemiah 11:1–36		The people settle in their respective towns, and several volunteer to live in Jerusalem to continue the rebuilding process.
Nehemiah 12:1–26		Nehemiah records the names of those who came with Zerubbabel in the first resettling and those who have worked alongside Nehemiah and Ezra.
Nehemiah 12:27–47; 13:1	Tishri, 445 BC (mid October)	Soon after the Feasts and the assemblies of the seventh month, the people celebrate the dedication of the wall with praise, singing, and the reading of the Word of God.
Nehemiah 13:1–3		All foreigners are excluded from Israel.
Nehemiah 13:6	433 BC	Nehemiah returns to King Artaxerxes in Babylon.
Nehemiah 13:4	433–430 BC (?)	Eliashib the high priest prepares a room for Tobiah in the Temple.
Book of MALACHI	ca. 433 BC–420 BC	Malachi prophesies.
Nehemiah 13:4–9	ca. sometime between 430 BC and 425 BC	Nehemiah returns to Jerusalem for a second term as governor. He evicts Tobiah from the Temple building and gives orders to cleanse those rooms.
Nehemiah 13:10–31	ca. 430 BC–415 BC	Nehemiah restores order in the Temple service, as well as in the day-to-day order of business, the Sabbath, marriage among the people of God, and the duties of priests and Levites.

With the completion of **Malachi** *and the last part of* **Nehemiah***, the Old Testament writings were complete, awaiting the promised coming of the Messiah, the Lord Jesus Christ, in the fullness of time (Galatians 4:4; see also Genesis 49:10; Matthew 1; Mark 1; Luke 1–2; John 1).*

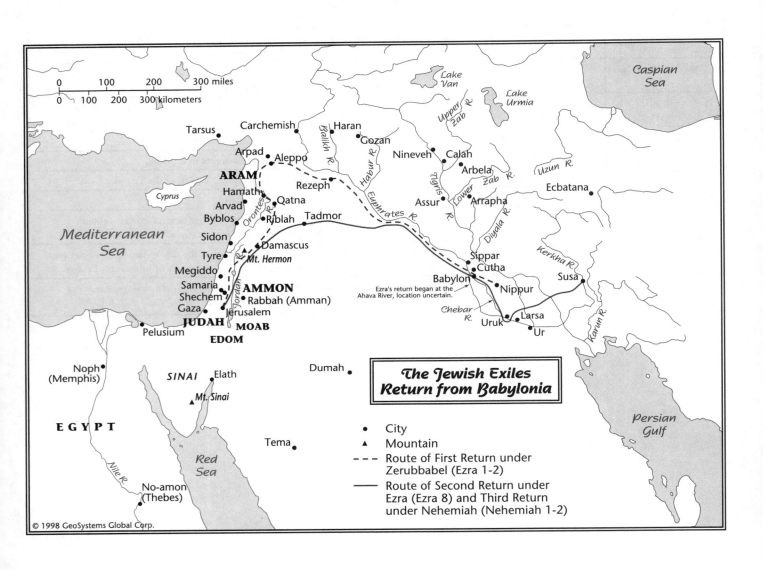

The Jewish Exiles
Return from Babylonia

- • City
- ▲ Mountain
- - - - Route of First Return under Zerubbabel (Ezra 1-2)
- —— Route of Second Return under Ezra (Ezra 8) and Third Return under Nehemiah (Nehemiah 1-2)

Ezra's return began at the Ahava River, location uncertain.

© 1998 GeoSystems Global Corp.

Notes

Notes

Nehemiah

LEADING BY FOLLOWING GOD

Nehemiah served as cupbearer to King Artaxerxes in Persia until 445 BC when he journeyed to Israel. There he served as Governor under the Persian regime from 445 to 433, returned to Persia for a time, and then came back to serve in Israel. Ezra the scribe served alongside him in leading the people of God. Most likely Malachi prophesied sometime during this period.

Leaders come in all shapes and sizes. They are chosen in any number of ways. Some are the popular choice of the people. Some are made leaders by their wealth, fame, or talent. Others work hard at becoming a leader. Some are given the responsibility of leadership in the role of a husband/father or wife/mother. Others are in some measure of leadership where they work. Some even "achieve" leadership status by deceit and craftiness. Then there are those leaders that God raises up, people who may walk into positions of leadership with many different attitudes. They may be fearful or reluctant, humble or grateful, with a sense of unworthiness, overwhelmed or ready to conquer all, or any combination of these. The one mark that should be common to all who are raised up by God is this: they know God has called and placed them where they are, and if the task is to be done right it must be done His way: by following Him. That is where we find Nehemiah. This week we will see what God taught Nehemiah about following Him and what he can teach us by way of testimony, example, and principle.

WHEN DID HE LEAD?

550	500	450	400
	HAGGAI **ZECHARIAH**	**MALACHI**	
	Zerubbabel 536—First Return 536—Rebuilding the Temple 516—Temple completed	Ezra 458—Second Return Rebuilding the people	
		Nehemiah 445—Third Return Rebuilding the walls and the city of Jerusalem	*The Jews are without a king or a prophet, living under the dominion of foreign rulers, and* AWAITING THE MESSIAH, THE TRUE KING OF ISRAEL.
586—Final Captivity Jerusalem and Temple destroyed			
	538–Decree of Cyrus to return		
	Queen Esther		
Amel-Marduk (Evil-Merodach) 562–560	Cyrus 539–530	Darius I 522–486	Xerxes 486–464	Artaxerxes 464–423	
			Socrates 470–399	Plato 428–348	Aristotle 384–322

LEARNING TO FOLLOW GOD THROUGH PRAYER

Solomon's Temple had been destroyed by the Babylonians in 586 BC. Work on rebuilding it began fifty years later with the first return from the Babylonian captivity, but it soon stopped. Sixty-six years after the Temple's destruction, Haggai and Zechariah were called by God to prophesy and call Zerubbabel to finish the work which had begun sixteen years earlier. It was finished in 516 BC, seventy years after its destruction. The remnant of the nation of Israel was still under the domination of the Persians when they returned.

Nehemiah was cupbearer to King Artaxerxes, ruler over the vast Persian Empire. We first meet Nehemiah in Susa, the winter residence of the Persian monarch. The time was 445 BC, some seventy-one years after the completion of Zerubbabel's Temple in Jerusalem. (For a complete overview of the dates surrounding Nehemiah, see "A Chronology of Ezra-Nehemiah-Haggai-Zechariah-Malachi" at the end of this lesson.)

When we open the book of Nehemiah, we find the people of God in great need and the report of a Jerusalem still in ruins and defenseless without walls or gates. (See the map "The Jewish Exiles return from Babylonia" at the end of the lesson on Zerubbabel and Ezra.) One problem: Nehemiah, the man burdened for this great need, is in Susa, over one thousand miles from Jerusalem—a four-month journey. The solution . . . follow God.

📖 Read Nehemiah 1:2–4. What was on Nehemiah's heart?

_____

_____

_____

What did he *do* about what he heard?

_____

_____

_____

The people of God were on Nehemiah's mind; specifically, the people who had returned to Jerusalem from Babylon. He was concerned with their mental, spiritual, physical, and material well-being. The news of their condition grieved Nehemiah. Because his focus was the God of heaven, he wept, mourned, fasted, and prayed for many days.

📖 Read Nehemiah's prayer in Nehemiah 5:1–11. What is Nehemiah's view of God (v. 5)?

_____

_____

_____

> **The people of God were on Nehemiah's heart. The God of heaven was Nehemiah's focus.**

Nehemiah addresses the *"Lord God of heaven, the great and awesome God."* "Lord" refers to Jehovah/Yahweh, the I AM, the covenant name for God, who is ever faithful and committed to fulfilling His Word concerning Israel. He is the God of heaven, there is none higher. This is who Nehemiah was focused on: the only One capable of restoring Jerusalem. The God of heaven is great and awesome. Nehemiah recognized the power and authority of God, and the fear, respect, and heart devotion due to God. God preserves the covenant because of His lovingkindness. He is attentive to those who obey. He hears the prayer of His servants.

📖 How does Nehemiah describe himself in verse 6?

_____

Nehemiah is *"Thy servant,"* and he includes himself among those who have *"sinned against Thee."* He is a son of Israel who bowed before a holy God with a humble, honest heart, wanting what God wanted for his life and for the people of Israel.

APPLY What does this tell you about being a godly leader?

_____

_____

Nehemiah beautifully illustrates the first, most foundational step in being a godly leader. He recognized that God is God, and he was not. The vision is God's: it has been shared with Nehemiah. And the ability to see it fulfilled is all God's as well. Nehemiah recognized his own inability to accomplish anything good apart from following God.

📖 What problem does he address in verses 6 and 7?

_____

_____

_____

Nehemiah addresses the sins of Israel. They *"acted very corruptly against"* God and did not keep His *"commandments, nor the statutes, nor the ordinances"* given to Moses. The idea of acting "corruptly" is one of working hard to carry out one's own way. It is wholehearted wickedness against God and His Word. The fruit of this brings pain, sorrow, destruction, ruin, and injury. It offends and spoils. It wounds and hurts.

📖 In verses 8–10, what is Nehemiah basing his request on?

_____

_____

What is his confidence in?

_____

_____

Nehemiah quotes from Moses and the Law God had given. Nehemiah was well aware of what God said, what He meant, and how it applied to the

Did You Know?

PRAYING TO THE GOD OF HEAVEN

The name *"God of heaven"* appears 22 times in the Old Testament with 16 of those occurring in Ezra, Nehemiah, and Daniel—books written when Israel was under the rule of a foreign nation. They each recognized that, in fact, it is heaven that rules (Daniel 4:26) and their God was the God of heaven, sovereign over all nations and fully able to care for His covenant people.

nation of Israel. The basis of Nehemiah's request was the clear will of God as revealed in the Scripture. His confidence was in God's commitment and ability to do what He had said He would do. And it was in this confidence that Nehemiah asked God to restore His people in the land of Israel.

📖 In his prayer, Nehemiah speaks of God's Word to Moses. Read Leviticus 26:30; Deuteronomy 12:5 and 30:2–4 and compare them with Nehemiah 1:8–10. What similarities do you see?

_____

_____

_____

_____

_____

Put Yourself in Their Shoes

A PATTERN FOR FOLLOWING GOD

Nehemiah was a man of devotion to God and His will, yet we see that he faced many distractions. In these times, he revealed his devotion in prayer and in following God's Word. Out of that devotion God always gave him direction. Thus in Daniel we find a pattern for following God through our trials:

•**DEVOTION**

•**DISTRACTION**

•**DEVOTION REAFFIRMED**

•**DIRECTION**

You will find that Nehemiah is speaking from what's on his heart, not from an exact quote. He had read God's Word and understood the heart of God. That Word was on his heart and comes out in his prayer.

APPLY Which of the following characteristics of Nehemiah's prayer are evident in your prayer life?

_____He went to God with his problem first.
_____No selfish agenda
_____A burden for others
_____Pure motives
_____He recognized God's holiness.
_____He recognized his own sinfulness.
_____Claiming God's mercy on his behalf
_____Made no demands on God
_____Requested from God what He had revealed in His Word

Nehemiah was cupbearer to King Artaxerxes, a position of great importance. He was responsible for everything the king drank and therefore held a position of great value, protecting the king from anything harmful. He would also be close to the king. With this special position came the responsibility of honoring the king at all times. In the courts of eastern monarchs, it was imperative that those in the king's presence seek only to please the king, and never show sadness or displeasure, an issue that comes up in chapter 2.

In Nehemiah chapter 2 we find the mention of the month Nisan (March-April). The time of the news of Nehemiah 1:1–4 was the month Chislev (November-December), four months earlier. For these months Nehemiah carried his burden for Jerusalem and prayed earnestly. Nehemiah 1:5–11 gives us the substance of his intercession over those months. In Nehemiah 2 we find him in the presence of the king and queen. Verse 4 reflects the reality of his continual attitude of "praying without ceasing," a short prayer of a few seconds to go with the intercession of the past four months. Let's listen in on this conversation with the king and queen.

📖 Read Nehemiah 2:1–8. What did Nehemiah do as a result of his praying and seeking the Lord?

_____

_____

List the four things he asked of the king.

_____

_____

_____

_____

As Nehemiah prayed and sought the Lord over the four months recorded in the Scriptures, it is evident he had carefully thought through everything he needed to do to rebuild the city of Jerusalem, and that is what he presented to the king when he asked to rebuild the walls. He knew the time he would have to be gone, the supplies he would need, and the letters of reference he would need to clear the way. The king granted his requests, and with that began his journey to Jerusalem. Nehemiah was learning to follow God through prayer.

FOLLOWING GOD IN THE MIDST OF DISTRACTIONS

It is evident in Nehemiah 2:8 that the source of Nehemiah's ability to lead was in his continual willingness to follow God. He knew that success came *"because the good hand of my God was on me."* But even though God's hand of blessing may be upon us, that doesn't alleviate problems and distractions.

📖 Read Nehemiah 2:9, 10. What was the first thing to greet Nehemiah on his journey?

_____

_____

_____

Even though God's hand of blessing may be upon us, that doesn't alleviate problems and distractions.

Sanballat and Tobiah, two officials who exercised some measure of control over the area, did not like the sight of Nehemiah coming to help the sons of Israel. Whatever their position, they were not concerned for the people of Israel. From the start Nehemiah began to face certain distractions.

This first encounter with Sanballat and company is not the last encounter. We learn from other passages that Sanballat is most likely a leader over Samaria (Nehemiah 4:2), and an ally of both Tobiah, the Ammonite official, and Geshem the Arab (a leader over the Arabs to the southeast of Judah). Together these officials represented enemy territory to the North (Samaria), the East (Ammon), and the Southeast (Moab, Edom, Arabia). The presence of a military escort with Nehemiah spoke volumes to these officials about their loss of control. They did not want the returned remnant to prosper or succeed in any way. Most likely this grew out of years of built-up prejudices against the once strong, now defeated and dominated, nation of Israel. These officials were all part of the Persian domination and quickly used their alliance as a power-play against the sons of Israel.

In addition, the Samaritans were a mixed breed of Jews and colonists planted by the Assyrians after they conquered the Northern Kingdom of Israel in 722 BC. The Jews despised them because they had intermarried with people from other nations. The Samaritans were determined to establish their position in the land. God was determined to reestablish His people for His purposes . . . but that did not come easily. More distractions loomed on the horizon.

📖 Read Nehemiah 2:11–18. What did Nehemiah do in response to this distraction?

_____

_____

_____

Why did he do this (vv. 12, 18)?

_____

Did You Know?

THE GATES AND WALLS

The city of Jerusalem in Nehemiah's day covered an area of about 200 to 220 acres. The wall's total length was about two to two and a half miles. There were Ten Gates—the Sheep Gate, the Fish Gate, the Old Gate, the Valley Gate, the Dung Gate, the Fountain Gate, the Water Gate, the Horse Gate, the East Gate, and the Inspection Gate.

Nehemiah first prayed. He listened to God to know what to do after he arrived in Jerusalem. He waited three days before he inspected the walls and the city and did so because of *"what my God was putting into my mind to do for Jerusalem"* (v. 12). His focus was on what God was doing and how God wanted him to proceed. He was following God, not some "How to Fix a Wall" handbook.

📖 What was the response of the neighboring governors in v. 19?

_____

_____

How did Nehemiah respond in v. 20?

_____

_____

The neighbors mocked them and despised them. They falsely accused them of rebelling against the king. That accusation goes back to the Babylonian siege over 150 years before, as well as to a more recent incident and letter to the king a little over ten years earlier when certain Samaritan officials had been able to stop an effort to rebuild and maintain their dominion in the area (Ezra 4:7–23).

In this incident Nehemiah knows he has the authority of God behind him, as well as the authority of the king. Nehemiah's response was God-focused. He saw himself and the people of Israel as the servants of God in their task. He also clarified the exact position of the enemy officials with regard to Jerusalem by pointing out that they had "no portion" (no part, nothing now), no "right" (no claim, nothing at any point in the future), and no "memorial" (nothing from the past that gave them any claim to any rule or say-so in Jerusalem). The next verses tell what Nehemiah and the people did in response.

📖 Read Nehemiah 3:1–32. What began to happen?

_____

_____

What kinds of people got involved?

_____

_____

_____

_____

How did they divide responsibilities?

_____

_____

_____

After Nehemiah clarified where everyone stood, the high priest led the way and began to work. Others joined in, and the wall began to go up. The list of people included priests, the men of Jericho, the Tekoites, goldsmiths, perfumers, government officials, sons and daughters of the people, Levites, temple servants, gatekeepers, and merchants. They wisely built section by section with certain people responsible for specific sections, especially the sections near their houses—an incentive to personal excellence and care. But some days it was "uphill all the way" and distractions were prevalent. That's what we find in chapter 4.

📖 Read Nehemiah 4:1–9. What kind of opposition do Nehemiah and the people face at this point?

_____

_____

What is the consistent *response* of Nehemiah and the people of God (vv. 4–6, 9)?

_____

_____

_____

Sanballat became furious and very angry and mocked the Jews. He consulted with the leaders of Samaria, and together they mocked the Jews. Tobiah chimed in with his own ridicule. Nehemiah and the people responded by calling on God to hear and deliver. Then they went back to the wall. The enemies responded with anger and a plot to attack and stop the work. Again Nehemiah and the people prayed. Then, they added guard duty day and night.

When we read the prayer in verses 4 and 5, it seems somewhat unforgiving. It is important to understand the perspective of Nehemiah and the people. Sanballat and company were opposing God in opposing the Jews. God judges the enemies of Israel. Joshua 1:1–9 gives the perspective of God. The land is theirs. They were to live and walk with God in that land. They were living in light of the Abrahamic covenant in which God said He would curse those who curse Abraham's children (Genesis 12:3). They were also well aware of the Mosaic covenant that said if the people sinned, they would be dealt with, and if they repented, God would restore them to the land, as Nehemiah prayed in 1:5–11. Everything they prayed in verses 4 and 5 agreed with what God had spoken to them through Moses in Deuteronomy 32:35, 40–43.

Think about your responses when distractions and attacks come your way. How do you tend to respond when the things you do are not approved of, or are even aggressively ridiculed?

_____I try to adjust or compromise to gain approval.

_____I get angry that people think they have the right to attack me.

_____I trust God's leading and continue to focus on Him.

_____I get offended and attack them back.

_____I cave in and assume God must not have been leading that way.

What can you learn from Nehemiah's response?

_____

_____

_____

_____

Nehemiah prepared the people to build and to fight, but he did not depend on his plans. He and the people depended on the Lord.

It is vital to see that God is the one who works out His vengeance. Here Nehemiah does not take vengeance. He leaves it with God and goes about doing what God had directed him to do: rebuild the wall. It is important to realize what the enemies are doing: they are mocking the covenant people of God. The Lord is committed to accomplishing His purposes with them and through them. God does not take that mockery lightly. Nehemiah's response is to go to God. He goes knowing he is one of the covenant children of God, and he prays that way. He is praying for the welfare of the people of God and for justice on the enemies of God (and enemies of the people of God).

📖 Look at Nehemiah 4:10–14. List . . .

. . . the problems.

_____

_____

_____

_____

. . . how Nehemiah responded.

_____

_____

_____

_____

The people were getting tired (v. 10). The work was far from complete. There was still *"much rubbish"* (v. 10). They saw no way to finish (v. 10). Their enemies were plotting to attack, kill them, and thus stop the work (v. 11). Their fears kept intensifying, and they saw no place to turn for safety (vv. 12, 14).

In response, Nehemiah did four important things. First, he recognized their fear, anxiety, and sense of hopelessness (v. 14). Second, he focused on the Lord and called the people to do the same (v. 14). Third, he prepared them by placing them in the right places to best defend the city (v. 13). And fourth, he focused them on their personal responsibility to defend what God had entrusted to them—their families and what belonged to each of them (v. 14).

📖 Read Nehemiah 4:15–23. Who got the credit for successfully spoiling the enemy's plan (v. 15)?

_____

List a few things that changed as the people continued to rebuild.

_____

_____

_____

_____

The cry of confident faith is "God will fight for us" (Nehemiah 4:20).

They gave the credit to God who "frustrated" the enemy plan. Nehemiah intensified the guard duty. The people worked as laborers and guards at the same time. They had a defensive strategy ready, but did not rely on that alone, because they knew *"God will fight for us"* (4:19–20). While they worked from dawn until dark they also spent the entire day and night on "alert" (4:21–23).

LEADING BY SERVING GOD AND OTHERS

Nehemiah **DAY THREE**

When we come to Nehemiah 5, we find that there were problems within the Jewish community, problems that were a distraction to accomplishing what God wanted for Jerusalem and for the people of Israel. Those distractions on the home front had to be faced and dealt with.

📖 List three complaints of the people found in Nehemiah 5:1–5.

_____

_____

_____

_____

A true leader has a servant's heart.

First, there was a famine in the land, and some could not buy grain. Others were mortgaging their property to buy grain, while still others sold their sons and daughters into slavery to survive. To add to the pressures, some of the leaders were *"exacting usury"* (charging interest) to their Jewish brethren (at a rate of 1% according to verse 11).

📖 Read chapter 5, verses 6–13. What solution did Nehemiah offer?

_____

_____

_____

_____

Nehemiah first went to the leadership and confronted them on the usury issue. Then, he called for a "great assembly," and he rebuked them for buying and selling their own kinsmen. He showed them that it was "not good." It was sin against God, and he rebuked them for not trusting God in the situation—they were not walking *"in the fear of God."* This was most evident in charging their fellow countrymen interest, a practice that had been clearly prohibited. The leaders repented agreeing to give back the interest and not enslave the people. Nehemiah required them to take an oath to fulfill their word: he held them accountable. The people agreed and rejoiced. *"And they praised the LORD"* and kept their word. It is important to note that Nehemiah stayed focused on the Lord and His Word in leading the people. He was following God and His Word.

We have seen in many instances that Nehemiah was a leader because he was a follower of God. Nehemiah 5:14–19 presents some characteristics of previous leaders of Israel.

📖 Read Nehemiah 5:14–19. What kind of leaders were the people of Israel accustomed to before Nehemiah came?

_____

_____

_____

Nehemiah gives an example of self-centered leadership: former governors *"laid burdens on the people"* and took food and money from them. Their rulership was oppressive with a heavy hand. Verse 15 notes, *"Even their servants domineered the people."* They exercised autocratic control, making sure that everything was done to serve themselves.

In contrast, what did Nehemiah do (vv. 17, 18)?

_____

_____

_____

Nehemiah did not act as the former leaders had. He understood that a godly leader is first and foremost a servant. He was a *giver* instead of a *taker*. He did not take the governor's food allowance for himself. He shared it with many (5:17–18). In 5:10 he also mentions lending money and grain to those who could not provide for themselves. He thought first of the people's needs and the heavy burdens they were already carrying. He was a servant-leader instead of a tyrant. He served the people in giving many food, as well as in working on the wall along with his servants. They did not buy land for themselves, but sought to do good for the people in any way possible.

Why did Nehemiah lead in this way (vv. 15, 19)?

_____

_____

_____

Nehemiah was God-centered. Verse 15 tells us he did what he did *"because of the fear of God."* He trusted God and walked according to God's Word. He also knew he had to answer to God and had the prospect of God's

"The fear of the LORD is the beginning of wisdom, And the knowledge of the Holy One is understanding."

Proverbs 9:10

reward for his faithful service (5:19). He did what he did out of a genuine love and concern for the people.

The wall was almost finished, but Sanballat and the other enemies still wanted to sabotage the work.

📖 Read Nehemiah 6:1–14. There were three plots against Nehemiah by his enemies. List each trap and how Nehemiah responded.

	The Plot	Nehemiah's Response
Nehemiah 6:1–4		
Nehemiah 6:5–9		
Nehemiah 6:10–14		

First, the enemies wanted a meeting on their terms in the plain of Ono. Nehemiah saw through their lies. He stayed focused on what God had given him to do and would not come down from the wall. The enemies then resorted to false accusations about him rebelling against the king. Nehemiah also saw through this fear tactic. He focused on God and asked for strength to follow what God had given him to do. Finally, the enemies hired a false prophet who used scare tactics to get Nehemiah to act out of fear of men rather than out of the fear of the Lord and trust in Him. A prophetess and some more false prophets also tried to frighten him, but he continued to focus on the Lord (6:14).

FOLLOWING GOD THROUGH HIS WORD

Nehemiah DAY FOUR

Nehemiah 6:15–19 brings us to the completion of the wall around Jerusalem. In the following chapters Nehemiah's attention is focused on getting the people back to following the Lord according to His Word. Their relationship with the God of Israel was the true wall of protection around them.

As he closes his account of the rebuilding of the wall, Nehemiah once again brings us to the central point of all that happened. Through everything that Nehemiah has faced in directing the rebuilding of the wall, his focus has remained consistent.

📖 Read Nehemiah 6:15–16. Imagine yourself in Nehemiah's place, and in your own words, write out what verse 16 is saying.

_____

_____

_____

_____

_____

Compare your paraphrase with this one: "The wall was finished, and our enemies heard all about it. Even the nations surrounding Judah heard all the details and saw that it was indeed finished successfully. As a result they lost confidence in themselves and in all their schemes. They knew without a shadow of a doubt that the God of Abraham, Isaac, and Jacob was still alive and active in the lives of His covenant people Israel. They recognized that it was more than man's leadership, organization, expertise, or skill. God Himself was at work, and we had followed Him."

Nehemiah and the people completed the wall in fifty-two days (6:15). After the city was secure they focused on the citizens. In Nehemiah 8, the people gathered in Jerusalem to hear the Word of God. Ezra read the Law to a great assembly and led them in worship. Along with Ezra were priests and Levites who explained the Law to the people assembled. According to chapter 8, verse 8, they read (told them what it said), _"translating to give the sense"_ (told them what it meant), _"so that they understood the reading"_ (told them how it applied). As a result, the people realized there were several things they had not done, and they began to weep. Nehemiah, Ezra, and others began to exhort them.

📖 Read Nehemiah 8:9–12. What did they say to the people?

_____

_____

_____

How did the people respond?

_____

_____

Nehemiah, Ezra, and others explained that this was the day for celebration (it was the date of the Feast of Trumpets—seventh month, first day) and called on them to celebrate. Because they understood the Law, they obeyed and celebrated. As a result they had great joy. When we understand how far short we fall from what God expects of us, our initial reaction may well be grief. But if we stay at that point, we dishonor God. As we turn away from our sin by turning to Him, we turn to the source of all joy, and the result will be lives marked by holy worship and praise to His glory.

On the next day the people gathered to gain further insight into the Word of God. As a result of what they learned, they prepared to celebrate the seven day Feast of Booths thirteen days later (7/15 through 7/21; the Day of Atonement would occur on the tenth day of this month).

📖 Read Nehemiah 8:17–18. What was their primary activity during the Feast of Booths?

_____

_____

During the time of the Feast of Booths or Tabernacles, they listened to *"the law of God daily"* (8:18). They followed that with a *"solemn assembly"* (8:14–18).

📖 According to Nehemiah 9:1–3, what followed this time of reading the Law of God?

_____

_____

_____

The people of Israel *"assembled with fasting, in sackcloth, and with dirt upon them"* to confess their sins (9:1–3). They read from the Book of the Law, and followed that with confession and worship (9:3). This is a beautiful example for us of how the Word of God should affect our lives. The study of God's Word should result in confession (agreeing with God about our sin), repentance (turning to Him away from our sin), and worship (praising and glorifying Him for His mercy and grace). Nehemiah 9:5–38 records the beautiful song of praise that resulted.

📖 Read Nehemiah 9:5–38. List the attributes of God which are referred to in these verses.

_____

_____

_____

_____

_____

_____

_____

_____

> **"I have treasured the words of His mouth more than my necessary food."**
>
> **Job 23:12**

Their confession and a covenant renewal is recorded in Nehemiah 10:28–39. They promised to follow what God said concerning marriage, business, the Sabbath, worship, and giving to the Temple service.

Think through what went on during those days. The Word of God led the people of Israel in following God (8:1–3, 5, 7–9, 12–15, 18; 9:3; 10:28–29, 34, 36). It was the Word which brought them to confession and led them into praise and thanksgiving.

APPLY How central is God's Word in your life?

_____I study every day, making it an integral part of my life.
_____When I'm worried or upset, I look to it for help.
_____I only read it when I'm at church or in a Bible study.
_____I like to listen to others teach, but I rarely read it for myself.

God's Word cannot direct your life if it is not a part of your life. Following God cannot be divorced from seeking His revealed will in His Word.

God is the Giver of great joy!

The dedication of the wall was a day of great celebration. Read Nehemiah 12:27–43 and picture the splendor and joy. What is central to all that happened? See 12:43 especially.

_____

_____

_____

The reason they could rejoice so intensely was *"because God had given them great joy"* (12:43). Nehemiah followed God, and that made all the difference. As a godly leader, the focus was not ultimately on him. His leadership continually brought the people back to God and His Word. In the end, the people did not exalt Nehemiah and his leadership—they exalted God.

Chapter 13 tells us Nehemiah served twelve years as governor then went back to Babylon. After some time he returned to deal with Tobiah once again and lead the people to *follow the Lord and His Word*. That is his legacy and that is his call and challenge to us.

Nehemiah　DAY FIVE

FOR ME TO FOLLOW GOD

Nehemiah followed God in the midst of many, many distractions and obstacles, much opposition and weariness, and numerous challenges to his faith in God and to his leadership as he followed God. We face the same kinds of things to one degree or another. What can we learn from Nehemiah?

When we first meet Nehemiah, God has put a burden on his heart about the plight of Jerusalem, defenseless without its walls.

Read Nehemiah 1:4–11. How did Nehemiah respond to this burden?

_____

_____

Nehemiah took his burden before the God of heaven in prayer. He poured out his heart to God and laid claim to the promises God had made in His Word. He talked about it to God.

Through His Word we increase our vocabulary in prayer, and we learn the heart of our Father—we learn how to speak, how to listen, how to ask, how to receive, how to surrender, and how to worship.

For many of us, prayer is either something we feel awkward and stilted doing, or that we're so familiar with, we just rattle off all the things for which we know we should pray. Prayer should be so much more than that! It should be conversation—talking with God heart to heart and listening for that still, small voice of His response.

 Think about your own life recently and the time you've spent in prayer. How would you describe a typical conversation with God?

_____

_____

_____

It's tempting to try to be "spiritual" when we pray, saying the right things and having the right attitude. But God knows how we really feel—who do we think we're trying to fool? He wants us to "spill our guts" and talk to Him about everything. That's one of the reasons He tells us to find an "inner room" in which to pray (Matthew 6:6), so we can get honest before Him! He will encourage our hearts and give us guidance and correction. The things in our lives that we're not willing to discuss openly with the Lord are often the things we're not willing to let Him change.

No part of our lives is too unimportant for God to be involved in, or too private for His loving interference. He wants us to bring it all to Him. If you feel like praying, pour out the praise and devotion of your heart to Him. And if you don't feel like praying, tell Him that too, asking Him to change your heart and give you a hunger for His company.

God honored Nehemiah's heart. As he continued to seek God in prayer, God made a way for Him to Jerusalem to begin the work of rebuilding the walls. But just because he was faithfully following God, that didn't mean everything was smooth sailing. Nehemiah seemed to face distractions and problems at every turn.

📖 What do each of the following verses tell you about how Nehemiah responded to the distractions and problems which confronted him?

Nehemiah 2:12 _____

_____

Nehemiah 2:20 _____

_____

Nehemiah 4:9 _____

_____

Nehemiah 4:14 _____

_____

Nehemiah 6:3, 4 _____

_____

Nehemiah 6:8, 9 _____

_____

Nehemiah 6:11, 12 _____

_____

When Nehemiah faced opposition or distractions, he stayed focused on God, His Word, and His call to rebuild the wall.

Following God does not mean that life's a bed of roses. We live in a world marred by sin, and we have to deal with the consequences of that sin continually. What's important is how we respond. We can't control our circumstances, but we can control our response to them.

Nehemiah gives us a strong example of following God in his responses to the problems he faces. He waited on God, following His leading in his heart. He sought God in prayer. He refused to be distracted from following God step by step. Nehemiah wasn't dealing with these problems and obstacles in his own strength and abilities. He tapped into God's wisdom and power.

Nehemiah exhibited an important perspective on everything that was happening: God is in control. God is God and we are not. The results aren't up to us—they rest in God's hand. Our only responsibility is to follow God step by step. Our faithful Lord will give us His grace and wisdom to deal with each trial or obstacle we come to.

God had burdened Nehemiah's heart with the task of rebuilding the wall, and Nehemiah followed God. Despite all that was against him, he saw that work accomplished. If Nehemiah had been like many of us, when the burden for the wall came to him, he probably would have prayed diligently that God would raise up a leader to spearhead the effort. He would have talked about it, and maybe even started a Rebuilding the Wall Aid Society. He would have given money to the cause and encouraged others to do the same. But he would never have gone himself. After all, he had a good job in a position of influence. He could do a lot right where he was.

But God isn't all that interested in the things we can do for Him. He's God; He doesn't need us to accomplish His purpose. But He does *want* to use us. That can be hard to understand, but let me give you a personal illustration. Last summer I needed to paint the fence along the side of our yard, and my three sons helped me. Now, I didn't really need their help. In fact, between cleaning up after them and repainting what they'd painted, the job probably took me twice as long as it would have if I'd done it by myself. But I did *want* their help. I love them, and I wanted to spend the time with them. I wanted them to be involved in what I was doing.

I think that God looks at us in much the same way. He doesn't need our help, and sometimes, from the human perspective, it may seem like we're more trouble than we're worth. But He loves us, and He wants us to be involved in what He's doing.

He is interested in our willingness to follow Him in every area of our lives, no matter where that may take us. Many times we pray diligently for a need God has placed on our heart, never stopping to think that God may want us to be His answer to that prayer.

APPLY What burden, big or small, has God laid on your heart recently?

_____

_____

How are you praying in that area?

_____

_____

_____

What would God have you do as He works to accomplish His purpose?

_____

_____

_____

Nehemiah followed God faithfully, and he saw His prayers answered—the wall was completed. As a strong and successful leader, He could have easily

> *God wants us to follow Him in every area of our lives, no matter where that may take us.*

accepted the gratitude of the people and the credit for a job well done. But Nehemiah's perspective wasn't just different in the hard times. His focus on God survived the good times too.

📖 Read Nehemiah 6:15, 16. Who received the credit for the successful completion of the wall?

_____

_____

It is obvious to everyone, even the enemies of Nehemiah and Israel, that God deserves the credit. At the celebrations that followed the completion of the wall, Nehemiah's strong focus on God encouraged the people of Israel to get back to the Word of God. When we acknowledge God's rightful place of sovereignty in our lives, the Bible is moved into a position of authority. In gratitude to God, Nehemiah and the people honored His Word.

📖 According to Nehemiah 8:9 and 9:1–3, what did the people do as a result of saturating themselves with the Word of God?

_____

_____

_____

When we see God's standard revealed in the Bible, the response of a heart seeking to follow God will be confession and repentance. The people of Israel mourned their sin. They didn't try to excuse it with ignorance. They simply agreed with God about their sin, and immediately turned away from their former way of living to God's standard of holy living. Nehemiah chapters 10 through 13 are chiefly concerned with this change in lifestyle.

Following God will always lead us to a proper response to His Word. Confronted with the holiness of God, we are overwhelmed by His grace and mercy. We are thus led to confess our failure to live up to His perfect standard and repent, turning to Him to change us and create His holiness in us.

Nehemiah's life was marked by prayer, the Word, and submission. He followed the path of a godly leader: following God and His Word. So, to sum up, what are some of the things that keep us available to God as we seek to follow Him?

✓ Opening our hearts continually to Him in prayer.

✓ Humbling ourselves to realize that God is God and we are not, and catching a glimpse of just how big a difference that is.

✓ Saturating our lives with His Word, allowing Him to bring us to a place of repentance and conform us to His image.

Take some time now to open your heart to God in prayer.

 God, I want to live a life marked by following You. As I walk through life, may others follow You in me. Teach me to trust You step by step as You lead me where You will. As opposition confronts me, as problems arise, as the burdens seem too great, help me to see Your mighty hand at work in all of it. Guide my heart in prayer, and give me a hunger for Your Word. And when You guide me to success,

Nehemiah followed the path of a godly leader: following God and His Word.

keep my heart ever focused on You, that You may be praised and lifted up in all Your glory. In Jesus' name, Amen.

Write out your own prayer to the Lord.

_____

_____

_____

_____

_____

_____

_____

_____

Notes

Notes

The True King in Israel

FOLLOWING THE KING OF KINGS

*P*salm 10:16 says, *"The LORD is King forever and ever."* He has always been and always will be the ultimate authority in life. Yet He has always wanted to share the glories of Himself and His kingdom. That's why he created Adam and Eve. He placed them as the first king and queen of creation and gave them clear responsibility to "rule" over all the earth (Genesis 1:28) in fellowship and harmony with Him. He wanted them to reign like Him, reflecting His image and bringing forth a family who would reflect His image—His love, His justice, His care, His wisdom—throughout all the earth. They were not to rule autonomously, but to rule under His rule. They were not to take the place of God in creation, but to make sure that God's will was followed in creation. What a wonderful kingdom that would be! What a wonderful place to live! Imagine having a ruler in the image of God with His character. Imagine a king who would reign with the wisdom of God's Word and will.

> Imagine having a ruler in the image of God with His character. Imagine a king who would reign with the wisdom of God's Word.

JESUS CHRIST: THE TRUE KING

4000 BC	2050 BC	1892 BC	1081? BC	6 BC	30 BC	Any Day!	1000 Years	Forever
Adam Eve	Abraham	Jacob	David	Mary	The King of Israel	The Returning King	The Reigning King	The True King Forever
Promise of the Seed of a Woman Genesis 3:15; Isaiah 7:14; Matthew 1:18–25	Promise of the Seed of Abraham Genesis 22:17–18; Galatians 3:16; Hebrews 2:14–18	Prophecy of the Scepter of Judah Genesis 49:8–12; Numbers 24:17–19; Hebrews 1:8; Revelation 5:5	Promise of the Seed of David 2 Samuel 7:12–17; Luke 1:31–33; John 7:42; Romans 1:3; 2 Timothy 2:8	The Seed is Born **Jesus** "Son of Man" "Son of Abraham" "Son of David" Matthew 1:1, 17; 16:27–28 Luke 1:26–38, 46–55; 2:1–40;	**Jesus Christ** Crucified Risen Ascended Reigning John 1:49; John 18—20; Acts 1:1–11; Romans 1:2–4; 1 Timothy 3:16; Hebrews 1:1–13	"When He comes to be glorified in His saints on that Day." 1 Thessalonians 4:15–18 2 Thessalonians 1:6–10; Revelation 19:1–16;	"They . . . reigned with Christ for a thousand years" Revelation 20:4–6	"The throne of God and of the Lamb . . . forever and ever." Revelation 21:1–27; 22:1–5

However, Adam and Eve failed. They chose to disobey God's Word and were expelled from the Garden of Eden. Instead of reigning, Adam and his children became enslaved to sin and selfishness. The first Adam failed to be the kind of king God wanted on earth. But that was not the end of the story. God was not through with man or His plans on earth. The Lord is King forever, and His kingdom stands forever. The rule he first placed in the hands of Adam will one day be placed in the hands of His Son, the second Adam.

True King DAY ONE

THE KIND OF KING GOD DESIRES

The period of the kings began at a dark time in Israel's history. It was birthed out of the dismal period of the judges when *"there was no king in Israel; everyone did what was right in his own eyes."* Mankind needed leadership. They needed authority and accountability. And yet, that leadership had to be exercised under the umbrella of God's rule and reign. In 1 Samuel 8:4–9 we see that God was not pleased when Israel asked for a king. It wasn't that it was wrong for Israel to have a king—they needed a ruler. But apart from a total commitment to following God, a ruler would not always be a blessing. You see, Israel wanted a king *"like all the nations"* (like the Gentiles). But the rulers of the other nations were not the kind of king God wanted. They ruled as autocrats, accountable to no one but themselves. God wanted Israel to have a king who would see himself as a servant of the people and a follower of God as the ultimate King. In 1 Samuel 8:7 the Lord says that Israel had *". . . rejected Me from being king over them."* God gave them Saul, the kind of king they wanted, so they would learn to want the kind of king He wanted. When they learned their lesson, God gave them David, a man with a heart after God's heart who would do God's will instead of his own. As we look back over the kings we have studied, it is obvious that those kings who ruled well are those who submitted themselves to God as king. Those who ruled badly are those who went their own independent way. God does not simply want people to rule, but people who will rule under His rule.

The first human king mentioned in Scripture is Adam. Though he is not called a king, clearly that is his function, for in Genesis 1:28 he is called to "rule" over creation. Yet he failed to rule as God intended, and by his rebellion, he forfeited part of his kingdom to Satan's control (1 John 5:19). Once sin entered the picture, God revealed a new facet of His plan for planet earth.

📖 Read Genesis 3:15; identify who God intended to use to deal with Satan.

_____

_____

_____

_____

_____

Immediately after mankind's fall, God communicated to Satan that from the woman would come a "seed" with whom his offspring would have enmity. Notice that the seed is singular. It points not to all of Eve's descendants, but to a specific individual. This is the first mention in Scripture of the Lord Jesus. Eve understood this, for when her first child was born, she named him

A true king should serve to provide, protect, and lead his people in righteousness. That means a kingdom fully supplied, at peace, and marked by purity in relationships. The Garden of Eden had all these characteristics at the start. The True King, the Lord Jesus, will bring these things to bear when He reigns on the earth. He wants us following Him as our True King so that we experience these things with Him right now.

Cain ("the gotten one") and what she literally said was "I have gotten a man, the Lord." She was looking for the promised deliverer. But Cain was not to be that deliverer. That would happen further down the line. When the promised seed finally arrived, Satan would one day "bruise" that seed on the heel. This foreshadows the crucifixion. He, in turn, would bruise (literally "crush") Satan's head. He would rid man of the curse of death, bring him eternal life, and reveal His power as Lord and King. All of that hasn't happened yet—but it will.

📖 Another of the first kings we meet is the king of Salem (later Jerusalem), a man named Melchizedek. His name means "king of righteousness." What can we learn from him, especially about following God (and about a king following the true King)? Read Genesis 14:14–24, the story of Abram's rescue of his nephew Lot. What do you discover about Melchizedek?

_____

_____

_____

_____

_____

Melchizedek was king of the city of Salem ("peace"). He was also a priest of El Elyon ("God Most High") possessor of heaven and earth. As king of Salem, Melchizedek acknowledged that it was God Most High who was king over all, and who gave victory to Abram. He blessed Abram by the name of God Most High. To bless someone in a name is to bring to bear the character of that name in a person's life. In this case, it was to speak the blessing of El Elyon for Abram, including provision and protection. Abram gave a tenth of all the spoil, acknowledging that El Elyon was indeed the possessor of heaven and earth and deserved to be honored as such. He would honor Him as his God. As a priest, Melchizedek served God and received the offering on His behalf. Abram was careful to take nothing from the king of Sodom. He wanted it to remain clear that he saw God Most High as his Provider, Protector, and King.

 Are you looking to God as your Provider, Protector, and King? Are you bowing to Him daily as Lord and King? Is there anything you need to turn over to His sovereign care?

_____

_____

_____

The promised seed of the woman would also be the seed of Abraham.

In Genesis 22:17–18, the Lord came to Abram and promised him a seed [singular] that would "*possess the gate of his* [masculine singular in KJV] *enemies*" and that "*in thy seed all the nations would be blessed*" (see Acts 3:25 and Galatians 3:16)—characteristics of God's kind of king, a victor and a blessing to others. After God entered into a covenant with Abram, his name was changed to Abraham. Isaac, was born to Abraham and Sarah, and became the father of Jacob and Esau. Jacob's name was changed to Israel, and Jacob (or Israel) had twelve sons, the heads of the twelve tribes of what became the nation of Israel. According to Genesis 49:10–11 the rulership—"the scepter"—of Jacob was to be seen in the tribe of Judah. This Ruler is worthy of obedience, and the scepter never departs from Him.

What do you find about the "scepter" and the place of Jacob (and Edom or Esau) in Numbers 24:17–19? [This is the prophecy of Balaam given in the presence of Balak, king of Moab (ca. 1405 BC).]

_____

_____

_____

_____

Did You Know?
"IN THE LAST DAYS"

According to Genesis 49:1, Jacob's prophetic blessing on his sons focused on what would befall them literally "in the end of the days." Judah was like a strong lion and like a warrior with the ruler's scepter who would rule in great prosperity (49:8–12). One born from him would have the power and authority to rule *"in the end of the days."* That One is Jesus Christ, the Lion of the Tribe of Judah (Revelation 5:5).

A star and a scepter shall come from Israel and crush the head of Moab. Edom (or Esau) will also be a possession—conquered by Israel. *"One from Jacob shall have dominion. . . ."* In other words, Jacob will rule as king through this "One" to come.

The Lord revealed His strong hand in bringing Israel out of Egypt and into the land promised to Abraham and his descendants, the land of Canaan. What did the Lord want for His people when He brought them into the land of Canaan? What revelation did He give through Moses before they entered the land, concerning a king for the nation of Israel? As we saw in the lesson on Solomon, Deuteronomy 17:14–20 (recorded by Moses around 1405 BC) gives us the guidelines under which a king should reign. Read that passage, and record the Word of the Lord in regard to a king in Israel.

_____

_____

_____

_____

If Israel would be what God desired them to be, they must be led by His Word. If they were to have the leadership they needed and that God wanted for them, they must follow Him in His choice of king. This was not an office a man would choose for himself. God wanted them to have the king He would choose. That was of utmost importance. **God's choice of king would lead the people in surrender to Him and in a true walk of faith and obedience.** The Lord gave other guidelines as well. He had to be an Israelite, not a foreigner. He was not to be a self-seeking man, seeking military might by multiplying horses, nor political might by the alliances that came with many wives. Neither should his goal be personal wealth. The Lord wanted a man who would seek Him, not money and power. That meant following Him through His Word and leading the people to do the same.

Around 1105 BC, Samuel was born and arose in Israel as the last of the judges and the first of the prophets. He ruled well and clearly spoke the Word of God to the people. When he appointed his sons to take care of some of the needs in Israel, they did not do well. They were corrupt and unjust (1 Samuel 8:3). At that point, the people of Israel came to Samuel asking for a king.

Read 1 Samuel 8:1–22, and record what you discover.

_____

_____

_____

_____

THE PRAYER OF HANNAH, SAMUEL'S MOTHER

"Those who contend with the LORD will be shattered; Against them He will thunder in the heavens, The LORD will judge the ends of the earth; And He will give strength to His king, And will exalt the horn of His anointed." 1 Samuel 2:10

The people of Israel certainly did not want Samuel's sons ruling over them. They wanted a king like the other nations. When Samuel brought their request before the LORD, God made it clear that they were not rejecting Samuel. They were rejecting God as their king. They would rather follow a man than follow God. They would rather walk by sight than by faith. They would rather be like the kingdoms of the world than like the kingdom of God. God gave them what they wanted, a man named Saul.

THE PROMISED COMING OF THE TRUE KING

Saul came to power and ruled Israel in the folly of his own wisdom. He had no heart for God. The Lord then chose David, a man after His heart who would do His will. First Samuel 16:1–13 tells the story of God's choosing David as king over Israel. As we look at the full picture of Scripture we recall that in Genesis 3:15, the Lord promised a "seed" [Hebrew singular] to come and deal with the evil on earth. In Genesis 22:17–18, He promised Abraham a "seed" [singular] who would rule and bless the nations of the earth. In the midst of David's reign God revealed yet another piece of the puzzle of His design for a king in Israel and a king on earth. God promised David a "seed," [singular] and He promised to establish the kingdom of that seed of David forever (2 Samuel 7:12, 16). In 1 Chronicles 22:7–13, we read that Solomon was God's choice to succeed David. God chose to rule Israel through the descendants of David.

Did You Know?

GOD CHOSE THE TRIBE OF JUDAH

David was from the tribe of Judah, but Jeroboam I was from the tribe of Ephraim. Psalm 78:67–68 made it clear: God *"did not choose the tribe of Ephraim, But chose the tribe of Judah, Mount Zion which He loved."*

📖 What do you discover about God's promise to David in the account of Ahijah the Shilonite and Jeroboam I in 1 Kings 11:31–39?

_____

_____

_____

_____

_____

The Lord told Jeroboam that He was going to tear the kingdom out of Solomon's hands and give ten tribes to Jeroboam. This arrangement of the division of Israel would not be forever—only for a time, in order to discipline Israel for the idolatry of Solomon and the people. In that message to Jeroboam, the Lord made it clear that David would always have *"a lamp before Me,"* a man ruling on the throne in Jerusalem to carry out the covenant He made with David.

📖 Over eighty years after Ahijah's words to Jeroboam, Jehoram came to the throne in Judah (848–841 BC). Read 2 Kings 8:16–19, and record what you discover about the Lord's ways in the line of David.

_____

_____

_____

_____

The promise to David that the Lord would *"give a lamp to him through his sons always"* was the basis of the Lord's actions in the life of Jehoram over eighty years later. The Lord revealed His covenant faithfulness in the life of Jehoram king of Judah. In spite of the wickedness of the king and of Judah, the Lord remembered His promise to David.

The kings of Israel and then of the divided Israel (Judah and Israel) ruled over a period of about 465 years (1051–586 BC). The first 120 years covered the united kingdom under Saul, David, and Solomon. The next 345 years saw the divided kingdom. In the time up to 722 BC, the Northern Kingdom (Israel) had 19 kings, all wicked in their reign. Over a period of 345 years (931–586), the Southern Kingdom (Judah) had 20 kings, eight of whom were righteous. In the midst of all this, God continued to show His faithfulness to the house of David and to the promise He had made. The promises remained—a righteous king would come.

📖 He also continued to speak through the prophets to the people of Israel and Judah about the true king who was coming. What do you find in Isaiah 9:1–2, 6–7?

_____

_____

_____

_____

At a dark time in Israel's life when the threat of Assyria loomed on the horizon, Isaiah spoke words of hope. Assyria first came and captured the land of Zebulun and Naphtali in the area of Galilee. Isaiah promised that one day a light would dawn in Galilee. A child would be born, specifically a son, who would rule in strength and peace. He would bring light to a people in darkness.

The prophet Micah, a contemporary of Isaiah, ministered in Judah and revealed several things about this coming king. Micah first warned of judgment against Samaria and Jerusalem because they refused to obey the Lord and His word. He also spoke of glorious days to come. His greatest word was the announcement of the birth of the ruler of Israel in the town of Bethlehem.

📖 Read Micah 5:2–5. What do you see about Bethlehem? About this ruler?

_____

_____

_____

_____

Bethlehem is too little to be among the clans of Judah—insignificant to all but God. The ruler would be born there. He will go forth *"for Me (the Lord)"* as ruler in Israel. *"His goings forth are . . . from the days of eternity"* (5:2). He will be a shepherd to His flock in the strength and majesty of the Lord. He will be recognized for His greatness to the ends of the earth, and this one will *"be our peace"* (5:5a).

Many other prophecies were spoken about the coming king, the Messiah of Israel. There are over 300 prophecies related to the first coming of the

The true King is the Word, the eternal expression of the mind and heart of God, God Himself: "In the beginning was the Word, and the Word was with God, and the Word was God" (John 1:1).

Messiah, and they were all fulfilled in exact detail in the person of Jesus Christ. We find those in the New Testament record of Jesus Christ. Just how does Jesus Christ fit in with the promises to David? After David had conquered his enemies and established his kingdom with the strength and wisdom of the Lord, God made a covenant with David that the throne of his kingdom would be established forever. David's throne was passed to his son Solomon, and to a descendant of his as long as Judah continued as a nation.

📖 Read Luke 1:31–33, and identify how Jesus relates to the throne of David, and where and how long His reign will be.

_____

_____

_____

_____

Did You Know?

❓ THE SAME PROMISE

In 2 Samuel 7:12, 16 the Lord promised David a seed, a house, a kingdom, and a throne . . . forever. This same promise was then made to Mary, the mother of Jesus, in Luke 1:31–33. The promise began to be fulfilled in the birth of Jesus.

It is evident that the line of David never died out. Both Joseph and Mary were descendants of David. When God meets with Mary, she is told that the son she will bear is to be called Jesus (from the Hebrew, "Joshua" which means "Jehovah is Salvation"), and that He will be given the throne of His father, David. She is also promised that Jesus will rule over the house of Jacob (Israel) and that His kingdom will have no end. That was the king God had in mind for Israel. He was from the tribe of Judah, the tribe given the scepter forever. His throne and His kingdom would be established forever, and He would reign as the Son of David.

📖 As we have seen, God did not leave Himself without clear witness as to His desires and His design. He spoke through many prophets about this coming King, the Messiah. Over 230 years after David, Isaiah spoke of a coming Servant-King who would bring forth justice to the nations. We have noted how He would be a descendant of David (2 Samuel 7:12; Matthew 1:1). Read Isaiah 42:1–4 and Matthew 12:9–23. Notice the connection Matthew and the people make to Jesus as the Son of David. What does this say about Jesus as the King? [John 1:35–51, especially verse 49 gives further light on the revelation of Jesus.]

_____

_____

_____

_____

Jesus fulfilled the prophecies of Isaiah and all the prophets. His ministry was aptly described by Isaiah. He had the marks of the long-awaited Son of David. Jesus was the promised king. In another incident, when Nathaniel met Jesus, he realized that this Jesus was the Son of God and the King of Israel.

The promise to Eve, Abraham, David, Isaiah, and Micah (and many, many others) came true. The seed of woman, the seed of Abraham, Isaac, and Jacob, and the seed of David, was born in Bethlehem. This Jesus grew up in Nazareth, and at age thirty came to be baptized by John the Baptist who was announcing the coming Messiah (Isaiah 40:3). Jesus began the ministry the Father had for Him (Isaiah 9:1, 6; 11:1–4a; 50:4–10; John 4:34; 5:19, 30; 8:15–18, 28–29), and many recognized that He was the Messiah. The Messiah, the Christ, the King of Israel, had indeed come. He was fulfilling

SON OF THE MOST HIGH

Jesus is the son of El Elyon, God Most High, the God that Melchizedek and Abram honored as their God and King (see Genesis 14).

the Father's will, but there was yet much to do and much to proclaim. Before the full revelation of the King's presence and power, He had to go to the cross to die for the sins of the world (Isaiah 53:1–12). Then, in His resurrection, He revealed the assurance of the forgiveness of sin and the cleansing He had purchased with His blood. By faith in Him and His finished work one could have His very life and His Spirit within their heart and life (Jeremiah 31:31–34 with Hebrews 8:8–12; Ezekiel 36:25–27).

We also learn from the New Testament record that He has chosen to rule the earth ultimately through the Son of David, Jesus Christ. God has not yet fulfilled **all** His desires for the kind of King He wants in Israel and on this earth. We can see that more fully when we discover some of the battles that have gone on in the war against the true King. Then we will see how He has worked and is working to bring the coming King to earth.

All rebellion is rooted in a desire to raise our own throne above God's so that we can be our own god.

THE WAR AGAINST THE TRUE KING

Spiritual warfare began when Satan decided to rebel against God's rule in his life. In Isaiah 14:13–14 we see his rebellious heart reflected when he says, *"I will ascend to heaven; I will raise my throne above the stars of God, And I will sit on the mount of assembly In the recesses of the north. I will ascend above the heights of the clouds; I will make myself like the Most High."* He wanted to replace God, and sit on the throne of his own life. Throughout time, he has sought to seduce man into joining his rebellion. The Serpent has not stopped fighting God nor man, and sinful man has joined in the war against the true King. We must see the reality of the opposition toward the throne, toward God's desire and plan for His king in Israel and on the earth. At its core, this rebellion is rooted in a desire to raise our own throne above God's so that we can be our own god.

The Serpent defeated Adam, the first king of the earth. Opposition to the Lord's kingship and true worship were seen throughout the years in men like Cain and in the men of Noah's day (see Genesis 4:1–17; 6—7). In Nimrod, king of Babel, we see further opposition to the true King. Nimrod, whose name means "rebel," was the founder of Babel and Nineveh (10:8–12).

📖 Read Genesis 11:1–9, and record what you find about the purpose of the people of Babel.

_____

_____

_____

_____

The main aim of the people of Babel was to make a name for themselves and to rule themselves in pride from their position of control. They had no thought of filling the earth as the Lord had directed both Adam and later Noah (Genesis 1:28; 9:1). Instead, they wanted to stay together in Babel and pursue their own will. God saw that their unified language had allowed them to go unrestrained in accomplishing their will in opposition to His will. Therefore, He confused their language, in part, to restrain them in their proud efforts and to get them to scatter over the earth.

This war did not stop with the confusion of the languages at Babel. It continued, and Babel became the foundation of the nation of Babylon, the enemy and destroyer of Judah, Jerusalem, and the Temple in 586 BC (2 Chronicles 36:5–21). Nineveh, which was also founded by Nimrod, was the capital of Assyria, the nation that conquered and scattered the kingdom of Israel in 722 BC (2 Kings 17). God decreed His judgment on both kingdoms, Babylon (Jeremiah 50—51) and Assyria (2 Kings 18—19; Nahum 1—3). In Revelation 17—18, we find the Lord bringing ultimate defeat to Babylon and all associated with it. The foes of the King of kings, Jesus Christ, will not stand.

Throughout history, Satan has attempted to destroy God's deliverer before he was old enough to deliver. He attempted this in Moses' day when the king of Egypt decreed that every male Hebrew child was to be put to death as soon as he was born (Exodus 1:16). He was fearful of the Hebrews and wanted to remove any possible threat to his throne and rule. But not only did Moses survive this scheme, but God worked it out so that Pharaoh paid to feed, clothe, and educate him. In the period of the kings we see another such attempt.

📖 Read in 2 Kings 11:1–3. What did the wicked queen, Athaliah, do to hold power? Why do you think she did this? What was Satan ultimately trying to achieve through using Queen Athaliah?

_____

_____

_____

_____

> **The foes of the King of kings, Jesus Christ, will not stand.**

Athaliah was the daughter of the wicked king, Ahab, and his evil wife, Jezebel. When her son, Ahaziah, died, she led a coup for the throne and had every one of the royal descendants of king David put to death. She wanted to be rid of anyone who could lay claim to the throne because she wanted to rule on her own. Through her, Satan tried to wipe out the line of David from whom the Messiah would come. If he had succeeded, there could be no deliverer to threaten his rule over the kingdom of earth. But God would not let his wicked plan succeed, and the priests rescued one infant son, Joash, and protected him until he could take the throne and continue the line of David.

There is another thread of opposition that runs through much of the history of Israel. Remember, the nation of Israel is simply the accumulated descendants of the man, Israel (Jacob). His twelve sons became the "twelve tribes" of Israel. But Jacob had a brother named Esau. When her twins were struggling in her womb, God told Rebekah that the older (Esau) would serve the younger (Jacob) (Genesis 25:21–26). Esau was not a willing servant. He didn't want anyone else ruling his life. The descendants of Esau, the Edomites, were often a grief and an enemy to Israel. Esau was often a challenger to the rightful rule of Jacob (Israel).

📖 Moses faced the opposition of the Edomites as he led the people of Israel in the wilderness. Read Numbers 20:14–21, and record what you discover about the people of Edom.

_____

_____

_____

_____

Did You Know?

JACOB AND ESAU

Isaac prophesied that his son Esau would serve his son Jacob, but would also break Jacob's yoke from his neck (Genesis 27:39–40). This was seen in the continual fighting of the Edomites against Israel.

Did You Know?

HEROD WAS AN IDUMEAN (EDOMITE)

Herod was known for his murderous ways. He called himself "king of the Jews" and zealously fought any threat to his throne, real or imagined. He executed hundreds of people during his reign: forty-five of the seventy members of the Sanhedrin when he first began to rule, his brother-in-law Aristobulus, his wife Mariamne (Miriam), her mother, her grandfather Hyrcanus, his two oldest sons, the children two years old and under within and around Bethlehem (because of the threat of a newborn king), and his oldest living son Antipater five days before Herod himself died. Finally, at his order, several prominent citizens of Judea were imprisoned to be executed upon his death, so that the people would mourn when he died. History records that his descendants continued their Edomite ways.

When Israel sought to go through the land of Edom, the Edomites stubbornly opposed them. They would not let them pass and even came out against them armed for battle—an example of Edom's opposition toward Israel.

When David ruled as king he conquered the Edomites for a time, and they were his servants (2 Samuel 8:14). David's son Solomon faced opposition from Hadad the Edomite who, as a descendant of the conquered king of Edom, sought to reestablish his authority and reign. In so doing he was an adversary to Solomon and caused much trouble (1 Kings 11:14–22, 25). Other kings faced opposition from the Edomites (also known as the sons of Mount Seir, where Esau had settled).

God raised up prophets to decry the ways and actions of Edom and to pronounce His judgment against them. During the period of the kings of Israel and Judah, we see the marks of the hand of God at work to fulfill His promises. Amos called all nations to an accounting with God (chapters 1—2). Included in that list was Edom whose slave trade included the selling of Israelites and whose warfare with Israel was marked with intense rage and no compassion (1:9, 11–12). The entire prophecy of Obadiah (21 verses) announces God's coming judgment on Edom for their pride and wickedness particularly against Israel. They rejoiced over the invasion of Jerusalem and the captivity of Judah. Edom joined in looting Jerusalem in 586 BC and hindered any escape by the Israelites (vv. 11–14). Obadiah assured them that in spite of their actions, Zion would be established by the Lord and would rule even over Esau (vv. 19–21). Isaiah 34:1–6 told of the Lord's judgment on the nations and on Edom. Ezekiel spoke of God's judgment on Edom (25:12–14; 35:1–15; 36:1–5). Psalm 137 lamented the days in Babylon and remembered the hatred of Edom during Jerusalem's destruction (v. 7).

Judgment came in the fifth century BC when the Nabatean Arabs invaded and defeated Edom. The refugees fled from the invasion to the region south of Judea. This area became known as Idumea, the Greek name meaning "land of the Edomites." Here is one historical fact we must not miss: King Herod was from Idumea. He was an Idumean—an Edomite. What would such a man think of the Israelites? Knowing that the prophets had declared that a king would be born who would reign in Israel, why should Herod be afraid? Herod's work and reign in Israel constantly revealed his jealousy for his throne and his honor and glory. Consider all his glorious building projects—the Temple and Temple Mount, the city and port of Caesarea, Herod's Palace in Jerusalem, the Palace and Fortress at Masada and the Herodian Palace near Bethlehem. In light of this it would be good to read the account of Herod and the wise men in Matthew.

Considering Herod and his background, what would the Bethlehem manger mean to him? Read Matthew 2:1–12, 16–18, and record your thoughts.

_____

_____

_____

_____

_____

_____

Jesus was born in Bethlehem in the days of Herod the king. Magi from the east came to worship Him. They had seen His star—a sign to the men who studied the stars that a king had been born. They considered Him to be the King of the Jews. The religious leaders knew and could quote the Old Testament prophecy about where the ruler/shepherd of the people of Israel was to be born. While Herod was busy investigating this, the Magi were busy seeking the infant king, Jesus, to worship Him. God led them, warned them and guided them. With Herod determined to squelch any rival ruler, Bethlehem became a place of mourning once again, for he was fearful of any threat to his place of rule. As it had mourned the death of Rachel, wife of Jacob, so now Bethlehem mourned the death of the male children two years old and younger from the city and surrounding region. The war continued against the "seed," the true King, but God would not let this wicked plan succeed. We must remember this: No attempt to dethrone the true King ever succeeds!

📖 One other incident will document this war against the true King. We pick up the story on the night before Jesus' crucifixion just after Gethsemane and the trial before Annas and Caiaphas. Read John 18:28–40; 19:1–22. See the war going on, the battle over who is king. What did Jesus say about the true King, His kingdom, and about following Him?

_____

_____

_____

_____

_____

_____

_____

Pilate questioned Jesus about being the King of the Jews. Jesus made it clear that He is indeed a king with a kingdom not like any in this world. He literally said, "My kingdom is not from here"—It's source is not the world and its evil system. He does not gain His kingdom like the world—no fighting, no political maneuvering. His kingdom is from above, from the Father, by the power and purity of His Spirit. He confidently declared *"for this I have been born, and for this I have come into the world"* (18:37). His purpose for leaving heaven as the Son of God and being born on earth as the Son of Man—the God-Man—was to be a king, the true King. As that true King His purpose is to reveal truth and lead His followers in truth, to reign in truth forever. All those who come to Him, who want to follow Him, who look to Him as their true God, their source of truth, walk with Him in truth. They hear His voice, and (the implication is) they follow Him as their true King.

Jesus died and rose from the dead as the triumphant Lord and King. We know from Scripture and from history that God has not fulfilled all His plans for the reign of the true King in Israel and on earth. The disciples knew that too. We can see that more fully when we discover how He has worked and is working to bring the coming reigning King to earth. That is why we still pray, *"Thy kingdom come, Thy will be done on earth as it is in heaven."*

No attempt to dethrone the True King ever succeeds!

"...You say correctly that I am a king. For this I have been born, and for this I have come into the world, to bear witness to the truth...."

John 18:37

THE COMING REIGNING KING

With the Babylonian captivity, the period of the kings came to an end. Though Israel would gain some measure of freedom, they ceased to be an independent nation. They watched as one kingdom after another ruled the known world, and ruled them as well. Babylon would give way to domination by the Medes and Persians, who were the main world power from 539–331 BC. Next, they watched as the Greeks stepped to the forefront under Alexander the Great. At Alexander's death in 323 BC, the Greek empire was divided among four of his generals. Jerusalem and Judea fell under the rule of the Ptolemies of Egypt and enjoyed some measure of liberty from 323–204 BC. Then Antiochus III conquered Egypt, and Jerusalem and Judea came under Syrian dominance with less freedom. When Antiochus IV (Epiphanes) took the throne, he set out to destroy Judaism and force Jews to worship Zeus. He outlawed all Jewish rituals. He destroyed copies of the Law and prescribed the death penalty for any found hiding one. He also desecrated the Temple by sacrificing a pig on the altar and erecting a statue of Zeus in the Holy Place. This led to the Maccabean revolt in 165 BC, a military action led by priests who eventually recaptured Jerusalem and restored the temple.

The descendants of the Maccabees ruled Jerusalem until 63 BC when it was conquered by Pompey of Rome. In 40 BC Herod was made "king" of the Jews as a favor from Rome. Herod's people, the Idumeans, had been forced to convert to Judaism during the Maccabean reign, but he was not devout, and lacked the respect of the people. They were waiting for the coming king who would throw off all foreign rule and return Jerusalem to its days of former glory. This is what the people expected Jesus to do when they shouted "Hosanna" at His triumphal entry to Jerusalem. A week later, He died on a cross, and their hopes were dashed. Even after the resurrection uncertainty abounded. What would the Messiah do? For forty days after His resurrection Jesus appeared to His disciples, to over 500 at one of those times (Acts 1:3–11; 1 Corinthians 15:1–8, see verse 6). On the fortieth day, Jesus met the disciples on the Mount of Olives. There they awaited further word from Him about the days ahead.

> "Lord, is it at this time You are restoring the kingdom to Israel?"
>
> Acts 1:6

📖 What was uppermost in the thinking of the disciples that day? Read Acts 1:1–6, and record their question. What does this tell you about their expectation?

_____

_____

_____

_____

_____

The disciples were expecting Jesus to begin His reign as the King of Israel. They wanted to know if today was the day. He had spoken to them for forty days about *"the things concerning the kingdom of God,"* and it was natural for them to ask this question especially in light of all they knew from the Old Testament scriptures about the promised Messiah and His kingdom.

📖 Jesus told them that the Father had fixed certain times and epochs to fulfill all the kingdom promises. To what can we look forward, and how are we to live today? What did Jesus tell His disciples? In the answer He gave them we find the answers we need for our daily walk. Read Acts 1:7–11, and record your insights.

_____

_____

_____

_____

_____

Jesus commanded that after they were empowered by His Spirit, they should bear witness to Him throughout the earth until He returns. Then He ascended, and the angels assured them He would return in the same way. The Holy Spirit did come ten days later on the Jewish holy day known as Pentecost, and the church was born. The early church knew the presence and power of the Lord through the indwelling Holy Spirit, and they proclaimed His gospel of forgiveness and new life (Acts 2:38–39; 4:33; 5:30–32; 9:31; 10:34–43; 13:52). They also spoke of the coming kingdom of the Messiah. They were sure He was coming back to earth to reveal the fullness of His Lordship to all the earth. He promised to complete His work and His promises to Israel, to judge the nations that rejected Him, and to establish His reign on the earth for one thousand years (the millennial kingdom). They read these truths in the prophets, they had heard them from Jesus Himself, they received revelation from the Holy Spirit, and penned those things in the New Testament.

📖 Read the Scriptures given, and describe the character and work of the Messiah.

In His First Coming—Isaiah 11:1–4a

_____

_____

_____

_____

Isaiah spoke of a shoot from the root of Jesse, David's father. In other words, a descendant of Jesse and David would be born and on Him would rest the Spirit of the LORD, *"the Spirit of wisdom and understanding, the Spirit of counsel and might, the Spirit of knowledge and of the fear of the LORD"* (11:2, NKJV). Jesus walked in the power of the Spirit and in the fear of the Lord, everfollowing His Father's desires and will. He ministered to the poor and needy, the physically and spiritually needy, and He did so with perfect righteousness.

In the Tribulation and Second Coming—

Isaiah 11:4b–5 _____

_____

_____

_____

> **The disciples were sure Jesus was coming back to earth to reveal the fullness of His Lordship to all the earth.**

Romans 11:25–27 _____

_____

_____

_____

Zechariah 12:10 _____

_____

_____

_____

Revelation 19:15–16 _____

_____

_____

(For further study see 2 Thessalonians 1:6–10; Psalms 2:4–9; 89:24–29.)

(For further study see 2 Thessalonians 1:6–10; Psalms 2:4–9; 89:24–29.)

The Scriptures are clear that the Lord Jesus will return to deal with the nations of the world, with the wicked, with all who will not bow to Him as Lord and King. But they are equally clear that God is not finished with Israel either. In the seven-year period of great distress on earth (the "seventieth week" of Daniel 9:24–27), He will deal with His people Israel so that they finally turn to Him as their true King. All the earth will see and know that the earth is rightfully His and that He alone is worthy to reign, though many will still stand opposed to Him as their king.

In the Millennial Kingdom—

Isaiah 11:6–10 (in light of verse 5) _____

_____

_____

Revelation 20:1–6 _____

_____

_____

_____

(If you want to study this further see Isaiah 2:2–4; 60:3–5; 65:20–25.)

(If you want to study this further see Isaiah 2:2–4; 60:3–5; 65:20–25.)

With Jerusalem as His capital, the Messiah and true King will reign over all the nations of the earth for one thousand years, a millennial reign. He will lead the nations in truth, judge with righteousness, and establish a lasting peace. Even the world's animal kingdom will live in peace and harmony, and children will be unharmed by any of them. The nations will rejoice over the reign of the true King, for He will order things on earth as they should be. Israel will prosper at the hands of the nations as the Lord Jesus oversees them. Many who are born in the millennium will come to the Lord Jesus to walk in His light. In addition, those born at this time will live long and fruitful lives protected by their King and enjoying the work of their hands. The people of the Lord will know a relationship with Him that is marked by wonder and awe.

Word Study

THE COMING OF THE LORD

In the first century, the Greek word *parousia* was translated "coming," "arrival," or "presence" (Matthew 24:3; 1 Corinthians 15:23; 1 Thessalonians 2:19; 3:13; 4:15; 5:23; 2 Peter 1:16; 3:4). This technical term referred to the official coming of a king or official to a region or town. At his coming he would right all wrongs and establish peace and order. Great preparations were made for his arrival including special gifts and a celebration of praise. Some cities proclaimed a holy day or even constructed buildings or minted a coin in honor of his coming. For many, expectations were high at the thought of his coming and expressions of joy abundant.

Because of Christ's First Coming we can live in confidence and expectancy day by day and rejoice in His Second Coming. Paul wrote in Romans 15:12–13, "*And again Isaiah says, 'There shall come the root of Jesse, and He who arises to rule over the Gentiles, in Him shall the Gentiles hope. Now may the God of hope fill you with all joy and peace in believing, that you may abound in hope by the power of the Holy Spirit.'*" Are you filled with joy in believing and abounding in hope? Think of your walk now as you apply what you have learned in this lesson about God's choice of King and how He is fulfilling His kingdom plans.

FOR ME TO FOLLOW THE TRUE KING, THE KING OF KINGS

True King **DAY FIVE**

Kings come and kings go. History records life as a constant change from one leader to the next. But behind it all, heaven rules. Nebuchadnezzar was king in Babylon while Israel was in captivity. It was he who brought the period of the kings of Israel and Judah to an end when he conquered what was left of the nation in 586 BC. He ruled over the most powerful nation on earth. His every whim was law, and Israel was subject to him. He had no respect for the God of Israel. But when three Hebrews, Hananiah, Mishael, and Azariah (renamed Shadrach, Meshach, and Abednego), violated his order to bow in worship before his golden idol, he learned that his was not the highest law. He witnessed first-hand the power of Jehovah supernaturally delivering those who would bow to no other God. Though he developed a higher view of God from this experience, his view was still not high enough. God warned him by a dream in which he was a magnificent tree which had to be chopped down in order to recognize that the Most High was the true ruler of the earth. A year passed, and yet he was unrepentant.

📖 We pick up the story in Daniel 4:28. Read 4:28–30, and write what you observe about Nebuchadnezzar's attitude and lack of reverence for God.

_____

_____

_____

_____

Even though Daniel interpreted his dream and called Nebuchadnezzar to repentance (Daniel 4:27), a year later we find Nebuchadnezzar patting himself on the back and glorying in his position, not recognizing God at all. In 4:30 we see all the manifestations of one consumed with self. We see self-will instead of surrender to God's will and way (He says, "*Is this not Babylon the great, which I myself have built. . . ?*"). We also see self-effort instead of trust in God ("*. . . which I myself have built . . . by the might of my power . . .*"). Finally, we see self-glory instead of giving the Lord the honor and credit He deserves ("*. . . for the glory of my majesty*").

Ask yourself: "Who is King of my life? Is my life characterized by self-will, self-effort, and self-glory?"

📖 Read Daniel 4:31–33, and identify how God deals with Nebuchadnezzar's pride and why.

_____

_____

_____

While Nebuchadnezzar's boasting was still in his mouth, God spoke, and his sovereignty was removed. He lost his mind and wandered like a beast eating grass like a cow for seven years. This judgment had one goal in mind: for Nebuchadnezzar to *". . . recognize that the Most High is ruler over the realm of mankind."*

📖 Take a moment to read through Daniel 4:34–37. What brought Nebuchadnezzar's humiliation to an end, and what lesson did he learn?

_____

_____

_____

_____

It was not until Nebuchadnezzar *"raised his eyes toward heaven"* that his reason returned to him. Further, it was after he *"blessed the Most High and praised and honored Him who lives forever,"* acknowledging that it is heaven, and not he, that rules. Once he recognized that he was accountable to God, his kingdom was restored. Now he could be the kind of king he ought to be, ruling under the authority of *"the King of heaven."* He learned a hard lesson about who was the true King, and that *". . . He is able to humble those who walk in pride."*

As we have studied these lessons on the kings, we have learned much about the right and wrong ways to exert our authority and influence. You see, each of us has a kingdom apportioned to us. It is the realm of our lives and influence. Some of us have others whom we are responsible to lead by serving. Yet however large or small our kingdom may be, it is not ours alone. It is our part of God's kingdom, and we must recognize that He is the ultimate ruler of all.

Take a moment to reflect on the list below, and identify the components that make up your own kingdom.

___ House	___ Job	___ Car
___ Spouse	___ Children	___ Grandchildren
___ Business	___ Employees	___ Subordinates
___ Church office	___ Community office	___ Governmental office
___ Other_____		

Now take the time to reflect on each one, and honestly identify which of them you rule and manage as Nebuchadnezzar did—with self-effort, self-will and self-glory.

_____

_____

_____

_____

_____

What about the components of your personal life? In the space provided, mark with an "S" those areas of your life that reflect a true surrender to God, and with a "W" those that are withheld from Him and controlled by self.

___ Friendships ___ Finances ___ Use of time
___ Hobbies ___ Use of talents ___ Family relationships
___ Possessions ___ Thought life ___ Plans for future
___ Work ___ Christian service ___ Other_____

Whatever we have, whatever we hold, whatever we do, whoever we are, we must all come to grips with the reality that heaven rules (Daniel 4:26). If we are living our lives independent of God, we may prosper for a time, but in the end we will fail. The most important application of this study is that everything must be surrendered to Him. In Luke 6:46 Jesus asks a penetrating question: *"Why do you call me 'Lord, Lord,' and do not do what I say?"*

In the life of every believer there is a throne and a cross. The throne is a place of ruling; the cross is the place of dying. The true disciple is called to *"take up his cross"* and follow Jesus. If Christ is to be on the throne of my life, I must be on the cross, dying to my own will and way. If I insist on sitting on the throne, ruling and reigning in my life, then Christ is not reigning, and I am not experiencing His resurrection life.

If you need to surrender, here are the steps:

1. Confess any sins of which God has convicted you in this lesson.
2. Repent of running your own life—do so area by area.
3. Yield each area of your life to Christ.
4. Trust Him moment by moment with the details of your life.
5. Deal with it quickly if you try to retake control over any area of your life.

Lord, I praise and exalt and honor You as the true King of heaven and earth. All your works are true, and all your ways are just. Your dominion is everlasting, and your kingdom has no end. Forgive me for those times when I have ruled my own life independent of You and Your will. Take Your rightful place on the throne of my life and lead me in Your ways. Help me to trust you with all of my worries, and help me to be quick to turn back to You every time I stray. Amen.

A Letter to the King:

_____

_____

_____

_____

_____

_____

_____

> *In the life of every believer there is a throne and a cross. If Christ is to be on the throne of my life ruling, I must be on the cross, dying to my own will and way.*

> *Lord Jesus, take Your rightful place on the throne of my life and lead me in Your ways.*

_____

_____

_____

_____

_____

_____

Jesus is the King who gave His life for us, that we might be a kingdom of priests to God the Father. He has given His life that we might walk with Him and reign with Him forever. Follow Him! Look up, for He is the coming King. Maranatha! (2 Corinthians 16:21–23; Revelation 1:4–7; 22:16–21).

Notes

Notes

How to Follow God

STARTING THE JOURNEY

Did you know that you have been on God's heart and mind for a long, long time? Even before time existed you were on His mind. He has always wanted you to know Him in a personal, purposeful relationship. He has a purpose for your life and it is founded upon His great love for you. You can be assured it is a good purpose and it lasts forever. Our time on this earth is only the beginning. God has a grand design that goes back into eternity past and reaches into eternity future. What is that design?

The Scriptures are clear about God's design for man—God created man to live and walk in oneness with Himself. Oneness with God means being in a relationship that is totally unselfish, totally satisfying, totally secure, righteous and pure in every way. That's what we were created for. If we walked in that kind of relationship with God we would glorify Him and bring pleasure to Him. Life would be right! Man was meant to live that way—pleasing to God and glorifying Him (giving a true estimate of who God is). Adam sinned and shattered his oneness with God. Ever since, man has come short of the glory of God: man does not and cannot please God or give a true estimate of God. Life is not right until a person is right with God. That is very clear as we look at the many people who walked across the pages of Scripture, both Old and New Testaments.

JESUS CHRIST came as the solution for this dilemma. Jesus Christ is the glory of God—the true estimate of who God is in every way. He pleased His Father in everything He did and said, and He came to restore oneness with God. He came to give man His power and grace to walk in oneness with God, to follow Him day by day enjoying the relationship for which he was created. In the process, man could begin to present a true picture of Who God is and experience knowing Him personally. You may be asking, "How do these facts impact my life today? How does this become real to me now? How can I begin the journey of following God in this way?" To come to know God personally means you must choose to receive Jesus Christ as your personal Savior and Lord.

- First of all, you must admit that you have sinned, that you are not walking in oneness with God, not pleasing Him or glorifying Him in your life (Romans 3:23; 6:23; 8:5-8).

- It means repenting of that sin—changing your mind, turning to God and turning away from sin—and by faith receiving His forgiveness based on His death on the Cross for you (Romans 3:21-26; 1 Peter 3:18).

- It means opening your life to receive Him as your living, resurrected Lord and Savior (John 1:12). He has promised to come and indwell you by His Spirit and live in you as the Savior and Master of your life (John 14:16-21; Romans 14:7-9).

- He wants to live His life through you—conforming you to His image, bearing His fruit through you and giving you power to reign in life (John 15:1,4-8; Romans 5:17; 7:4; 8:29, 37).

You can come to Him now. In your own words, simply tell Him you want to know Him personally and you willingly repent of your sin and receive His forgiveness and His life. Tell Him you want to follow Him forever (Romans 10:9-10, 13). Welcome to the Family of God and to the greatest journey of all!!!

WALKING ON THE JOURNEY

How do we follow Him day by day? Remember, Christ has given those who believe in Him everything pertaining to life and godliness, so that we no longer have to be slaves to our "flesh" and its corruption (2 Peter 1:3-4). Day by day He wants to empower us to live a life of love and joy, pleasing to Him and rewarding to us. That's why Ephesians 5:18 tells us to "be filled with the Spirit"—keep on being controlled by the Spirit who lives in you. He knows exactly what we need each day and we can trust Him to lead us (Proverbs 3:5-6). So how can we cooperate with Him in this journey together?

To walk with Him *day by day* means ...
- reading and listening to His Word day by day (Luke 10:39, 42; Colossians 3:16; Psalm 19:7-14; 119:9).
- spending time talking to Him in prayer (Philippians 4:6-7).
- realizing that God is God and you are not, and the role that means He has in your life.

This allows Him to work through your life as you fellowship, worship, pray and learn with other believers (Acts 2:42), and serve in the good works He has prepared for us to do—telling others who Jesus is and what His Word says, teaching and encouraging others, giving to help meet needs, helping others, etc. (Ephesians 2:10).

God's goal for each of us is that we be conformed to the image of His Son, Jesus Christ (Romans 8:29). But none of us will reach that goal of perfection until we are with Him in Heaven, for then "we shall be like Him, because we shall see Him just as He is" (1 John 3:2). For now, He wants us to follow

Him faithfully, learning more each day. Every turn in the road, every trial and every blessing, is designed to bring us to a new depth of surrender to the Lord and His ways. He not only wants us to do His will, He desires that we surrender to His will His way. That takes trust—trust in His character, His plan and His goals (Proverbs 3:5-6).

As you continue this journey, and perhaps you've been following Him for a while, you must continue to listen carefully and follow closely. We never graduate from that. That sensitivity to God takes moment by moment surrender, dying to the impulses of our flesh to go our own way, saying no to the temptations of Satan to doubt God and His Word, and refusing the lures of the world to be unfaithful to the Lord who gave His life for us.

God desires that each of us come to maturity as sons and daughters: to that point where we are fully satisfied in Him and His ways, fully secure in His sovereign love, and walking in the full measure of His purity and holiness. If we are to clearly present the image of Christ for all to see, it will take daily surrender and daily seeking to follow Him wherever He leads, however He gets there (Luke 9:23-25). It's a faithful walk of trust through time into eternity. And it is worth everything. Trust Him. Listen carefully. Follow closely.

Other Books in the *Following God*
Bible Character Study Series

Life Principles from the Old Testament

Characters include: Adam, Noah, Job, Abraham, Lot, Jacob, Joseph, Moses, Caleb, Joshua, Gideon, and Samson
ISBN 0-89957-300-2   208 pages

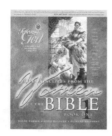

Life Principles from the Women of the Bible (Book One)

Characters include Eve, Sarah, Miriam, Rahab, Deborah, Ruth, Hannah, Esther, The Virtuous Woman, Mary and Martha, Mary the Mother of Jesus, The Bride of Christ.
ISBN 0-89957-302-9   224 pages

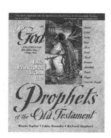

Life Principles from the Prophets of the Old Testament

Characters include: Samuel, Elijah, Elisha, Jonah, Hosea, Isaiah, Micah, Jeremiah, Habakkuk, Daniel, Haggai, and "Christ the Prophet."
ISBN 0-89957-303-7   224 pages

Life Principles from the New Testament Men of Faith

Characters include: John the Baptist, Peter, John, Thomas, James, Barnabas, Paul, Paul's Companions, Timothy, and "The Son of Man."
ISBN 0-89957-304-5   208 pages

Life Principles from the Women of the Bible (Book Two)

Characters include Hagar, Lot's Wife, Rebekah, Leah, Rachel, Abigail, Bathsheba, Jezebel, Elizabeth, The Woman at the Well, Women of the Gospels, The Submissive Wife.
ISBN 0-89957-308-8   224 pages

Other Following God™ books are also available, including Leaders Guides!
Call for more information (800) 266-4977 or (423) 894-6060.
Log on to **amgpublishers.com** for more information about these books.

Available from AMG Publishers

Life Principles for Worship from the Tabernacle

ISBN 0-89957-299-5

This Bible study is designed in an interactive format, incorporating important scriptural points of interest and will help you understand all that God says to us through the components found in Israel's Tabernacle. Important historical and symbolic details will leap from the pages and into your heart. Inside the pages you'll also find the special helps sections you've come to rely on from the best-selling "Following God" series; Word Studies, Doctrinal Notes, Did You Know?, and Stop and Apply. Each help section will add to your understanding and ability to share these new-found truths with those you know and/or teach.

In the pages of this "Following God" study on the Tabernacle you'll learn to:

✓ Focus on the fence, the gate and the outer court with the bronze altar and bronze laver;

✓ Focus on the Holy Place with the golden lamp stand, the table of showbread, and the altar of incense;

✓ Move into the Holy of Holies through the veil, and look at the ark of the covenant with the golden jar of manna, Aaron's rod that budded, the tables of the covenant, the mercy seat and, ultimately, the cloud of glory.

Most importantly, you'll discover how God has provided a way for man to draw near to Him.

To order, call (800) 266-4977 or (423) 894-6060.
www.amgpublishers.com

Leader's Guidebooks for *Life Principles for Worship from the Tabernacle* also available. Watch for new Following God titles to be released soon!

Available from AMG Publishers

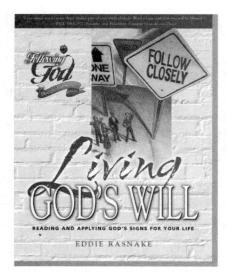

Living God's Will

ISBN 0-89957-309-6

How can I follow and identify the signs that lead to God's will? *Living God's Will* explores the answer to this all-important question in detail. It is Eddie Rasnake's deeply-held conviction that the road to God's will is well-marked with signposts to direct us. Each lesson in this twelve-week Bible study takes a look at a different signpost that reflects God's will. You will be challenged to recognize the signposts of God when you encounter them. But more importantly, you will be challenged to follow God's leading by following the direction of those signposts.

In the pages of this "Following God" study on finding and obeying God's will, you will find clear and practical advice for:

✓ Yielding your life to the Lord

✓ Recognizing God's will through Scripture, prayer and circumstances

✓ Seeking godly counsel

✓ Discovering how God's peace enters into the process of following His will

✓ Determining God's will in areas not specifically addressed in Scripture, such as choosing a wife/husband or career path.

Throughout your study you will also be enriched by the many interactive application sections that literally thousands have come to appreciate from the acclaimed **Following God** series.

To order, call (800) 266-4977 or (423) 894-6060.
www.followingGod.com

Leader's Guidebook for *Living God's Will* also available. Several newer Following God titles have also been released!
Log on to www.amgpublishers.com for more details.

Following God